Pure Land

A True Story of Three Lives, Three Cultures, and the Search for Heaven on Earth

Annette McGivney

AUXmedia
Detroit, Michigan

Pure Land: A True Story of Three Lives, Three Cultures, and the Search for Heaven on Earth

AUXmedia, a Division of AQUARIUS PRESS
Aquarius Press
20615 Fenkell, # 23096
Detroit, MI 48223
www.AUXmedia.studio

Cover photograph of Grand Canyon by James Kay
Kanji illustrations by Austin Frick

ISBN 978-0-9985278-8-8

LCCN 2017952493

Printed in the United States of America

For my sisters,

Elizabeth and Maria,

with love

CONTENTS

Tomomi Hanamure and her dog, Blues, Muir Beach, California, January 2002

WIND

FIRE

EARTH

WATER

Prologue

"Is this a crisis?"

The woman at the reception desk of the Guidance Center in Flagstaff, Ariz. needed to know.

"Yes!" my friend Mary responded for me as she pushed paperwork my way. I could not read because my vision was blurry with tears and my hands were trembling so violently I struggled to hold a pen.

The Guidance Center was the only place in northern Arizona, besides the hospital emergency room, where a person could see a psychiatrist without an appointment made weeks in advance. But treatment was available only to those experiencing a full-blown mental breakdown that required immediate attention.

"Yes, yes, yes," I whimpered, just to confirm the urgent nature of my visit. I was terrified. If I did not get help right there, right then, I believed I would lose my mind.

I was, I thought up until that day in July 2010, a pillar of unshakable mental health. At age 49, I was the rock that everyone else leaned on. I was the determined journalist, the family breadwinner, an attentive mother and caregiver for my parents with Alzheimer's. I could pull late nights working to meet a story deadline and get up the next morning to make the perfect school lunch for my son. I could push myself, and then push harder.

But now something was very wrong with me. I had not slept even for one hour in the last 10 days and had collapsed in a sobbing heap in my doctor's office that morning. The doctor, a general practitioner, said she could not help me.

"You've got to see a psychiatrist right away," she advised, handing me an address for the Guidance Center and asked her nurse to call someone to drive me there.

In the weeks prior to my sleeplessness, I had been shaken by nightmares. In these dreams someone was looming over me, killing me. There was no escape. Then I was a spirit floating over my body, bumping up against the windows and ceiling of a dark room. I would awake startled and gasping for air, part of me still stranded in the black fog of death.

For the first time in my life, my willpower was failing me. I had been working non-stop the past year and pouring much of myself into a story about a woman who was murdered in Grand Canyon. I reasoned that knowledge about her violent death, combined with all my other life stresses, must have pushed me to the breaking point and be the reason for the insomnia, the nightmares, the trembling and unchecked adrenaline surges. As Mary and I were ushered into a waiting room, I rehearsed in my head what I was going to tell the psychiatrist about why I was a mess.

We sat on a sinking plaid couch beneath blinding white fluorescent lights. The musty smell of the couch and old magazines filled my nostrils as I struggled to breathe between sobs. After 20 minutes, the psychiatrist knocked. He stepped into the room and stood there sizing me up as I sat holding Mary's hand. I opened my mouth to utter my plausible excuses. But before I had a chance to speak, the psychiatrist asked me a question.

The crisis, what seemed like a nervous breakdown that I had been experiencing over the past few weeks, was just a warm-up to this moment. And in the darkness of my subconscious, I had been creeping toward this terrifying place for years, even decades, until finally being ushered to the brink by two strangers: Tomomi Hanamure and Randy Wescogame. Now it was time.

The question swung at me like a giant wrecking ball. Six words. Boom. My world was reduced to rubble.

Birth in the Pure Land is an event that takes place while we are still living in this life... A student asked a teacher, "A bird freed from the cage—what does he eat?" The teacher replied, "You come through the cage yourself, then I will tell you."

— D.T. Suzuki

PART I

1

Hiking In

The path to Havasu Falls begins at the edge of the Earth. Here, at the dead end of Indian Road 18, which is 80 miles from the closest gas station, the modern world is swallowed in one big gulp by the Grand Canyon. The trail cuts steeply down a series of switchbacks descending some 3,000 feet through colorful layers of geologic time. Then it rambles over a wide, dry wash and squeezes in between the narrowing walls of Havasu Canyon where the blue-green waters of Havasu Creek first bubble up from the red earth.

After eight miles, the trail reaches the Native American village of Supai on the Havasupai Reservation and follows the main road through town, past horse corrals, plywood shacks, a tribal community building, store, school and two-story tourist lodge. Located deep in the Grand Canyon, Supai is notoriously remote for a world-famous tourist destination; it has no paved roads, no cell phone service and can only be reached by foot, horseback or helicopter.[1]

Just beyond the village, the path is lined with willow and cottonwood trees, following the meandering creek as it picks up velocity on its way to the Colorado River. Rushing waters crash through green thickets of willow and, suddenly, the trail emerges at Havasu Falls. The pulsing creek cascades 100 feet over travertine ledges into turquoise pools that are surrounded by fern-decked grottos. It is the most beautiful place in the Grand Canyon, if not the entire United States. The spot is often described as a Shangri-La in travel articles that feature spectacular photos of the falls and gushing descriptions of natural beauty. Some 25,000 tourists a year venture here, lured by the promise of a real life paradise.

On May 8, 2006, Tomomi Hanamure hiked the path to Havasu Falls. She went alone. She had traveled halfway around the world from her home in Japan for this trek. It was her 34th birthday and seeing the falls was going to be a birthday gift to herself. But she never made it. After a lodge cleaning woman found Tomomi's bed untouched on May 9, a search crew discovered her body four days later along the creek in an eddy above the falls. It was submerged in the blue-green waters and riddled with 29 stab wounds.

~~~

My journey began where Tomomi's ended. On Jan. 9, 2007, I found the hand-painted sign "Supai, 8 miles" at the corner of the dirt parking lot that marked the way down. On assignment for *Backpacker* magazine where I work as Southwest editor, I intended to investigate the story behind Tomomi's death and rumors of violent crime at a popular hiking destination.[2] A month earlier, the FBI had announced that an 18-year-old Havasupai tribal member named Randy Redtail Wescogame was charged with murder in relation to the case. It was the culmination of a six-month-long investigation that was conducted mostly in secret despite hungry reporters from around the world trying to sniff out the details of the killing in Grand Canyon, an unlikely location for violent crime.

Over the last decade, I had hiked numerous times in the Grand Canyon, always in the national park, and always for positive stories about outdoor adventure and the unspoiled wilderness of a natural wonder. During these explorations into the depths of the 17 million year old chasm I had witnessed the unleashing of rockslides, the fury of flash floods, a mountain lion darting across a ledge and sunsets so spectacular they made me cry. Grand Canyon had become a beloved touchstone for me that I kept returning to again and again as a way to recharge my spirit with its limitless beauty and wildness. But this was my first trip to Supai; the Havasupai reservation was new territory for me, as was the subject of murder. Yet, as I made my way down the switchbacks on the trail to Supai, I felt the space of the Grand Canyon wrap around me like a favorite warm blanket. The familiar rainbow of rock unfurled before me: white Kaibab limestone, green Toroweap Formation and red Hermit shale. Then I noticed something red on the white rocks beneath my feet. At first I wondered if it was a mineral deposit, but as I kept hiking and the spots got bigger and more numerous, I knew it was something else. Blood.

Because the murder case was expected to go to trial, authorities had shared few details with the media about Tomomi or her accused killer. The only picture of Tomomi to appear in hundreds of stories about the murder was her passport photo, in which she stared blankly at the camera. It was used by Coconino County Sheriff's detectives on "wanted" fliers during their hunt for her killer.

But journalists, including myself, had obtained the coroner's report on Tomomi's autopsy. What reporters did know and publicized widely was that this murder was shocking for its brutality. Performed by Coconino County Coroner Lawrence Czarneki, the report listed in gruesome detail all of the injuries to Tomomi's body. Of the 29 stab wounds, 22 were to the head and neck, a number of which, all by themselves, were severe enough to result in death. With a single blade that was approximately four inches long and one inch wide, Tomomi was stabbed repeatedly. The carotid artery on the left side of her neck was sliced; her lung was punctured; her skull was chipped from blunt force. The cuts were deep, penetrating the skin, organs and bone. Many of the stab wounds were described by the coroner as "gaping." Cuts on her arms and hands showed she fought back.[3]

"Clearly the murderer was in a frenzy," surmised Tom Myers, a Flagstaff physician[4] whom I had asked to evaluate the report several weeks before my Supai hike. Myers is co-author of *Over the Edge: Death in Grand Canyon,*[5] which chronicles all known deaths in the natural wonder. "The killer must have been so psychotic or incoherent, he couldn't appreciate what he'd already done. He was still stabbing her even though she was unresponsive, basically dead.

"This is the most brutal killing in the Grand Canyon in modern times," he added. "There is no other incident that is so horrific."

After about a mile of hiking and not passing a single soul, the explanation for the blood exploded past me. A young man on a horse, probably a Havasupai tribal member, was driving two mules loaded with tourist backpacks. He was charging hard up the trail kicking his horse to go faster and whipping the mules. I jumped to the side of the narrow trail in a cloud of dust. As the animals passed, I could see their ribs sticking out and the saddle straps digging into raw skin. The blood of saddle sores dripped onto the rocks.

I continued down the switchbacks and spotted just below me two more mule trains headed in opposite directions that were each being driven by Native American men. They had stopped, were blocking the narrow path, and appeared to be visiting with each other. But as I approached, I could see that these young mule drivers wearing black t-shirts, baseball caps and MP3 earbuds had pulled their horses up next to each other so they could pass a pipe back and forth. Not exactly the kind of friendly, Camelbak-sipping, Patagonia-wearing travelers I was used to encountering on Grand Canyon trails; they were sharing a hit of something. I shrank on a distant rock and waited for them to finish their business so I could resume my trek. And I questioned the wisdom of my covert reporting strategy, which was to retrace Tomomi's footsteps, witness what she might have experienced, and piece together clues about what had happened on her birthday.

Most of Grand Canyon is located within Grand Canyon National Park and afforded the protections and visitor accommodations that come with being a crown jewel in the richest country in the world. But the slice of Grand Canyon that encompasses Havasu Canyon and its iconic waterfalls is in a different world altogether. Like many small, economically impoverished countries still reeling from the effects of colonization, it is a third world, and it lacks the basic safety and public services taken for granted in much of the United States.

Hiking the path to Havasu Falls means entering the sovereign nation of the Havasupai,[6] the *Havsuw 'Baaja* — "people of blue-green water" — where there is great natural beauty but life can be brutal for both humans and animals. Randy Wescogame had such a life; he spent much of his childhood in Arizona's juvenile corrections system.[7] Law enforcement officials said that in the months before Tomomi's murder, when Randy was living in Supai and getting into trouble, he was using drugs and had become addicted to meth.

~~~

Entering the village, I walked over a wooden bridge crossing the swift waters of Havasu Creek where graffiti of a giant marijuana leaf was spray painted on a concrete berm. Sheer orange sandstone walls rose 500 feet framing the broad canyon bottom and gray, winter-bare cottonwood trees rattled against the wind. Horses snorted and nodded along fences as I walked by, and the steel drums of reggae music pulsed from open windows.

I was visiting in the off-season, but the residential paths and yards seemed eerily empty. Windows were blown out everywhere and covered with plastic or plywood. This combined with a whirlwind of trash to create the sense that a tornado had touched down just minutes ago and I was following the path of its destruction. Lining the main dirt road and plastered against barbed wire fences were empty cartons of Pampers, U.S. mail crates, old saddles, Backpacker's Pantry packages, Clif Bar wrappers, CDs, horse tack, abandoned furniture, and lots of plastic Gatorade bottles. Ravens as big as turkeys picked through overflowing bins of garbage. The pungent smell of sewage wafted from an open ditch.

As I walked farther into the village, the canyon became crowded with homes. A maze of dirt paths branching off from the main road led to closely-spaced small structures that appeared to be slapped together with whatever wood was available. And attached to nearly every roof was a satellite TV dish. There were also trampolines; in tiny backyards everywhere children silently bobbed up and down like fish hitting the surface of a lake.

Like Tomomi, I planned to stay at the tourist lodge, a 25-room hotel run by the tribe at the edge of the village and fortified with a 20-foot high, embassy-style concrete wall and an iron gate that was locked at night. I had booked two nights at the lodge and checked in after a group of hikers who arrived with an outfitter. The quiet in the village gave way to the excited chatter of tourists inside the compound. They were the type of travelers who appreciated the opportunity to visit an authentic Native American community and likely saw the unkempt village setting as simple, rustic charm.

"What brings you here? Are you going to the falls?" asked one of the hikers cheerily as we sat on picnic tables waiting for our rooms to be readied. He was assembling a camp stove on the table so he could brew tea for his group. Meanwhile a pack of 10 stray dogs squeezed through the gate and panhandled for bites of pastrami and Clif bars.

"Oh, I'm just visiting," I said, feeling somewhat paranoid because journalists were not supposed to be in Supai. The Havasupai Tribal Council had banned the media from the reservation since Tomomi's murder. Publicity about a brutal killing was bad for business. And, so far, I had been unable to get any tribal members to talk to me for the *Backpacker* story.

"What will you get out of this story?" responded Roland Manakaja, the tribe's director of cultural resources, when I had called him before my Supai visit to ask if he would agree to an interview. "And what will we get? Nothing! We don't even have a fire truck that works down here. Buildings burn to the ground."

A steady tourism business from the lodge, campground, café, store, entrance fees, and mule packing earned $2 million a year for the 500-member Havasupai tribe, most of whom lived in the village for at least part of the year. Yet, according to the most recent census, two thirds of Havasupai children lived below the poverty level.[8] And there were other problems: epidemic diabetes, lack of education (the village school only went through the 8th grade), alcoholism (even though alcohol was illegal on the reservation), drug abuse, and, lately, violent crime. In addition to Tomomi's murder, there were 10 violent assaults under investigation by law enforcement during the six months after her death, which was a 200 percent increase over previous years.[9] Most incidents were drunken tribal members attacking each other, usually with knives and baseball bats. Reports of child abuse had also risen sharply in the last few years.

The two Bureau of Indian Affairs police officers stationed in Supai were exhausted and eager to talk to me. They blamed the spike in crime on a group of juvenile delinquents in the tribe who were committing petty thefts in the village and campground to buy booze and drugs. After these young men got wasted, they would get into fights. Because Supai had no high school, kids were sent to government-funded boarding schools in faraway places like Oregon and California. The majority dropped out by 11th grade and returned to Supai. "Sometimes they help their parents with the family packing business, transporting tourist cargo and village goods up and down the canyon," said BIA officer Kendrick Rocha who had been working in Supai since 1992. "Mainly these dropouts just lurk around town getting liquored up and looking for tourists to rob." He said they were responsible for the broken windows and graffiti in the village. But Randy did not hang with these bad boys.

"Randy was a special case," Rocha added. "His whole life, he was the black sheep of the tribe. He was a loner."

~~~

There are two streams flowing through Supai. One is the traditional world of the original inhabitants of the Grand Canyon, the ways of the *Havsuw 'Baaja*. It emanates from the depths of the Earth and speaks a language that only the Havasupai understand. The other stream contains everything else; it arrives by helicopter, satellite dish, and fleeting visitors who expect Starbucks, ATM machines, exceptional customer service and being able to buy anything they need, or don't need.

Steve Hirst, author of the book *I Am the Grand Canyon: The Story of the Havasupai People,* has an anthropological explanation for this paradox. "In addition to the four cardinal directions (north, south, east, west), the Havasupai have two other ways of orienting themselves: In the canyon and away from the canyon."[10] Hirst says in the Havasupai culture there are two realities, two worlds: in or out; down or up.

Sometimes, one of the streams overflows its banks and intermingles with the other in comical or wonderful or cataclysmic ways. But generally, each stays in its own channel, flowing side by side, and the tribe, tourists and police seem to prefer it this way.

After unpacking my things and letting some of the stray dogs nap on my bed, I walked to the café, hoping I would be able to strike up conversation with tribal members willing to talk about the murder. Sitting on a stone wall outside the restaurant, I watched the parade of Down Here and Up There flow by: hikers in bright colored fleece jackets on their way to the campground followed by dogs looking for scraps; young Havasupai women speaking to each other in their native language and carrying children on their hips; a white woman in heels asking about a cab to the falls; transgender tribal teenagers giggling behind their press-on nails; a white handyman shaking his hammer about the recently broken café windows; and old Havasupai men sitting on an aluminum bench sipping coffee and watching people step off the helicopter as it landed in the middle of town.

Emerging from a whirlwind of noise and dust were tribal members who used the helicopter to go on grocery runs and loaded cases of eggs and bottles of Mountain Dew into a wheelbarrow to push home. A BIA cop appeared with a stack of Pizza Hut boxes to take to the elementary school DARE (Drug Abuse Resistance Education) meeting. There was also a black Rasta guy wearing sunglasses, and a red, green and yellow knit hat over elbow-length dreadlocks who was quickly ushered away by tribal members waiting to greet him. And a group of white attorneys wearing business suits and carrying briefcases stumbled through the sand into the nearby tribal office building.

"Where's your husband?"

The question jarred me from my trance. It came from a middle-aged Havasupai man standing in front of me dressed in a camo jacket with an American Indian Movement patch and red, yellow and green Rasta stripes on the sleeve. His hair was in one long braid down his back and he carried a stack of Hirst's book *I Am the Grand Canyon*, which he was selling to tourists. He introduced himself as Damon Watahomigie and took a seat next to me on the rock wall.[11] He said he was a medicine man and also the official sergeant at arms for the Havasupai Tribal Council.

"Oh, my husband is working," I said. "He couldn't come with me." This was a lie. My husband, Mike, and I had just split up. Several months before my visit to Supai, Mike had told me that he had quit his job although I suspected he had been fired. He had started going on drinking binges again. It was the latest in a long line of jobs lost while I held down multiple jobs to support the two of us along with our 10-year-old son Austin. On top of that, I had been trying to care for my ill parents, both of whom had become increasingly incapacitated as they slipped into the clutches of Alzheimer's disease. The only thing that felt right about my life at that moment was being a journalist, finding reasons to hike in Grand Canyon, and an unexplainable if not unreasonable determination to uncover the whole story behind what had happened to Tomomi. So, despite the gag order from the Havasupai Tribal Council, I decided to tell Damon that I was writing a magazine article about the murder. I offered to buy him a cup of coffee and we went inside the café.

When I asked Damon about the vandalism around the village, he said it was caused by the youth in the tribe who had lost their traditional ways. "The kids go to boarding school and bring back negative influences." Damon talked so softly, his voice was barely audible as he looked beyond me at some tourists walking to their seats with baskets of fries. "TV has become our culture, not the elders," he whispered. "The dominant culture tells our kids: buy, obey, consume. Their parents are under the bad influences too, getting drunk and addicted to meth. I am trying to educate our people about ways to fight the dominant culture, about how to politicize their ideas like Leonard Peltier did with the American Indian Movement."[12]

The Havasupai had endured a long history of betrayals by the dominant culture. One of the latest, and the reason for the attorneys' visit, involved genetic researchers from Arizona State University who obtained blood samples from tribal members in the 1990s under the auspices of trying to help the tribe stem a diabetes epidemic. Instead of using the blood samples for the research that the donors thought they had agreed to, the professors conducted studies and published papers on genetic inbreeding and schizophrenia within the tribe. Tribal members believed misuse of their blood, especially that taken from those who had since died, was not only deceitful but put the tribe spiritually out of balance. The tribe filed a lawsuit against the state of Arizona's university system in 2003 demanding financial damages as well as the return of the blood samples.[13] When I was there in January 2007, the attorneys visiting Supai reported that the case was still making its way through the judicial system (having been appealed to the Arizona Supreme Court), and the vials of Havasupai blood were still in the genetic researcher's freezers on university campuses in Phoenix and Tucson.

Damon said he did not think Randy murdered Tomomi. "He is not capable of that." He believed the murder was part of a covert campaign by the U.S. government to destroy the Havasupai tribe in order to claim the world-famous waterfalls. Damon whispered that he suspected the murderer was an Irish guy named Neil who was living as a transient in Supai the previous summer and that Neil had been planted there by the feds. He was a drug addict who hung out with the tribe's meth dealers, and his body was covered in satanic tattoos.

"I have been praying that someone would come down here and put the puzzle pieces together about what is happening," Damon said, looking me straight in the eye. "And now you are here."

The journalist in me was pleased with this news. It looked like I might be able to pull off the story after all. Yet another part of me felt trepidation about what I might be falling into—the other stream with an unfamiliar current that could sweep me to a place I should not go. But I quickly pushed these fears aside, dismissing them as silly superstitions, and pressed on with my reporting.

Damon told me to come back in a few weeks. There were other tribal members who he thought would be ready to talk.

~~~

The first person to break rank was Billy Wescogame, Randy's father. Like an undercover spy, I returned to Supai in February hoping I could sneak over to Billy's house for an interview without being noticed by the tribal council.

"I want the world to know what is going on here, and I want to speak out against the bootleggers and drug dealers who are destroying our tribe," Billy told me.[14] We sat on plastic milk crates in front of his small, weather-beaten house next to the helicopter landing pad. A baby shoe was nailed above the doorway and a couch, bookcase and foosball table were against a chicken wire fence and covered with tarps. White cottonwood blossoms swirled through the air like snowflakes.

Billy's eyes darted back and forth, looking up and down the path to see who might be watching him. "I am not speaking up because of Randy," he said. "Whatever Randy did is on him." Billy, who was 50, a convicted felon and the father of 11 children, said he was coming forward to protect his other children from the village juvenile delinquents. "They're trying to beat up my [adult] daughter and my other kids. They go to parties and come home all bloody. One boy recently attacked another boy with a machete."

Billy came from one of the longtime Havasupai families that just a century ago had nearly the entire Grand Canyon to themselves. He said his great grandfather (and Randy's great, great grandfather) was Billy Burro who protested the creation of Grand Canyon National Park in the 1920s by refusing to leave his homestead and move to the 518-acre reservation. Burro, the last "Indian" living at Indian Garden along the Bright Angel Trail, operated his farm for more than a decade after the park's creation in 1919 until officials threw him out. Even a geologic layer in the Grand Canyon's Supai formation bears the name Wescogame.[15]

As the village tattoo artist, Billy's arms and chest were covered with his handiwork, including Sanskrit swastikas on his forearms and the letters l.o.v.e. on his fingers. He liked to sit on his front stoop and carve pieces of cottonwood while listening to reggae. He said he had whittled a memorial cross and put it at the murder site last May before he was told by the police that his own son might be involved. "Randy was a known thief, no doubt about it. He would always steal from the tourists, from anybody and everybody, to get money to buy drugs and booze," he said. "But Randy is not a murderer. He is not a bad kid."

Billy was once a police officer (until he was fired for committing a felony), and he said he had also spent a lot of time studying psychology. "In the psychology books it states there is a line between murder and thieving," he explained as he dragged his boot tip across the sand. "A thief will not cross that line and murder somebody to get what he wants. Randy's intentions were to steal, not to murder." He paused. His defiant tone melted into faint words that choked with emotion. "If Randy did murder, it was because of that meth."

Over the course of our three-hour conversation, Billy's demeanor swung from smiling and friendly to excited and agitated. When he talked about crime in the village, he became especially angry. He said the police were afraid to enforce the laws in such a closed, isolated community, and the meth dealers roamed freely because they were related to tribal council members. He said no one — not tribal members or tourists — had any civil rights in Supai.

"If I went into my house right now and got my gun and said, 'Give me all your money, right this minute. I want everything you have.' And then you give it up and you go to the nearest police and tell them I robbed you. Well, they would just laugh at you. You know why? Because this is a sovereign nation! We are self-governed! We do as we please! Even the president of the United States can't do nothing about it."

I was already well outside of my comfort zone and Billy's hypothetical threat only heightened my paranoia. Although I did not understand why then, I reacted as I always had when I thought things might take a turn for the worse: I steeled myself. "Huh," I said nonchalantly, trying to appear unfazed.

Then Billy's mood brightened and he walked into his yard to point out an ancient ancestral cliff dwelling high on the canyon wall. The sound of the helicopter landing nearby forced him to raise his voice. "What you need to understand about this tribe is we have a lot of stories!" he shouted. "We used to get a lot of power from these stories and beliefs! We had the ghost dance! We had black magic! But now all that power is gone."

Billy said he had not had a drop of alcohol since he got out of prison a decade ago. He blamed Randy's problems on Randy's mother, who he said was "boozing and drugging all the time" when Randy was a young child. Billy became visibly agitated with this topic; his jaw clenched and his eyes narrowed. Suddenly, his wrath turned toward me. "I don't like the way you are asking these questions. You don't believe me?"

"Well, yes, but…" I stammered.

Billy stood up and disappeared into his house. And I waited, wondering if it might be smarter to leave.

Five minutes later Billy emerged with a 10-inch high stack of file folders that he handed over to me. "Here, I have all the papers to prove it," he said, a bit more calmly.

These photocopies chronicled years of custody fights, restraining orders, child support disputes and other battles waged by Randy's parents in Supai tribal court. The files from Billy were the beginning of what would become a research obsession for me, eventually taking up an entire room in my house for document storage and nearly a decade of my life. As I sought to understand Randy's motivations in the coming months and years, my questions multiplied like mosquitoes in a stagnant pond. The hunt for explanations would lead me to also explore Billy's life, the Havasupai tribe's history, and the plight of all of Native America.

Billy next showed me a cottonwood root with a whittled handle he kept propped inside the front door. He held it up like a samurai sword. "This is to fight off the drug dealers!"

He said that shortly before Tomomi's murder, Native American medicine men performed an exorcism in the village. "There are bad spirits here. We may need to close this place down to the public to get things straightened out. It is our tribe's destiny that we will hit bottom and then we will get help." He sat the cottonwood root back in its spot and stood in his doorway, the tiny baby shoe above his head.

Thanks to Damon's help, Roland Manakaja also decided he would talk to me. In addition to his official job as the tribe's cultural resources director, Manakaja was a Havasupai medicine man who was often described as "the spiritual voice of the tribe." He is the great grandson of Chief Manakaja, the last man to serve as chief before the tribe converted to a council form of government in 1934 to comply with U.S. government-imposed reservation regulations. Modern-day Manakaja also commanded respect throughout the community and seemed almost like a de facto chief.

Damon escorted me to Roland's homestead at the edge of the village. He had a small, tidy house, a sprawling yard and nine children. A big man, full of sage-like protestations, Roland sat in a small school chair in his yard. His long hair was pulled back in a ponytail, and he was wearing a black "Homeland Security" t-shirt that had a picture of Geronimo and his Apache warriors on it. Roland was gazing out at the rock formations at the top of the canyon, "the deities," that talked to him.[16]

"We are struggling to survive here, fighting against a lot of things brought in from the white man's culture—uranium mining, alcohol, meth," he said.[17] "These things are impacting our youth and throwing our world—the whole world—out of balance. Out there, in the white world, you have all these problems, too. But they are magnified down here."

Roland said he was worried about how far his tribe had strayed from their cultural traditions and family support systems. "The kids involved in this violence and drugs, they don't have family love. They are scared and angry.

"The Havasupai are an endangered species on the verge of extinction," he added. "This is the history of America that is at stake here."

Always looking up at the canyon buttes where the sun was sinking, Roland spoke with a soft, steady cadence that was like water trickling over rocks. His train of thought was serpentine and frequently digressed into tribal stories from the past. "We make offerings at every spring in Grand Canyon because water is our most sacred thing. The Earth is our house."

When he talked about the destruction of the Grand Canyon or how bad he felt about the murder, he started to cry. "Before the murder, there was a dark aura down here. I could feel it," he said, his voice breaking into sobs as he thought of Tomomi. "But I believe that our oriental sister who suffered here enjoyed this place — before the demons on that side of the creek rolled with the flow and kept going."

~~~

It was not until my second visit in February that I finally hiked all the way to Havasu Falls. On my first trip in January, I had set out from the village and was soon followed by a tribal man who said his name was Goofy. I thought I would be able to spot suspicious people before they got close, but as Goofy popped in and out of the brush and attempted to make conversation, I realized that there was a network of private trails around the main tourist path. Two streams. Feeling vulnerable, I turned back.

On this second attempt, I passed the familiar marker at the edge of town — a concrete drainage channel that was painted with graffiti reading, "Fuck the police."[18] About a half-mile outside the village, houses disappeared as the trail paralleled the creek, following a steady flow of 28,000 gallons per minute. Coupled with the beauty, there is a certain fury to this creek, the potential for an unbridled rage that is wildly destructive. These beautiful yet unpredictable waters are at the center of Havasupai spiritual beliefs. Here, the Grand Canyon is much more than a tourist attraction. It is an omnipotent being.

Off in the distance, beyond a thicket of willow, I could hear Fifty Foot Falls. A few tribal members and tourists passed me as they headed in the opposite direction and offered friendly hellos. Then I came to the 100-foot cascade of Navajo Falls, and just beyond that, I stood in the icy spray at the foot of Havasu Falls. The waters spilled over the cliffs and into deep pools that vibrated blue and green and turquoise, like the plumes of peacock feathers. Swimmers shrieked as they plunged into the frigid waters, and two photographers were setting up their tripods on the ledges at the base of the falls to get that postcard-perfect shot.

On my hike back to the village, I thought of Tomomi, and just before reaching Fifty Foot Falls, I noticed tattered yellow crime scene tape tied to the bushes. It was lining a side path that led to the creek and in a place where the tumbling water rumbled like a passing freight train and a steep cliff fenced in the main trail. I wandered into the dense thicket of willow and oak. I stood there, alone, listening to the blood curdling screams of swimmers off in the distance. This was where the murder happened. But why?

From my perspective, juvenile delinquency, even the use of meth, did not explain such brutality. Nor did the tribe's assertion about the invasion of a "dark spirit." When announcing the charges against Randy, law enforcement officials offered only that his motive in killing Tomomi was to rob her, "to steal her cell phone, credit cards and cash."

And then there was the matter of Tomomi hiking to the falls by herself and the implication that, if only she had not gone alone, the murder would not have happened. "Most Japanese tourists who visit northern Arizona and Grand Canyon travel in large groups, often by bus," noted Coconino County Sheriff's spokesman Gerry Blair during a December 6, 2006 press conference when charges against Randy were announced.[19] "But Tomomi Hanamure usually traveled by herself." The Japanese press had even scolded Tomomi's father for allowing her to travel alone in America.

Before my February visit to Supai, I met with an attorney for the U.S. Attorney's Office in Flagstaff, Arizona who brought the charges against Randy. All the details and evidence from the murder investigation remained sealed by the courts in anticipation the case would go to trial. Still, this woman was an avid Grand Canyon hiker and there was something about Tomomi that stoked a sense of kinship—between her and Tomomi and ultimately the two of us. Although she couldn't tell me anything, she wanted me to keep digging. While working as an attorney over the years, she had dealt with numerous tragic cases involving crimes on Southwest Native American reservations, but Tomomi's murder really got to her.

"It could have been me," she said, as she handed me a copy of Randy's indictment. "Or it could have been you."

Soon after Randy was charged, the media coverage of Tomomi's murder stopped. If the killer had been found, and law enforcement officials said they had solid physical evidence linking him to the crime, then it seemed the story was over. But it wasn't over for me. I was caught in the current. Lingering there, amid the crime scene tape along the path to Havasu Falls, I sensed something powerful and painful, forces unseen that can move water, carve a canyon, make people do terrible things to each other. Well beyond the professional curiosity of a journalist and for no apparent reason, I longed for real answers, for the truth.

When I returned home from Supai, I tried to contact Tomomi's family through the official channels of the U.S. Japanese Consulate's office in Los Angeles. I wanted to know more about her and what she was seeking when she hiked to Havasu Falls. But I was told her father would not grant any interviews to the media, in the United States or Japan, under any circumstances. "He is very, very distraught," the consulate's public affairs director said.

Eventually, I would be entrusted with Tomomi's travel journals, letters to family, and the most intimate details in her diary. But in January 2007, as I continued to report on the *Backpacker* story, the only personal information about Tomomi came, sadly, from her autopsy. In addition to the many injuries, it described what Tomomi was wearing on her birthday.

"The body is received clad in a brown short sleeve shirt, a dark blue short sleeve shirt, a brown bra, two brown boots, two socks from the right foot, two socks from the left foot, green shorts, a belt, and black panties. Personal effects include a ring from the left index finger, a leather band from the left wrist, and a green bellybutton ring from the umbilicus." Under identifying marks, the report noted: "1 by 1/8 inch color tattoo of a heart on the left lower quadrant of the abdomen and a 3/4 by 7/8 inch dark ink tattoo of a Japanese symbol on top of the left foot."

A Japanese TV station in Tokyo that had covered the murder and also obtained a copy of the autopsy report, quoted one of Tomomi's friends in a June 2006 story. The friend said the tattoo on Tomomi's left foot was the kanji character for *"hana,"* the first part of her last name. In Japanese it means "flower."

2

Earth and Sky

Agnes Gray lives in a trailer in the middle of Monument Valley. It sits like a lighthouse on the shore of a vast ocean of space. Travelers drifting down from Utah or up from Arizona can see the white metal structure from 10 miles away, glinting in the sun, standing out against the red dirt and blue sky. As they get closer, they can read Agnes' hand painted sign: "Bed and Breakfast in a Traditional Hogan." Many people stop, but few decide to stay.

"They look at the dirt floor inside the hogan and over at the outhouse and they ask, 'So this is where we would sleep?'" said Agnes.[1] "And I tell them, 'That's right. You are in a different country now. This is how we live on the Navajo Nation.'"

In December 1997, Tomomi Hanamure knocked on the door of Agnes' trailer. Tomomi was 25 and with her boyfriend, Mako, a Japanese citizen she met the year prior while attending an English language program at the University of Southern Mississippi. They had returned to the U.S. over the Christmas holiday to visit school friends in Mississippi and make a road trip through the Southwest. They drove all the way across Texas and were now on the last leg of their journey, headed for a motel in Flagstaff 140 miles away, then the airport in Phoenix to catch a flight back to Tokyo. Mako was driving 90 miles an hour as tumbleweeds blew across the road and distant, oddly shaped rock buttes flew by.

"Stop!" Tomomi shouted. She couldn't resist Agnes' sign.

"They stayed for two nights and then they went on their way. I thought that was it," Agnes recalled years later. "Then, maybe three days passed, and Tomomi was at my door again. This time by herself."

Mako had boarded a plane in Phoenix, wanting to return to Japan in time to attend a family New Year's celebration. But Tomomi called her father and said she was changing her ticket and extending her stay. She had to go back to Monument Valley, to Agnes' place, right away. This urge wasn't explainable to her father, and Mako didn't understand, either. Yet, as crazy as it even seemed to herself, Tomomi was convinced something special was waiting for her there, like a gift still wrapped.

~~~

In the Navajo language, hogan means home. But for the Navajo, the traditional round structure with its domed roof is much more than a place to sleep; it embodies the tribe's belief system and their spiritual connection to the Earth and the cosmos.[2] The structure is circular because the Earth is round and a single door faces the east to greet the rising sun. The floor is dirt to embrace Mother Earth. The conical roof with a smoke hole at the top offers an entrance to the universe and a connection to Father Sky. Structural posts holding up the roof are placed like a compass at the four cardinal directions of east, south, west and north. A wood stove in the center of the hogan represents the central fire of life, and the stovepipe reaching up through the roof is the link between the Earth and the sky. Inside a hogan, there is harmony, symmetry and the constant reminder that a human being is part of something much bigger, a single star in an infinite universe.

The family hogan of Agnes Gray is about 40 feet in diameter and 20 feet tall at the apex of the smoke hole. The interior walls and roof are built from the trunks of large juniper trees, and the exterior is a thick stucco of red earth. Like many Navajo on the rural 26,000 square mile reservation, Agnes prefers the convenience of a trailer—with its sink, toilet and generator-powered electricity—for day to day living. But the culturally correct hogan is the family's traditional home, a spiritual sanctuary—and sometimes she will rent it out to strangers passing through.

"A lot of miracles have happened here," she said. "Traditional weddings, including my own, healing ceremonies, birthdays, peyote meetings, Christmas ceremonies."

There are no furnishings in the hogan during ceremonies, but Agnes tries to offer "bed and breakfast" guests some comforts. She puts an airbed on the red dirt floor and covers it with thick fleece blankets. She brings in a round plastic table, some folding chairs, an oil lamp as the only light, and a five-gallon water jug and large bowl as a way to wash. She also keeps the tiny, plywood outhouse 50 yards away as aesthetically pleasing as possible by hanging a bag of dried lavender on the wall and putting a padlock on the door to make it for guests only.

"I only open the hogan to people who are willing to listen and who appreciate it," Agnes explained, sitting at the plastic table as her two grandchildren jumped on the airbed. "For people who are not with it, I can feel the energy in everything around them, and so I back off. I tell myself those people don't need to know, they won't understand. But for people who do understand, I can talk to them. Once in a great while, people like that, who really understand, will come here." Her voice softened from defiant to nostalgic to silent as the memory of Tomomi's visit filled the hogan.

~~~

When Tomomi awoke that first morning after returning to Agnes' place, the temperature in the hogan was near freezing and she could see her breath. Lying atop the airbed, beneath three blankets, she stared up at the circular ceiling and wondered if she was dreaming. It was different without Mako; they had slept in, not wanting to leave the warm bed. But light creeping through the doorframe beckoned Tomomi to get up. She wrapped herself in blankets, walked across the red dirt floor, opened the east-facing door and greeted the dawn.

Sitting on the picnic table in front of the hogan, shivering against the cold, she watched her first Monument Valley sunrise. Spreading out from where she sat and extending to the east as far as she could see was an infinite emptiness filled with color. There was the black ribbon of State Route 163 and two buttes—called the Mittens for their hand-like shape—

rising against the horizon, but, except for the buildings of Agnes' family, there was not a single structure or person within view. Only earth and sky, changing from purple to red to pink to gold.

At her back, far to the west, beyond Arizona, California and the Pacific, was Tomomi's home in Yokohama. On the other side of the world, she had grown up in a three-room high rise apartment in metropolitan Tokyo, a 5,200 square mile area with more than 35 million people. It is one of the most densely populated places on the planet. Industrial smog hangs in the humid coastal air, pavement is always underfoot, and the sky is blocked and blinded by the insatiable metropolis. She had spent all of her 25 years living in Yokohama, except for the year she was in Mississippi going to English school. The southern United States was an exciting change of pace from Yokohama—refreshingly strange—but this isolated, windswept desert in the far corner of northeastern Arizona was something different entirely. Here, she not only saw the sky, she also felt it.

No longer able to stand the cold, Tomomi went inside the hogan and started a fire in the wood stove with freshly split juniper. The crisp, sweet aroma of the burning wood filled the room. Tomomi sat at the table and began to write a letter to her cousin Konomi who lived in southern Japan near the Hanamure family homestead. Tomomi rarely visited Konomi, but they had a strong, almost psychic relationship. They looked like twins and shared many of the same interests, including an intense curiosity about Native American culture.

Dear Konomi,

How are you? I am visiting Monument Valley and staying with a Navajo Indian family. I am sleeping in a traditional house called a hogan. You can see the stars through the chimney hole in the roof. It is so beautiful! You may have seen pictures of Monument Valley in TV commercials or on those western cowboy movies. Well, I am actually here!

Every morning and evening the sky is a different color. Sometimes it's purple; sometimes it's orange. There's just something about the huge open spaces that's amazing. You've got the red earth and the gigantic sun and all this air. On the Navajo reservation there is no running water or electricity, so they use oil lamps and propane that they get from a store. You wake up with sunrise and go to bed with sundown. I feel like, THIS is America![3]

Soon Agnes appeared at the door with breakfast. It was a thermos of coffee and a covered plate of scrambled eggs, bacon, and toast. She had never hosted a guest from Japan before and wasn't sure if Tomomi would eat this food. Back home Tomomi drank iced green tea and ate mostly rice, noodles, miso soup, fish and dried spinach. But here, she was hungry for the eggs and bacon, anything that tasted of America rather than of Japan.

Although Agnes usually kept her distance from non-Indian visitors, she could not help but quickly warm up to Tomomi. Despite Tomomi's petite five-foot stature, there was a certain pluckiness about her that Agnes liked. "She was not afraid of anything," Agnes recalled nearly 13 years later. Tomomi's black eyes sparkled when she talked, and her broad, toothy smile was filled with a sincere exuberance that pulled people in.

And Tomomi was in awe of Agnes, who was 11 years her senior. Here was a woman who grew up in Monument Valley, as had her two sisters and seven brothers and the many generations of her family before her. She lived close to the land, just like her mother did, grandmother, great grandmother and so on. Her first language was Navajo. She tended chickens, sheep and horses. She split wood with a single swing of the ax. She took care of three young children and her husband. She ran spiritual ceremonies. She wove beautiful Navajo baskets. And, more than anything, she was deeply connected to her native landscape and her culture. For the weeks that Tomomi stayed in the hogan, Agnes was like her big sister.

"Tomomi was very curious about everything. She wanted to know what we did in our day-to-day lives," Agnes said. "She told me that during the time she was here she wanted to make a basket. So I brought my supplies into the hogan and showed her how to do it."

The ancient art of basket making is something that has been passed down to the women in Agnes' family for many generations. It is how her mother and her grandmother earned money for the family. The craft is tedious and painful. Sumac twigs for the basket are torn apart with the teeth, sometimes causing the gums to bleed, and the fingers are rubbed raw pulling rough fibers through the weaving pattern. Agnes and her sisters are known in the Southwest for their ornate baskets that are used in Navajo ceremonies and also sold by art dealers. It takes them at least two weeks of steady weaving to make a basket that is about 15 inches in diameter.

Tomomi was determined to do it, too.

"It was at least 10 days, maybe two weeks, that she worked on that basket. She would not leave until she finished it," said Agnes. "She sat in the hogan weaving for five hours a day. Sometimes it was eight hours. I'd periodically go in and check on her and if she had made a mistake, I would correct it for her. Most people would have given up, but not her."

On most days, Tomomi would take a break for a few hours and go for a hike or a drive. "She liked to walk around by herself and do things on her own," recalled Agnes. "She would go down into the valley and then come back saying she had a great time just lying on a rock listening to the wind. She said she felt so good with nothing around. I think Mother Earth was speaking to her."

Tomomi also entertained Agnes' three children and made origami animals for them out of her stationery. One day the family took her to Mesa Verde National Park in southwestern Colorado to view the ancient Anasazi cliff dwellings. On another day Tomomi watched the butchering of a sheep for the family to eat. Adhering to traditional Japanese manners, Tomomi never asked prying questions and was careful not to impose on Agnes' family or request that they go out of their way for her.

"I said to her, 'I don't know if you are going to like mutton,' " recalled Agnes, laughing. "For us people, when we butcher, we eat everything—the intestines, the feet, the legs, the head. There is no waste. And Tomomi ate it all; the blood sausage, everything. She said it was the best food she ever had. Whatever we were eating or whatever we were doing, she just wanted to go along with that."

Tomomi never talked of her life in Japan. She never told Agnes that she was an only child. Or that she had not seen her mother since she was four years old. But Agnes could tell that Tomomi was thinking about people back home.

At night Tomomi sat at the table in the hogan writing letters by the dim yellow light of an oil lamp. "I would see her writing and writing," said Agnes. "She had a pile of papers, all of it her writing in the Japanese symbols."

Dear Konomi,

Okay, so here is Part 2 of my letter. I am learning how to make a Navajo basket. I am also eating Navajo tacos. At the place where I am staying there are lots of cows, horses and sheep. I am hoping to ride a horse if the weather warms up. Get this: I was scratched on the leg by a chicken.

I heard you want to be a teacher? I think that would be a very hard job. I could never do it. But I guess we all have our own paths don't we? If you do become a teacher, be a passionate one. I don't feel like there is anything out there I want to do for a career. I don't have dreams like you do to become a teacher or a nurse. Except I think it would be cool to be some kind of artisan – to weave rugs or make jewelry or pottery. And I would want to live somewhere in the States, in the Southwest, where I could have a dog and horses. I might have cows and sheep, but I would not eat them. Did you see that movie "Babe"? It is really good; go out and rent it right now.

Anyway, why am I living in Yokohama? When I am in the States there isn't a time when I can't get sleep; I don't get cold; I don't feel any kind of stress. In Japan, I get tired just being at home. Sometimes I wonder if Dad and stepmother are not getting along. But that is not my business. They have their own lives to live. I have my life to live. We all just need to be free to make our own choices.

~~~

The earthly world of the Navajo is bounded by four sacred mountains that correspond with the four cardinal directions: Mount Blanca, Colorado in the east; Mount Taylor, New Mexico in the south; the San Francisco Peaks, Arizona in the west; and Mount Hesperus, Colorado in the north. The tribe migrated down from the northern plains some 500 years ago and began farming and herding on this breathtakingly beautiful but unforgivingly harsh high desert landscape. The Navajo (called Dine´ "the people" in their native language) is the second largest American Indian tribe in the United States with nearly 300,000 members, two-thirds of whom live on the reservation. And the Navajo reservation, encompassing 17 million acres, is the largest in the country.

But because it is located hundreds of miles from any metropolitan area that could supply a job base, the Navajo nation has one of the highest poverty rates of any American Indian tribe in the United States. According to the 2010 U.S. Census, more than one third of tribal members live in extreme poverty. Much of the reservation is without electricity, running water and telephone service, and there are few paved roads except for the state highways that ferry non-native travelers across the area as quickly as possible. Life has always been hard on this land, but most tribal members agree that it got a lot harder 100 years ago when the federal government stepped in, first attempting to relocate the Navajo and wipe out the tribe, and then trying to repair the damage by providing government handouts. Rates of alcoholism are high and life expectancy is low. And the situation on other Southwest Indian reservations surrounding the Navajo Nation is just about as grim.

There are tight-knit families like that of Agnes Gray who, despite their poverty, manage to persevere with various odd jobs, living off the land as much as possible and clinging to the life-line of their spiritual traditions. These tribal members say the key to survival for the Navajo—and other Southwest Indian tribes—trying to cope with the modern world is to swear off alcohol and drugs, to greet the sunrise and not be hung-over.

"Native Americans can't tolerate drugs or alcohol," said Agnes. "We always overdo stuff. What happens is we get so drunk or so high that we go out of our minds. Then the next morning we realize we did something to someone that was horrible." Agnes kept her three children from getting into trouble by being strict and having the family participate in regular religious ceremonies of the Native American Church. But outside the Gray hogan, problems swirled like dust devils randomly touching down and destroying anything in their path.

In the late 1990s the Navajo reservation had a violent crime rate that had doubled in less than a decade and was higher per capita than that of any U.S. city. In 1997 the homicide rate on the Navajo Nation was four times the overall national average and double that of Los Angeles. A report released by the U.S. Department of Justice in October 1998 drew attention to what it called an escalating law enforcement crisis on the Navajo and other Southwest Indian reservations.[4] The report noted most of the violent murders were against fellow tribal members and committed by young males between the ages of 25-35. Based on the government statistics, people living on Southwest Indian reservations were twice as likely to be the victim of a violent crime, compared to the overall U.S. population.

In 1996 and 1997 there were more than 60 homicides annually on the Navajo reservation. And many of these murders were shocking, even to seasoned reservation law enforcement officers, for their randomness and brutality. The victims were usually strangers, there was rarely a motive beyond petty theft, and the manner of death was typically by bludgeoning or stabbing, often upwards of 20 times. Such violent behavior was not only highly out of character for the traditional Navajo culture, but also unheard of for any area so sparsely populated; just 50,000 households on the reservation were spread across an area the size of West Virginia.

There were many theories on the cause of the frightening trend that was infecting the Navajo Nation. Some said it was due to the influence of urban gangs, or the increasing use of meth, or the loss of traditional values and a breakdown of the family. An April 1998 article in *Harper's* quoted a philosophical Navajo police officer who theorized the rash of brutal murders was caused by "an overwhelming and cumulative sense of frustration and despair."[5] But whatever the cause, the random violence was spreading like a slow moving fog that would infiltrate other reservations. By the turn of the century, murder rates would double and triple on the White Mountain Apache reservation, the Ute, the Tohono O'odham, the Gila — even on the tiny Havasupai reservation at the bottom of the Grand Canyon, where a troubled boy named Randy Wescogame was desperately struggling in a very twisted world.

~~~

Entirely oblivious to the chaos elsewhere on the Navajo reservation, Tomomi spent New Year's Day 1998 sitting on the red earth floor of the hogan weaving her basket. By now, after more than a week without a proper Japanese bath, her skin and clothing had an orange tinge from a thin coating of dirt that covered everything. Outside, the icy wind howled and the constant spray of blowing sand against the hogan sounded like rain. Sometimes, big gusts would cause sand to blow under the door.

Inside, the wood stove crackled with burning juniper and filled the hogan with a radiant heat. A single shaft of sunlight reached down through the roof and moved around the circular structure like the needle of a compass marking the rotation of the Earth as the day progressed. The warm, windowless shelter was like being inside a womb. Tomomi sat cross-legged next to the stove, pulling the split sumac through the basket, looping a single strand dozens of times. Over and over. And something kept eating away at her. It was something she had never talked about to anyone, far more serious than anything she might broach in her chatty letters to Konomi.

"She asked if I could take her to see a medicine woman," explained Agnes. "She felt like there was something wrong with her."

Agnes drove Tomomi to a Navajo spiritual healer who lived nearby. Tomomi had a question for the medicine woman that had been burning inside of her most of her life. "She asked about her mother," said Agnes. "She asked if her mother ever thought about her.

"Tomomi had a lot of sadness about her mother. But the medicine woman told her, 'Your dad doesn't want your mom near you because she abandoned you. But as you live your life, your mom is watching you from the crowd. She still cares about you.'"

Then the medicine woman performed a prayer ceremony to heal Tomomi's pain and bring her spirit back into balance with the rest of the universe, according to the traditional Navajo belief system. This state of harmony is called *hozho* in Navajo, which translates to beauty in English. The *Dine'Be'linå*, or Navajo way of life, is to "walk in beauty"; it is the living path to a happy, healthy and meaningful existence.

"Tomomi just wanted to be happy," said Agnes. "She wanted to find the right path."

Tomomi finally finished the basket. It was about 17 inches in diameter, and the circular shape was slightly lopsided. But the weave was tight and the geometric design in the center was perfect. She would carry it on the plane back to Tokyo to make sure it was not damaged.

On her last morning at the hogan, Tomomi wrote the names of each of Agnes' three children in kanji (Japanese characters) and gave it to them. She told Agnes she would return. And Agnes said she would be waiting.

Before leaving, Tomomi sat on the picnic table in front of the hogan to take in the landscape one last time. The wind blasted and sand stung her face. Fast moving clouds cast shadows that drifted like black puddles across the desert floor. She hurriedly finished the letter to Konomi so she could put it in the mail on her way to the airport.

Part 3: Konomi, here's my plan. On my next trip to America I want to visit the Black Hills of South Dakota and then, after that, Yellowstone in Montana and then the Grand Canyon. I've decided I really want to learn more about various Native American cultures. I want to see buffalo and the Rocky Mountains. There is something about nature here that is so amazing. In Monument Valley I feel like, "I'm alive. I am here, on Earth." If I could see Monument Valley out my kitchen window, then I think I could deal with anything. I'm not really interested in going to New York or LA.

I've also decided that if I get married I'm going to ask the Navajo or the Sioux to perform the ceremony.

I am sending you a dream catcher I bought from a Navajo woman at a stand along the highway. Hang it above your bed to catch bad dreams.

Promise me we will go to Monument Valley together. Save your money for this. I am sending you pictures of Monument Valley. Put them up on your wall to inspire you. More later!

As Tomomi drove out onto the highway, she was upbeat. She now knew where she was going; she would walk in beauty. It was a path that would shape the rest of her life, and the end of her life.

3

The Nation of the Willows

During much of the 19th century, as forced relocations to reservations devastated Native American tribes in the Southwest, the Havasupai existed in a sort of bubble, remaining largely untouched by the intruders thanks to their remote location and small size. In 1864, U.S. Army Col. Kit Carson led 8,000 Navajo on a forced march called the Long Walk from Arizona to a New Mexico reservation. Hundreds died along the way. Also in the 1860s and 1870s, the Hualapai and the Yavapai Apache in north/central Arizona went to war with the U.S. Army and experienced brutal retaliation from a federal government that was intent on getting this unruly part of the West settled once and for all. Unbowed, the Apache and Hualapai had a reputation for raiding wagon trains, stealing cattle and horses, and waging a ruthless, guerilla-style warfare to protect their homeland.

But when 24-year-old anthropologist Frank Cushing descended into the Havasupais' home at the bottom of what was then called Cataract Canyon in June 1881, he discovered a welcoming Shangri La. Cushing was on assignment for the Smithsonian and was one of the first Anglos to visit the tribe in order to document Havasupai culture. He called the tribe "the nation of the willows," and he chronicled his experiences in two lengthy articles for *Atlantic Monthly* magazine that were published in 1882. Cushing wrote that his first glimpse of the canyon bottom "revealed numerous cultivated fields of corn, beans, sunflowers, melons, peaches, apricots, and certain plants used in dyeing and basket making...Everywhere these fields were crossed and re-crossed by a network of irrigating canals and trails."

Cushing went on to describe how his party was taken to the home of a tribal headman. "He welcomed us with jolly cordiality; gorged us with succotash; cleared the principal portion of his hut of women, children, and dogs, for our use; and soon after summoned a council, which kept us blinking, jabbering and smoking until past midnight."[1]

In what was likely one of the first descriptions of Havasu and Mooney Falls in a general audience magazine, Cushing offered this: "It is useless to try to paint these falls, with their crown of perennial verdure, their three hundred feet of crystal glory, their footstools of eternal, circling rainbows, which sink far into the clear green depths of the fathomless pools, or rise on the clouds of mist, and turn to ashes and lime on the leaves of trees around them." Cushing then went on to recount his gravity-defying scramble below Havasu Falls and how he came upon the tribe's sacred burial ground above Mooney Falls where the Havasupai cremated their dead along with burning all the deceased's possessions. He also added that Mooney was the name given by Anglo prospectors and that the Havasupai called the falls "Mother of the Waters," a place the tribe believed "the spirits of...ancestors sometimes float up and down amid the mists and rainbows, or that animistic demons lurk in the green, shadowy depths of the chasm."[2]

The Havasupai world that Cushing witnessed was much the same as it had been for millennia. While the neighboring Navajo and Apache migrated to the Southwest from the northern plains in the 15th century, the Havasupai, who speak a Yuman-based language that is connected to the oldest known dialect in North America, had been in the region for at least 1,000 years.

And for as long as the tribe could remember, their traditional and undisputed home had encompassed almost all of the 280-mile long Grand Canyon, but also hundreds of square miles of upland plateaus south of the canyon. To the Hopi tribe, who had also been in the region for thousands of years, the Havasupai held an honored role as the guardians of Grand Canyon, the place the Hopi said humans first emerged. The Havasupai lived in the home of the Hopi fire god *Ma'sauwu*; it was a most sacred and powerful place. [3]

As for the Havasupai origin story that was told to Cushing and has since been retold in various tribal anthologies, the Havasupai came to the Grand Canyon with instructions to be both farmers and hunters, to live along streams in the summer and on the plateaus in the winter. "Only during the summer do we live in the home of the Mother of Waters," Cushing recounted of the story from the tribe's headman. "But in winter we have to follow the deer with our father, the Coyote, and live only as he does." [4]

Havasupai life revolved around the seasons, around farming and hunting, with knowledge passed from one generation to the next about how to survive in the arid, high desert environment. In winter, small family-centered bands would scatter across the plateau above the canyon and hunt large game like deer and antelope. Hunting also allowed the tribe to obtain deer hides, which the men sewed into exquisite buckskin clothing that was valuable currency and traded throughout the Southwest. The winter uplands not only provided plentiful big game, but also pinon nuts, forage plants, juniper for firewood and snow to melt for water. In summer, the Havasupai relocated to homes in Grand Canyon along reliable water sources to grow corn, squash, beans and fruit. Willow supplied materials for the women to weave water-tight baskets that were also prized and traded throughout the Southwest. Perennial streams in Grand Canyon allowed for irrigation systems that produced enough food to feed the Havasupai during the summer months and extra that could be dried and stored in cliff granaries for access during other times of year. Most families farmed in what is now called Havasu Canyon, but they also occupied drainages throughout Grand Canyon.

"The non-Indian descriptions of [the Havasupai] as a canyon-dwelling people miss the essential character of the Havasupai, who conceive of themselves as a people of space," writes Stephen Hirst in his book *I Am the Grand Canyon.* [5]

While European immigrants brought to the West their notion of home that was tied to one fixed location, home for the Havasupai was not so much about attachment to a place but to a way of life. This seasonal pattern of hunting and farming intimately tied them to the cycles of nature, to the stars, the animals and all that shaped the thousands if not millions of acres that sustained them. Instead of the mechanical Anglo practices of raising fenced-in domestic animals and tilling the land with a plow, the Havasupai relied on spiritual ceremonies, "power songs," and staying in balance with the natural world in order to produce successful hunts and crops.[6] This was Randy Wescogame's ancestry. His father, Billy Wescogame, and mother, Carla Crook, were both from longtime Havasupai families.

Early census rolls taken two decades after Cushing's visit recorded multiple family members with the name Wescogame. Like other Havasupai family names such as Manakaja, Watahomigie, Sinyella, Tilousi and Putsoy, Wescogame was a phonetic English pronunciation used by the census taker who did not speak Havasupai. Others, like Crook (probably after the U.S. Army General George Crook), were names of Anglos whom tribal members encountered in the 1800s. The 1906 census also recorded a 40-year old Havasupai man by the name of Grover Cleveland. [7]

~~~

Even though the Havasupai were not impacted by European immigrants in the early to mid-19th century the way their Native American neighbors were, the tribe was being increasingly invaded by prospectors who thought nothing of setting up shop in the middle of the Havasupais' summer home. So when a military party from Fort Whipple in Prescott was dispatched in June 1881 (just before Cushing's visit) to mark the boundaries of the new Havasupai reservation, the tribe was relieved. They had been told the previous year that President Rutherford B. Hayes had established a reservation for the tribe in Havasu Canyon. The tribe was tired of the prospectors trespassing on their territory. Havasupai Chief Navajo not only welcomed Lt. Col. W.R. Price and his men, but he assisted in deciding where the reservation boundary markers should be placed. A reservation was roped off at the bottom of the canyon that was approximately 12 miles long and five miles wide. [8] It was a mere 518 acres, the smallest reservation in the United States.

The Havasupai thought that clarifying the boundaries of the reservation was the best way to protect their rich agricultural area from intruders. What they did not realize in 1881 was that they were also being asked to live year-round within those boundaries and give up their winter homes and hunting grounds on the plateau. In the coming years, as the Havasupai continued to migrate to the plateau in winter, they experienced increasing conflicts with ranchers who had moved into the area. The new homesteaders were fencing off the grass-rich plateau lands, building cattle tanks at the Havasupais' long-time water sources and allowing livestock to overgraze the tribe's traditional hunting area. Within a decade, the tribe that called itself a "nation of hunters" in its origin story witnessed the disappearance of large game from the plateau and their own banishment from an area that was at the core of their identity.

The Havasupai were not only deprived of meat but also of the buckskins they used for trading. According to one account, "Visitors to the tribe in 1890... reported that instead of dining on deer and antelope, the Indians were eating 'rats and mountain squirrels which they dug from their dens.' The following winter, others noted that because of the scarcity of game, the Havasupai were 'killing and eating their horses and burros.'"[9]

The Havasupais' loss became official and enforceable in 1893 when the U.S. government created the 1.8 million acre Grand Canyon Forest Preserve which banned the tribe from hunting or living anywhere on the Coconino Plateau. "The Grand Canyon of the Colorado River is becoming so renowned for its wonderful and extensive natural gorge scenery and for its open and clean pine woods that it should be preserved for the everlasting pleasure and instruction of our intelligent citizens as well as those of foreign countries," wrote regional forest supervisor W.P. Herman to his superiors in 1898. "Henceforth, I deem it just and necessary to keep the wild and unappreciable Indian from off the Reservation and protect the game."[10] To achieve this, Herman instituted regulations that not only made it illegal for the Havasupai to hunt on the plateau, but also to set foot on the Forest Preserve for any purpose. Because the massive preserve completely surrounded the tiny reservation, the tribe was suddenly, as one government official noted, "prisoners within the [canyon] walls... Two hundred and fifty souls are deprived by law of all contact with the outside world."[11]

Rather than restoring access to the tribe's traditional hunting grounds, the federal government tried to counter the Havasupai plight by teaching them to adopt Anglo agricultural methods. "The introduction of the plow did not meet with as much approval as I had anticipated," lamented Bureau of Indian Affairs instructional farmer John F. Gaddis in an 1892 report. The tribe also shunned the domestic livestock they were encouraged to substitute for wild game. "They will not have them [the goats] nor will they look after them," continued Gaddis.[12]

Starvation, along with epidemics of measles, small pox and influenza—diseases for which Native Americans had no immunity—nearly wiped out the Havasupai completely by the end of the 19th century. Most of the deaths were women and children. Census takers in 1905 counted only 115 tribal members and just 40 women of child-bearing age. This was down from 293 members in 1898 and perhaps one-tenth of the pre-European population.[13]

With the tribe teetering on the brink of extinction, the Havasupai joined other western Native American tribes practicing the Ghost Dance in a desperate attempt to return to the life they knew before Europeans arrived. In 1890 the Havasupai along with their Hualapai neighbors sent representatives on an exploratory mission to meet with the Northern Paiute tribe in central Nevada. There, a prophet named Wovoka was teaching a peaceful practice that involved dancing to summon the dead. This messiah promised not only the return of lost loved ones, but also the restoration of balance to the earth and the exodus of Europeans who would sail back across the ocean. The Lakota took the practice to their starving tribe in North Dakota, which would bring tragic results at Wounded Knee Creek later that year.

The Havasupai began holding their own Ghost Dances led by Chief Navajo and continued the practice for nearly a decade. The tribe quit cremating their dead and buried them at a cemetery above the falls so the bodies could be resurrected. In the winter of 1892-1893, Ghost Dance ceremonies were held on the Coconino Plateau at Sheep Tank and Black Tank. Dances were also held in Havasu Canyon and were observed by Bureau of Indian Affairs representatives in 1900 and 1901.[14] The tribe danced for hours and sometimes days around a pole. Participants climbed the central pole and touched eagle feathers, the "medicine" at the top. Exhausted dancers collapsed and were removed from the circle. But the others continued on, praying, shouting, often hysterically, asking for the return of all that had been taken from them.[15]

The final blow to the Havasupai came in 1919 with the creation of Grand Canyon National Park. Up to that point, tribal members had continued to farm throughout Grand Canyon in riparian areas like Indian Garden and Santa Maria Spring that were outside the reservation. But with the park and its ever-increasing visitors and ranger patrols came a mandate to not only keep the Havasupai off the plateau, but also out of the rest of Grand Canyon. A few years before the park dedication, President Theodore Roosevelt visited the canyon and rode a mule down the Bright Angel Trail. He stopped at what Anglos called Indian Garden, and, with much fanfare, personally informed Billy Burro and other Havasupai families that they would need to move out to make way for the park.

For countless generations, the family of Billy Burro farmed the oasis the Havasupai called "the place below the spruce trees" along the Bright Angel Trail.[16] The Havasupai had created trails throughout Grand Canyon to access their farms and granaries and winter dwelling sites scattered across the plateau. While the others abandoned their summer homes at Indian Garden and relocated to Havasu Canyon, Burro refused. He and his wife Tsoojva stayed in their mud and wood wikiup until 1928 when park rangers physically removed them and tore down their home. Havasupai tribal members recalled that once he was on the South Rim, Burro looked down one last time at "the place below the spruce trees" and cried over what had become of it. He died on the reservation one year later at age 80. Tsoojva died in 1935.[17]

~~~

Over the span of little more than a single generation, the world of the Havasupai had been completely transformed from one that followed long-held traditions and natural cycles to a life that required adapting to a cash economy in order to avoid starvation. In the early 20th century, the best place for the guardians of Grand Canyon to earn money to feed their families was by working low-paying service and construction jobs at the national park. Growing numbers of tourists were arriving by rail and automobile to visit the natural wonder, and they expected the comfortable accommodations the Fred Harvey travel brochures promised. Ancient trails needed to be improved, utility infrastructure built, hotel rooms cleaned and restaurant food cooked. It was back breaking if not soul crushing work, but the steady wages gradually allowed the tribe to move away from the brink of extinction.

Park projects built in the 1920s and 1930s, mainly by crews of Havasupai men, included a suspension bridge across the Colorado River, a sewer line through Grand Canyon Village and a pipeline that pumped spring water from Indian Garden up to the South Rim. Most were temporary, menial jobs, but National Park Service payroll records show that some Havasupai tribal members were involved in more skilled work. Dallas Wescogame worked as a projectionist at Kolb Studio where he showed the Kolb brothers' infamous motion picture about their river trip through Grand Canyon.[18] Jim Crook worked as a "powder man" and was responsible for setting the dynamite blasts used to clear routes for trails and pipelines within the canyon's steep rock walls.[19]

The Havasupai had established a kind of de facto village called Supai Camp on the South Rim that gave tribal members working in the park a home base. Family and extended family also moved into these traditional wikiups to be closer to the breadwinner and other amenities unavailable to them at the bottom of Havasu Canyon. But in 1955 the Park Service deemed Supai Camp in Grand Canyon Village an eyesore. Park officials burned the wikiups to the ground, including all the tribal members' possessions that were inside. The Havasupai were informed that only tribal members who were employed by the park could live within park boundaries, and those individuals had to live in authorized housing they could rent from the Park Service.[20] As for the others, mainly women, children and elderly tribal members, they were driven by the Park Service to Topocoba Hilltop west of Grand Canyon Village and told to hike 14 miles and down 2,300 feet, to their reservation in Havasu Canyon. It was winter and the trail was covered with snow. "Those abandoned at Topocoba were too tough to freeze," writes Stephen Hirst. "They were also too angry to forget."[21]

Meanwhile, the village at the bottom of Havasu Canyon known as Supai was under the management of various federal programs, all aimed at getting Native Americans to be self-sustaining. But crops were often destroyed by floods and little could be grown in winter. The canyon bottom was also stripped of firewood. Unlike the energy-efficient wikiups, poorly constructed government housing was cold in the winter, hot in the summer and filled with mold in the perpetually damp village, which remained cut off from the rest of the world with no utilities or roads. And, yet, an ever-growing stream of Anglo tourists was passing through the village en route to the falls. Missionaries also arrived and attempted to convert tribal members to Christianity, always with the promise of giving them food. One such mission was documented in a 1938 article in *Life* magazine that showed Havasupai member Jim Crook, Randy Wescogame's great grandfather, being baptized at Fifty Foot Falls.[22] Some 68 years later, Randy would invite Tomomi Hanamure to follow him off the trail to see these falls.

Federal policies also required that the tribe's children be sent to boarding schools far from home. Even children as young as six were ripped from their families and placed in an environment that was often not only alien but also abusive. The relentless goal was to get the Havasupai to assimilate with the European American culture and discourage them from using their native language and spiritual practices. According to the federal Indian Relocation Act of 1956, Native Americans of all ages were to be encouraged to move to urban areas and abandon their native land and traditions in order to make a successful life for themselves.

In their cramped quarters at the bottom of Grand Canyon, the Havasupai attempted to farm and remain self-sustaining for several generations, but gradually fields and orchards were replaced by tribal home sites. There was an increasing reliance on store-bought food that was packed in on horses. Havasupai spiritual tradition had long encouraged boys to "run toward the dawn," so they would be fit, strong hunters. But life on the small reservation discouraged physical activity; obesity, which was previously unknown, became common. So did alcoholism. Resentment toward the federal government and Anglos in general was becoming part of the tribe's DNA, now running two to three generations deep.

The waterfalls down canyon from the village that were technically part of the reservation were off limits to the Havasupai during much of the 20th century. Claims under a 19th century mining law allowed miners to live in cabins between Havasu and Mooney Falls, occupying the tribe's "Mother of the Waters." In 1957, the National Park Service bought out the mining claims, fenced off a 62-acre area to separate it from the reservation and established a park-run campground between the falls on the tribe's sacred cremation site. [23]

"Morale was extremely low," writes Stephen Hirst about Supai in the 1950s and 1960s. "Drinking and fighting became rampant in the little canyon village...Suicide, an act almost unknown among the Havasupai, began to occur...Gas and glue sniffing became widespread among young people, and their despairing parents ceased offering them any direction."[24]

Some Havasupai families turned to a cash-driven packing business and competed for tourist dollars, while others had no means of income in the isolated village. The once strongly communal tribe started to split apart, and sometimes children fell through the cracks. In the early 1960s, representatives from Arizona's child welfare department were called to Supai to investigate a young Havasupai boy who had apparently been abandoned by his parents. Billy Wescogame, aged 5 or 6, and the great grandson of Billy Burro, was found living in the bushes by the creek.[25] Billy was removed from the reservation by the state and eventually placed with a foster family in Tempe, Arizona who was already looking after four other Native American foster children. Spanish replaced Havasupai as the language he spoke at home, and Catholicism became his religion.[26] Billy was teased in public school for being Native American and disciplined for his frequent and angry outbursts. Yet, Billy believed he was better off in Anglo culture and shunned the reservation. Soon after dropping out of high school in Tempe, he married an Anglo woman and they had a son named Billy Junior.

But when Billy was 18, his father died and he returned to Supai for the first time in years to attend the funeral.[27] Billy would recall years later that the tribe "seemed really screwed up" to him on that trip, and he was thankful for his upbringing in Tempe.[28] Yet, he also felt the undeniable pull of his ancestry, his language and his traditions. When he was a young man, Billy answered the call. After splitting with his first wife, he abandoned the Anglo world in the city. He moved back to rejoin his tribe in the nation of the willows.

PART II

4

Nature Traveler

Immediately upon returning to Yokohama in January 1998 after her stay in Monument Valley, Tomomi started plotting her next adventure to the United States. It would be an epic road trip across the West that would hit the scenic high points she had been collecting pictures of all her life. Grand Canyon. Yellowstone. Grand Teton. The Black Hills. Devil's Tower. Badlands. That it required she drive long distances across vast, unpopulated country was no deterrent. Nor was the fact that she was planning to visit these places alone, and in the deep of winter. Tomomi wanted to visit America during Japan's most celebrated holidays, Dec. 23—the Emperor's Birthday—and New Year's Day, which was also the time when she could take off more vacation days from work.

"Bokkemon!" said her grandfather Fumitomo when Tomomi told him of her plans. "You have no fear." A slang word from the rural Kagoshima dialect in southern Japan, *bokkemon* was most often used to describe macho men in Japan's Kyushu region who had courage and were not easily intimidated.[1] Fumitomo, a decorated World War II hero, and Tomomi's father, Tetsushi, were both called *bokkemon* by friends and family.

Tetsushi shook his head as Tomomi described at a family gathering how she was going to hike in America's national parks and drive thousands of miles on rural highways. He and Tomomi were visiting Fumitomo at the long-time Hanamure family home in the small village of Takarabe on the island of Kyushu in southern Japan. Tetsushi and his father were from the old school Japanese way of thinking, which was suspicious of outsiders and especially of the West. Neither of them had ever even left the country to go on a vacation. But Tomomi was different. She wanted to see buffalo, towering mountain peaks and the very depths of the Grand Canyon. Tomomi's boyfriend Mako didn't understand her fascination either.

"Wasn't the two weeks she spent sitting in the dirt in Monument Valley enough?" he asked.

But Tomomi felt like she was just getting started on her journey, her walk in beauty. Cousin Konomi was the only family member who shared Tomomi's attraction to America. Except that Konomi was most interested in Elvis and liked to hear Tomomi's stories of walking through the gaudy rooms of Elvis' mansion in Memphis and of visiting jazz clubs in New Orleans. Konomi was also tickled by clothing Tomomi had purchased in Mississippi thrift shops and brought back as gifts. One was a t-shirt given to cousin Sali that said "Baldwin Family Reunion 1995" (on the front); "The family that prays together stays together" (on the back).[2]

Friends and family would recall years later that in middle school Tomomi loved sports and animals. She played basketball, wrote poetry and had pet marmots. Her dream in middle school was to one day marry her boyfriend Hiruta and play on Japan's national women's basketball team. Then in high school, Tomomi became increasingly interested in whatever she could find to read on the American West and Native American culture. Pictures of larger-than-life landscapes like Grand Canyon and Yellowstone fascinated her. Tomomi clipped articles about America from Japanese newspapers and hung them on her bedroom wall. She attended American Indian-related presentations in the Tokyo area. She read books about Native American history that told of how tribes like the Lakota, Navajo and many others were driven from their homeland as part of the economic ambitions of the U.S. government. Soon after graduating from high school in 1990, and with no money for college, Tomomi began to research what it would take to attend English language school in the United States. After saving up enough money, she enrolled in the most affordable option: University of Southern Mississippi.

"I told Tomomi she could learn English in Japan," recalled Tetsushi some 15 years later, laughing at the memory of his daughter's stubbornness.

"She said she wanted to learn English in America."

Four years after completing that ESL (English as a second language) program in the Deep South, Tomomi was a seasoned U.S. traveler. She studied road maps online and pored over guidebooks about western national parks. She also continued her research into Native American history with a special interest in the Plains Indian tribes (especially the Sioux)[3] of Montana, Wyoming and South Dakota. Since high school, *Dances with Wolves* had been Tomomi's favorite movie and she had watched it a dozen times. She also bought a book at the Monument Valley park visitor center called *Stories of the Sioux*, by Luther Standing Bear. Published in 1934 when Standing Bear was in his late 80s, the book is an oral history of tribal stories passed down to Standing Bear, an Oglala Lakota chief, from his parents and grandparents that told of life on the prairie before the Lakota were corralled onto reservations.[4]

On a February day in 1998 Tomomi was reading *Stories of the Sioux* while riding the train to Tokyo to go to work. A couple visiting from Montana named Tim and Lonnie Morin, were sitting across from Tomomi on their way to watch the winter Olympics in Nagano. Surprised to see a Japanese woman reading a book in English about a Native American tribe from his home in Big Sky Country, Tim couldn't resist asking Tomomi about it. Soon after, Tomomi wrote a letter to Konomi describing the encounter and her trip plans for the following year.

Dear Konomi,

It was great to see you at Grandpa's. Seems like us kids have all grown up. I wanted to tell you that I will be going to the States over New Year's. I think I have saved up enough money to stay for several weeks. Also, I just met a couple from America who actually invited me to visit them at their ranch in Montana! I was on the train and reading an English book called Stories of the Sioux. This couple said it was a good book, and next thing I know they are showing me pictures of their ranch. They have a horse named Pearl and said I could ride her if I visited them. Isn't that cool! And they showed me a picture of the Rocky Mountains, which are beautiful, but they said even more beautiful in real life than in the picture. Hard to imagine, isn't it? They live near Yellowstone where there are lots of buffalo. They promised I would

*definitely see buffalo! I can't wait to go. I will bring you something back from
the Sioux. Next time, you must go with me! Anticipation!!*

Years later, Tetsushi would sum up Tomomi's single-minded
determination this way: "When she wanted something, she figured out
how to get it. There was no stopping her."

He would never tell her, but he was proud of his daughter for carrying
on the Hanamure family tradition of being *bokkemon*.

~~~

After flying from Tokyo to Los Angeles and stopping at an Orange
County outlet mall to buy Timberland hiking boots, Tomomi arrived
at the South Rim of Grand Canyon on Dec. 23, 1999, the birthday of
Japan's Emperor Akihito. Tomomi had promised herself that on this most
important Japanese national holiday and on her own birthday, May 8, she
always wanted to be in America, preferably somewhere amazing like the
Grand Canyon.

She spent the night on the lip of the South Rim at Bright Angel Lodge
and watched a gentle snow shower dust the canyon cliffs like a sprinkling
of powdered sugar. On Christmas Eve day, Tomomi descended into the
canyon on the Bright Angel Trail. She was glad she had bought real hiking
boots because the steep path was slippery for the first few miles and
covered with packed snow, mud and patches of mule droppings. As she
walked by herself, smiling at hikers and mule riders passing on their way
up, Tomomi was excited to see deer near the rim and a hawk that rode
thermals overhead.[5] About halfway down she stopped for lunch at Indian
Garden and sat next to the creek where Billy Burro and other Havasupai
tribal members had farmed a century ago. Except for the name Indian
Garden, any obvious signs of Native American history had been erased by
decades of park improvements.

After hiking nearly 10 miles and descending 5,000 feet elevation
through the most rugged landscape she had ever traversed, Tomomi stood
at the bottom of the Grand Canyon. She walked over the steel suspension
bridge that crosses the roaring waters of the Colorado River and into the

shaded respite of Phantom Ranch, a historic and tidy national park lodge where she had scored reservations for two nights in a dormitory style cabin. She would join park visitors from all over the world who had a personal tradition of being at the bottom of Grand Canyon on Christmas. Among the people she quickly befriended was a middle-aged, outdoorsy couple from Tucson named Tim and Luana Nelson.

"My wife had been assigned a top bunk and didn't want that, so Tomomi offered to switch with her," Tim recalled years later. "Tomomi was very pleasant but Luana and I were thinking, 'What is this woman doing down here on Christmas Eve all by herself?'"[6]

The next day, Tomomi joined Tim and Luana on a 12-mile round trip hike on the North Kaibab Trail to Ribbon Falls. Then they gathered in the Phantom Ranch dining hall with all the other guests for a family-style Christmas dinner of turkey and dressing. Afterward, Tomomi played checkers with other guests and attempted to answer their questions using her halting English and ear-to-ear smile. Even though Tomomi could often not find the exact English word to describe what she wanted to say, Phantom Ranch visitors remember how her exuberance transcended the language barrier.[7]

On her way to the bunkhouse that night, Tomomi stood next to the creek and took a long look at the stars. The distant, jagged edge of the South Rim formed a silhouette against an inky sky that sparkled with diamonds. Directly overhead, the Milky Way arched across the heavens from rim to rim and infinitely beyond. In Japanese Shinto tradition, this was so much *kami*. The outdoors was not just beautiful, but also full of animated spirits; the stars, the rocks, the wind, everything in nature possessed unique powers that were once worshiped by the Japanese. But in America, unlike Japan, nature was also so very big—the sky, the canyon, even the friendliness of fellow travelers was massive. For this the Japanese had a special word: *Daishizen*. Great nature.

Tomomi had begun keeping a travel journal and she pulled out the small notebook while lying under the covers on the top bunk. She wrote neatly in English, and probably because she preferred the real America to the textbook version, she made a special effort to drop the letter g at the end of her words and replace it with an apostrophe like the lyrics to a country western song. The English language school she had attended a few years earlier in Hattiesburg, Mississippi had taught her formal grammar, but this was not how Americans she met in the Deep South and everywhere else actually talked. Tomomi wanted to write and live what was real. She wanted the authentic American experience.

Dec. 25, 1999: Hiked to Ribbon Fall with Tim and Luana. Gettin' in to the nature is feelin' great!! I want to live this kind of place.

"As we got to know Tomomi better, we came to understand that she just really had a genuine enthusiasm for the Grand Canyon and seeing other places like that. And she was a very savvy traveler," recalled Tim. "It's not like she set out to hike in the Grand Canyon alone, but she just really wanted to be there and going alone seemed to be the only way for her at the time. When I tried to find out more about what her life was like in Japan, she just said she liked seeing the stars, and that is why she came to Grand Canyon. She said she couldn't see any stars where she lived in Yokohama."

Compared to the countryside in southern Japan that her father roamed as a boy, Tomomi's childhood environment in Yokohama was completely paved and extremely crowded. In the 1970s, the population density of Yokohama was 8,000 people per square kilometer as it grew into a booming Tokyo suburb. The sprawling blocks of high-rise apartments where she and her father lived had no yard; sidewalks, trains, schools and public spaces were all packed with people. Even the school playgrounds were paved. As Japan's economy became the third largest in the world by the late 1970s, the nation had transformed from a poverty-stricken, post-World War II disaster zone to a cosmopolitan super power. Nowhere embodied this change more completely than the shining metropolis of Yokohama, Japan's second largest city. Salarymen wearing identical suits and carrying identical briefcases filled the sidewalks as they walked to their offices in glass towers. New shopping malls were built in what used to be rice paddies. The night sky, along with the old Shinto beliefs about nature, had become largely irrelevant in modern Japan and viewed with nostalgia, if thought about at all.

On the morning of Dec. 26, Tomomi said goodbye to the Nelsons, and the couple made plans to visit her on a vacation to Japan the following summer. Tomomi headed back up the Bright Angel Trail, determined to hike 10 miles and then drive to Las Vegas in a day. Trekking steadily uphill to the top of the canyon was, physically, the hardest thing she had ever done in her life. But hiking mile after breath-taking mile, up and up, felt right to Tomomi. She felt pure, inside and out.

Dec. 26, 1999: Bright Angel Trail. Took 8 hours. My legs hurt. I didn't think I could make it! But I did make it!! I proud by myself.

From Las Vegas, Tomomi hit the highway headed for Yellowstone and then South Dakota. She wanted to spend New Year's Day at the site of the Wounded Knee Massacre, which is, perhaps, the most broken-hearted place in authentic America.

~~~

Like the abundant herds of bison they hunted, the Sioux had roamed the Great Plains for thousands of years, moving their communal teepee camps every few months to be close to water and an abundant food source. They knew how to survive brutal winters and driving winds, but the onslaught of the white man was a blizzard they were not prepared to weather.

In the beginning, these tribes fought the encroachment of Anglo settlers, trappers and miners on their home range that encompassed what is today all of North and South Dakota as well as much of Wyoming, Montana and into Canada. Sioux tribes called Lakota and Oglala Lakota claimed the Dakotas and, especially the Black Hills, an area they considered sacred. Just as they had gone to battle with the Crow and Cheyenne over territory, the Sioux waged war on the wagon trains of white settlers crossing the prairie. In response, the U.S. government pressed the Sioux to sign peace treaties in exchange for promises the various tribes could keep their land if they allowed safe passage for travelers on the Oregon Trail en route to California.

In 1851, the Lakota signed the first of several treaties at Fort Laramie,

Wyoming. This one acknowledged sovereignty of the Lakota over a vast area of the Great Plains and guaranteed that the tribe would retain their homeland without encroachment from white settlers "as long as the river flows and the eagle flies."[8] But the U.S. government did not enforce the restrictions against westward expansion into Lakota and Oglala territory, and thousands of eager sodbusters sought to establish farms on the windswept prairie only to have their homes and livestock raided by the Sioux who considered the Anglos intruders. Sioux chiefs Red Cloud, Sitting Bull and Crazy Horse led the opposition against broken promises by the U.S. government. After a series of bloody "Sioux wars" with the U.S. Cavalry, the federal government and Lakota leaders signed another Fort Laramie Treaty in 1868. The agreement set aside 60 million acres in the Dakotas as the Great Sioux Reservation and exempted the Black Hills from ever being settled by whites.[9]

Yet, just six years later in 1874, a U.S. Army expedition led by General George Armstrong Custer went into the Black Hills on behalf of the U.S. government in search of gold and other natural resources. Custer reported back with lavish descriptions of untapped wealth in the Black Hills—abundant gold to be mined, timber to be harvested, lush streams and land for farming. For the Lakota, however, the Black Hills were the tribe's spiritual stronghold. The 5,000 foot-high granite peaks that shot up from the western Dakota prairie and parched desert badlands harbored numerous sacred sites. They believed the tribe's well-being had long relied on performing ceremonies at these sites as well as drawing sustenance from the area's plants and animals.

But after Custer's widely-publicized report, the Black Hills region was stampeded by settlers who aspired to get rich quick. This earned the white man the name *wasicu,* which literally means in Lakota "takes all the fat." And the federal government did nothing to enforce its promise to keep the Black Hills free of whites.[10] The Lakota, again, fought back and briefly seemed to be winning with their June 1876 victory at the Battle of Little Bighorn where Custer made his infamous "last stand" just before being killed. Nearly 300 of 700 U.S. 7th Cavalry soldiers were killed during the battle along the Little Bighorn River in Montana, just east of what is today Yellowstone National Park. The number of Native American warriors killed during two days of battle was estimated to be only 30 to 60. Stories published in East Coast newspapers about the death of Custer and the U.S. defeat at Little Bighorn fueled a public bias against Plains Indian tribes as "savages." On the eve of the United States' centennial celebration, politicians wondered aloud if the nation's divinely-inspired doctrine of Manifest Destiny was failing.

The United States retaliated by sending 2,500 7th Cavalry soldier reinforcements to the Dakota Territory, and in 1877, the government withdrew nearly 8 million acres of the Black Hills from the Sioux reservation. Federal negotiators then attempted to buy the Black Hills from the Sioux for pennies per acre, but the tribes refused to sell their sacred grounds for any price. In response to the blatant breaking of the Fort Laramie treaties and taking of the Black Hills by the U.S. government, Henry Benjamin Whipple, the Episcopal Bishop for Minnesota, said in an 1877 plea on behalf of the Sioux: "I know of no other instance in history where a great nation has so shamefully violated its oath. Our country must forever bear the disgrace and suffer the retribution of its wrongdoing. Our children's children will tell the sad story in hushed tones, and wonder how their fathers dared so to trample on justice and trifle with God."[11]

In order to accommodate Anglo homesteaders and commercial development of the Black Hills, the Great Sioux reservation was further separated into five smaller reservations in which the Lakota and other tribes were left with only the most arid desert plains and relegated to become wards of the federal government. Like the Havasuapi during that time period, the Sioux were required by U.S. law to stay within the boundaries of their reservation and instructed to support themselves with agriculture, even though the land was impossible to farm and they had no tradition as farmers. And just as the Havasupai were cut off from deer on the Coconino Plateau, the Sioux were also robbed of their primary food source. The buffalo herds that had long been at the center of the tribes' existence were slaughtered to near-extinction by Anglos. While bison once numbered in the tens of millions across the Great Plains, the species was reduced by the end of the 19th century to a single herd of 25 to 30 animals in the preserve of Yellowstone National Park. The government's goal was to force the Plains tribes to the reservations by eliminating the animal that was their life-blood.[12] Shooting sprees that killed bison for sport were carried out by homesteaders, hide merchants, U.S. soldiers and even passengers sticking their rifles out the windows of passing trains.

By 1890 the Sioux, like the Havasupai, felt they had exhausted all their options, both peaceful and otherwise, for protecting against the intruders. In a last ditch effort to recover their sacred lands and hunting grounds, some Lakota tribal members began participating in the Ghost Dance movement. Several hundred Lakota left the Pine Ridge and Rosebud reservations in December 1890 to hold a multi-day Ghost Dance ceremony at Stronghold Table in what is today Badlands National Park. Word about the ghost dancing "cult" made some U.S. government officials paranoid that the Lakota would rebel and cause trouble for white settlers and business interests in the Dakota Territories. Responding as if the Ghost Dance was the equivalent of an act of war, the U.S. Army dispatched approximately 200 7th Cavalry soldiers equipped with rifles as well as four Hotchkiss machine guns to break up the ghost dancing activities.

On the morning of Dec. 29, 1890, the Lakota were camped along Wounded Knee Creek after the dance. The Cavalry entered the camp with the intention of confiscating the Indians' rifles and dispersing the group. A skirmish with a deaf Lakota man caused a rifle to be discharged into the air. The tense U.S. soldiers erupted into attack mode, and the machine guns were fired indiscriminately on the mostly unarmed campers. An estimated 250 Lakota men, women and children were killed.[13]

Snow fell on the dead bodies scattered across the field and journalists documented the slaughter—frozen corpses of old women, young children, many shot in the back as they ran. In order to avoid further negative publicity about the incident, Army soldiers dug a 12-foot deep pit at the site and buried the bodies in a mass grave. Word of what happened at Wounded Knee traveled through Native American tribes in the West as quickly and lethally as smallpox. It brought an anger and hopelessness that infected reservation life.

At least the Plains Indians who fought in the Sioux wars knew what was lost and why they were angry. Their descendants would have the same anger but with no memory to anchor it, so the rage and despair would wildly thrash about, like an unmoored ship in a storm. Alcohol would be used to temper the despair, but it would more often just fuel the rage and lead to a slow death, a kind of spiritual starvation.

~~~

By Dec. 28, 1999, two days of hard driving brought Tomomi to the foot of the Grand Teton. The Rockies, as Tim and Lonnie Morin had promised, were far more spectacular than any of the most beautiful photographs she had ever seen. As she approached the mountain skyline on US 89, the jagged granite spires shot straight up 7,000 feet from the sagebrush prairie. It was late afternoon, and the low-slung winter sun bathed the grassy fields in gold, while the snow-covered mountains radiated in pastel hues of pink and lavender. Near the pointed summits, where wind had swept the rock clean, exposed, granite crags shimmered silver. Even though she knew her photographs wouldn't capture the majesty of the scene, Tomomi kept pulling over to the side of the road every 10 minutes to take another picture of the Tetons at sunset. She pulled into Jackson Hole just before dark when there was still enough daylight to gawk at the entrance to Jackson Park—a giant arch made of elk antlers. She spent the night at The Hostel in Teton Village. The rustic hotel was packed with ski bums looking for a cheap place to crash close to the slopes. During her travels, Tomomi always stayed in cheap hotels because she thought it was safer than camping.

Tomomi left Jackson Hole early the next morning, driving north on US 287 and around Grand Teton National Park toward Yellowstone. She discovered that most roads were closed in Yellowstone for winter, but she could enter the park from the north entrance at Gardner, Montana. A sign along the highway near the Montana border warned: "chains required." She did not know what this meant since learning how to drive in snow was not part of her English education in Mississippi or part of her life in Japan.

Seeing the Rockies glimmering white was mesmerizing. Tomomi thought it was like a dream as big white flakes, steadily increasing in size and number, began to float in front of the windshield. Soon the snow was sticking to the highway. Maybe it was partly because she was looking out into the meadows for wildlife, but Tomomi's rental sedan slid off the road and went bumper first into a frozen embankment. She was stuck. It was late afternoon, maybe 15 degrees, and the snow kept coming down. Montana locals know you never drive anywhere in winter without a sleeping bag in your truck, along with extra jackets and a full gas can in case of the unexpected. Motorists who are stranded in winter on these windswept plains freeze to death. By the time the State Highway Patrol shows up it is often too late.

But Tomomi always seemed to get lucky. Within 10 minutes of sitting there in the snowstorm wondering what to do, two Good Samaritans appeared. The Montana ranchers wasted no time in fetching a tow strap from the back of their truck, which they hooked to the car bumper and pulled the lightweight sedan back onto the road.

"Where is this woman headed in this storm?" they wondered.

Tomomi beamed with gratitude, but she did not stick around to chat. What had she learned? Drive slowly in the snow. And, compared to the more reserved Japanese culture, Americans were just so friendly, outgoing and helpful.

Dec. 29: When I was drivin' to Yellowstone, I slipped and couldn't move my car. But two cowboys came to rescue me!! Thank you!

Dec. 30: Yellowstone N.P. I saw wild Buffalos. They're huge!! They're cool!! Got more snow today.

Tomomi wondered how she could convey to Konomi the astonishing size of the American bison. So she decided to take a picture of a buffalo turd with her foot next to it for scale. Somewhere along the highway where buffalo were grazing, she pulled over and walked within 20 feet of the bulls. In the mud was a round turd as big as a dinner plate. She put her Timberland hiking boot (women's size 6) next to it and snapped a few photos. Then she smiled at the buffalo and ran back to the car, bracing against a bone-chilling wind.

Tim and Lonnie Morin were away for the holidays, so Tomomi did not linger in Yellowstone. She wanted to keep moving on to South Dakota and, more than anything, she wanted to spend New Year's Day at Wounded Knee. On New Year's Eve day, she cruised along I-90, leaving the Rockies in the rearview mirror and descending into the vast prairie of the Dakotas. The view was so big from the highway that Tomomi could see the curve of the Earth. The land went on forever. So much wide open space was soothing, like taking a long, deep breath.

Tomomi pulled into Mount Rushmore National Memorial around 3 p.m., when the last of that day's tour buses were unloading in the parking lot. The national park located in the heart of the Black Hills features the faces of George Washington, Thomas Jefferson, Abraham Lincoln and Theodore Roosevelt carved into a granite cliff face. Tour groups, including a bus full of Japanese, slowly filed through the visitor center and up the paved ramp toward the iconic stone monument. Tomomi rushed around them, especially avoiding the Japanese group, as the tour leader spoke through a megaphone and people snapped pictures.

Dedicated as a national memorial in 1936, the "colossal statues," as the Park Service describes them on its website, are intended to be a "shrine to democracy."[14] Tomomi stopped and read the bronze plaque written in 1934 by William Andrew Burkett and located on a balcony overlooking the grandiose tribute to America's political giants:

"Almighty God, from this pulpit of stone the American people render thanksgiving and praise for the new era of civilization brought forth upon this continent. Centuries of tyrannical oppression sent to these shores, God-fearing men to seek in freedom the guidance of the benevolent hand in the progress toward wisdom, goodness toward men, and piety toward God... Holding no fear of the economic and political, chaotic clouds hovering over the earth, the consecrated Americans dedicate this nation before God, to exalt righteousness and to maintain mankind's constituted liberties so long as the earth shall endure."[15]

The American history that is missing from the guided tours or park displays at Mount Rushmore is the fact that the mountain on which the statues are carved was stolen from the Lakota and turned over to prospectors and homesteaders who sought to mine the Black Hills' riches. It is a history that flies in the face of the democratic ideals Mount Rushmore sets in stone. This injustice was formally recognized in 1980 when the U.S. Supreme Court ruled that the Black Hills, including Mount Rushmore and Badlands National Park, were taken illegally from the Lakota in 1877 in violation of the Fifth Amendment and treaties that the U.S. had signed with the Native American tribes. The court settlement awarded $106 million in damages to nine Sioux tribes. But the poverty-stricken tribes have so far refused to accept the money and insist, instead, that their sacred lands be returned.[16]

While Tomomi had taken dozens of photos of buffalo and the Great Plains on her drive through South Dakota, she snapped just one obligatory photograph of Mount Rushmore. It was something in which she was just not that interested. But she figured the visitor center would be a good place to ask for directions to Wounded Knee, which was a National Historic Landmark.[17]

"Why would you want to go there?" an interpretive ranger asked, incredulous.

Tomomi couldn't explain why, but the ranger was not going to change her mind. She knew the history of the place and that was a draw for her, not a deterrent like it was for most tourists.

While about 3 million people a year visit Mount Rushmore, maybe only a few thousand (no one is there to count) visit Wounded Knee. The two national memorials are 130 miles apart but in two completely different worlds. One is a highlight on the tour bus circuit and has every national park amenity, including a museum, paved interpretive trails, dramatic night lighting, a snack bar and even a fake Sioux village.

Wounded Knee National Historic Site is a cement marker in a field somewhere off secondary roads on the Pine Ridge Reservation. Home of the Lakota, Pine Ridge has 28,000 residents, 50 percent of whom live below the federal poverty level. It is the poorest reservation in the United States, and Shannon County where the reservation is located has the lowest per capita income in the country.[18] Violent crime, especially gang-related, is common as are alcoholism and diabetes. One in four babies born on Pine Ridge has fetal alcohol syndrome. The average life expectancy for a male tribal member on Pine Ridge is 47 years; for women it is 52—which is about the same as in Somalia.[19]

Spending New Year's Eve alone in her room at the Kings X Lodge in Rapid City, Tomomi performed a nightly ritual to document her travels. She took her stuffed teddy bear that she had brought from her bedroom in Yokohama and put it on the motel bed. The bedspread was a printed quilt design of feathers and Native American shields, and the headboard was made from lodgepole pine. Tomomi positioned Teddy so he was sitting up against the headboard and surrounded by South Dakota travel brochures that she had picked up that day at Mount Rushmore and Devil's Tower National Monument. She knew that once she was back in Japan, she would look at this photo to fondly remember this night and this place. *"So sweet by myself."* Sometimes on the road she would also photograph Teddy in the car's passenger seat as she was *"just drivin'"* across the mountains and prairies.

On New Year's Day, Tomomi rang in the new millennium lost in a maze of unsigned, rutted roads on the Pine Ridge reservation. Teddy rode shotgun. While there was a sign for Wounded Knee Memorial posted on South Dakota 27, once she turned onto the reservation roads, the signs vanished, as did any gas stations, stores or other open place where she could ask for directions. She drove up and down, past trailers with tires on the metal roofs to keep them from blowing away. Abandoned cars sat in fields, and trash was piled high outside the windows where it had been tossed. Many houses were boarded up and had been spray painted with gang graffiti. Drifting against fences and all along the roadside was a flotsam of empty beer cans.[20]

Tomomi easily looked like she could be Lakota or from another Plains Indian tribe like the Navajo that had crossed the Bering land bridge from Asia around 9,000-11,000 BC. But as Pine Ridge residents noticed her driving up and down the same muddy roads several times, they did not smile or wave. The California plates—and perhaps Teddy in the passenger seat—gave her away as not from there. On this day she was not getting lucky. Maybe it was just too cold, she thought, or were the people she passed along the road unfriendly? Tomomi decided to drive all the way back to Mount Rushmore to find someone who could give her better directions.

Jan. 1, 2000: Mount Rushmore again. I tried to go to Wounded Knee Massacre but I lost the way and couldn't get there.

Tomomi was determined to get to Wounded Knee the next day. She had to. It was like the compulsion to return to Agnes Gray's hogan in Monument Valley. She felt that something special was waiting for her there.

5
Dad

My desire to become a journalist was a seed that was planted early. And it was watered every time I listened to my father tell a story. One of my first memories is of lying in the "way back" of our Rambler station wagon in the early 1960s, looking up at the blue sky through the rear window, and asking Dad an endless stream of questions, coaxing a fantastical story from him as he drove.

"Can clouds talk?" I might ask.

"Well, that depends if there is a wizard nearby who can fly," Dad might say.

And the yarn would spin on from there as I lobbed increasingly outrageous questions to Dad and he responded without pause, incorporating the answer into the next twist of the tale. The volley between his expansive imagination and mine would amuse the entire family. It seemed there was no limit to the possibilities and no question Dad would not answer. My older sister Elizabeth, sitting in the middle seat, would finally look up from her book and laugh while my little sister Maria, lying next to me in the way back, would giggle and ask nonsensical follow up questions.

"What a story!" Mom would often exclaim from the passenger's seat to cap off another well-told tale. She was not a storyteller like Dad but she was always an enthusiastic listener.

This is how we passed the time on the two-hour drive from where we lived in Houston, Texas to visit Dad's family in Galveston where he grew up. There were also stories during dinner and before bed. Sometimes they were purely imagined tales inspired by my silly scenarios, but there were also often repeated true stories rooted in family history that illustrated how fortunate we were.

Dad's grandfather, Philip McGivney, had survived the Great Famine in Ireland while more than 1 million others perished.[1] He immigrated as a child in the 1850s to New Orleans from Cavan County, Ireland, one of the hardest hit regions during the potato blight. Dad's father, Felix McGivney, was orphaned, raised by his older siblings, and had no formal education. He moved as a young man from New Orleans to Galveston in 1900 to help build a sea wall after the island was devastated by the Great Galveston Hurricane.[2] In 1901, amid the destruction and disease that followed one of the deadliest hurricanes in history, he met my grandmother and married her. And, now, after all that poverty and hardship, here we were, living the high life in booming Houston.

"Isn't that something!" Dad would always exclaim after a good luck tale.

There was the story of how math saved Dad's life. When he was drafted into the Air Force during World War II, his knowledge of basic college math allowed him to get a job teaching pilots how to calculate where to drop the bombs on Germany and Japan. He was not naturally inclined toward numbers, but it was math, he told my sisters and me as we agonized over our homework, that kept him from having to go into battle where he would have surely been killed.

And then, there was the story of how Dad rescued Mom. After going to the University of Texas medical school on the GI bill following WWII, Dad was doing his residency in Houston. He was also an amateur tennis champion and, still unmarried at 38, an eligible bachelor. He was dashingly handsome: tall and broad shouldered, with jet black hair, hazel eyes and a strong chin. Before the war, he had dreamed of becoming a journalist, to make a living telling stories, but his mother convinced him he should pursue something with better pay and more prestige. Meanwhile, Mom's first husband, an accomplished psychiatrist, had left her for another woman.

Mom was an only child who grew up in a small Illinois farming town.

Her mother gardened, canned, and hosted ladies' bridge parties in their modest but spotless home. Mom's father worked as a manager in the town's only department store, and he liked to play golf on the weekends at the local country club. Although it was common during that era for women to get married right after graduating high school, Mom's parents wanted to improve their daughter's prospects by sending her to college.

By 1950, Mom had earned a master's degree in psychology from Penn State. With eyes so blue they were almost turquoise and an hourglass figure that caught the attention of every man when she entered a room, Mom could have gotten by on just her looks, Dad said, but she had greater ambitions. After her husband abandoned her, Mom got a job as one of the first child psychologists for the Houston public school system. But when Elizabeth was a toddler, Mom was struggling to make ends meet in a culture that looked down on divorced women.

"She and Elizabeth were all alone," Dad said, pausing for emphasis. Then, as luck would have it, Mom and Dad's dentist set them up on a blind date. Not long after, "Elizabeth asked me, 'Would I be her father?'" was how Dad told it. And Dad said he would.

"Now, isn't that something!" Dad remarked in the re-telling, his voice elevated by excitement and a broad smile.

My parents got married in 1960, and they set up medical offices next to each other in the Hermann Professional Building. Fed by a steady flow of oil profits, Houston was thriving, and that prosperity produced shining new urban icons including NASA, the Astrodome and the Texas Medical Center. I was born in 1961 and named after my father's mother. My sister, Maria, came along in 1963. I had my father's hazel eyes, dark hair and tall, lean build; Maria favored my mother with dreamy blue eyes and light brown hair. Elizabeth, five years my senior, had Mom's heart-shaped face but the dark brown eyes of her phantom father, whom Mom never uttered a single word about. Maria and I took ballet lessons and went to Catholic pre-school. Elizabeth got involved in theater and played Brigitta von Trap in *The Sound of Music*.

Shortly after Maria was born, we moved into a bigger house near the Texas Medical Center that was perhaps more fitting for a successful doctor who worked in the Hermann Professional Building. The house had two very long halls, a "play room" where we kept all our toys, and a fenced backyard with a patio that was shaded by a large mimosa tree. But this house was located at the intersection of two streets that were becoming increasingly busy as Houston grew into one of the largest cities in the United States. Between 1950 and 1970 Houston's population would more than double to reach 1.2 million.[3] The traffic made it too dangerous for my sisters and me to play in the front yard or to even ride our bikes in the driveway because we might accidentally roll into the street. So we rode in circles around the patio and mostly played indoors, pushing our Barbies in their orange convertible down the long hallways and building houses out of Lincoln Logs in the playroom as a steady stream of cars could be heard roaring by just outside the window. A city bus stop was even placed in the far corner of our front yard.

When Dad came home from work, I would run up and jump in his lap, eager to show him a picture I had drawn that day in pre-school or a story I had written. "Oh my, this is wonderful, honey!" he would exclaim. "You have certainly inherited the McGivney story-telling gene!"

Mom and Dad sometimes hosted lavish cocktail parties in the new house and hired a bartender who wore a black tuxedo to serve the drinks. On the weekends, Mom took sewing lessons, and Dad played in tennis tournaments at country clubs. Most of Mom's clothes came from Neiman Marcus. Like the many striving, white, upper-middle class families in Houston at the time, we had African-American "help" who cooked and cleaned and cared for us when Mom was working or taking her lessons. Our housekeeper's name was Laura Overshone and she called me her "baby."

I don't remember Mom holding me, or feeding me, or singing to me when I was little. Instead it was Laura, cradling me in her arms as I drank a bottle or pushing me in a stroller down the sidewalk while I gazed up at the trees overhead. She told me that "the boogeyman" lived high in the branches.

"I don't see any boogeyman," I would say, fascinated and a little scared.

"Child, don't you know anything! He only comes out at night," she would reply matter-of-factly.

~~~

Dad had two older brothers, John and Merlin, and an older sister, Estelle. They all lived in Galveston, along with Dad's parents. Dad was the baby of the family by a long shot, 14 years younger than John, the second youngest sibling. He was an accident, born in 1919 when his mother was 40. The good thing about this, he said, was he got a lot of attention from his mother. Uncle John was also a physician and became a renowned specialist in proctology. Merlin was a dentist. And Estelle married a doctor. The college educations and careers of Dad and his siblings were remarkable considering their father never attended school and supported his family by working as a longshoreman unloading cargo ships at the Port of Galveston. They grew up as working-class Irish Catholics on the lowest rungs of Anglo society,[4] but my grandmother was "a snob for no reason," according to Estelle's daughter Ann. Estelle and Ann lived with my grandparents for a few years when Dad was a teenager and Ann was a little girl. Ann recalled many years later that Grandma McGivney, who, like her husband, was descended from peasant Irish potato farmers, longed to be part of Galveston's wealthy aristocracy instead of a longshoreman's wife. She pushed her children to achieve the social status and material wealth that she would never have. "She was horrible to your father," Ann said, "just pushing him around all the time." And Ann noted that Grandma also spent a lot of time sitting on the front porch sipping whiskey.

When I was young, we made the pilgrimage to Galveston every Thanksgiving and Christmas. Uncle John and his wife Beth always hosted the McGivney clan in their palatial home. My sisters and I were decades younger than a few other cousins and, like my parents, seemed to have absolutely nothing in common with anyone there. Aunt Beth, along with her grown daughter Bibby and her visiting mother, Mrs. Wagner, all dressed as if they never planned to leave the house. They wore floral print muumuu dresses and gold house slippers that I had only seen on the TV show, *I Dream of Jeannie*.

By then, Uncle John had likely reached the epitome of his mother's aspirations for her children. He was one of the wealthiest doctors in Galveston. He was a member of the elite Artillery Club where Bibby had been presented as a debutante. He owned a second home along Galveston

Bay, and he served on the boards of numerous charities. Uncle John would often grill Dad about how things were going with his practice in Houston and give Dad advice on how he, too, could climb the ladder of high society.

While Elizabeth chose to sit with the adults as they visited before dinner, Maria and I roamed freely, sneaking from room to room in the large house. Bibby, who would later be diagnosed with schizophrenia, lived upstairs. In Uncle John and Aunt Beth's downstairs bedroom, there were twin beds that could be elevated under the head or feet. And two televisions were mounted high on the walls, just like in a hospital, for optimal viewing from bed. John and Beth each had their own bathrooms where the counters were covered with pill bottles. In the study, a special instrument invented by Uncle John that revolutionized hemorrhoid surgery hung on the wall.[5] It was gold plated and encased in glass. Maria and I stood in front of it, mesmerized, as we tried to imagine how the instrument might be used.

Visits to Uncle John's involved a lot of alcohol. Liquor bottles lined the wet bar and ice buckets with tongs were strategically placed in the living areas. Before, during and after dinner, all the adults had a drink in their hands. Eventually, after hours of drinking and talking and eating, it would be time for Aunt Beth to play the organ in the formal living room. With her gold slippers dancing over the organ pedals, and her hands pounding on the keys, Catholic hymns were belted out in slurred words. Sometimes Aunt Beth would cry as she sang.

After Uncle John's, we would visit Dad's parents who lived in a small, dilapidated house on the poor side of town. Grandpa McGivney was always sitting on a donut cushion and three feet away from the TV, which was turned up loud. They called Dad "Junior" since he was named after his father. Grandma McGivney would offer my sisters and me old candy from dusty tins on top of the piano. And she would inevitably point to the round dining room table with a dark stain in the middle of it. "This is where Junior was born!"

If our Galveston visit fell on the weekend, we would also go to Catholic Mass with Aunt Beth, Uncle John and Bibby. Whether is it was in Galveston or Houston, Mass specifically, and being Catholic in general, was a very serious affair. My sisters and I learned that punishment was certain and often extreme for anyone on the wrong side of the law. For example, the only way Dad could have married Mom and saved her was if she converted to Catholicism. And one time, when I wet my pants during Mass, causing enough of a stir that the woman in the pew in front of me turned around and looked, Dad immediately yanked me up and hauled me outside. He smacked my bottom while we stood on the front steps of the church as punishment for interrupting Mass. After Dad took Communion, he would always rush back to the pew, stone faced, to pray, sometimes pushing others out of the way if they were walking too slowly. The only person more serious during Communion than Dad was Aunt Beth, who would cry as she walked back to the pew, dabbing at her eyes with a handkerchief. Staring up at the giant crucifix above the altar, I thought maybe Aunt Beth felt bad about what happened to Jesus, the way nails were driven into his feet and hands and blood dripped from the crown of thorns on his head. Or maybe she felt bad about her sins, and Dad felt bad about his. I wondered what their sins were.

As for me, my sins were always the same. During our family's monthly visits to Confession before church, I would go into the wooden booth, close the door, kneel down and whisper to the priest on the other side of the dark screen. "Bless me Father for I have sinned. It has been one month since my last confession… I have been mean to my sisters. I have been selfish. And I have done things that made my father mad."

~~~

In 1965, when I was four, the good luck tale of our fortunate family took a dark turn. The story from Dad—and this one did not have a good ending—was that Mom, then 39, had a "nervous breakdown." (The actual medical diagnosis was more likely severe depression.) To calm Mom's nerves, she received electric shock treatments and took Valium, considered a new miracle drug at the time, especially for women.[6] She was also plagued by migraines that caused her to spend much of the day shuttered in her dark bedroom. On the bright side, Mom's illness meant that our housekeeper, Laura, stayed longer during the day and did not leave until she had made dinner for my sisters and me.

"Can I go with you?" I would plead as she gathered her gloves and hat and shoved her apron into her purse.

"Oh, my baby!" she would say, kissing me on the cheek. "You need to stay here and help your momma."

After Laura walked out the front door, I would climb on top of the fancy, gold-embroidered couch in the formal living room and press my face against the window. I would watch her stand with the other hired help at the bus stop in our front yard. Sometimes she would wave at me. I would not leave until the bus pulled up and took her away.

When Mom was in the hospital for the electric shock treatments, she disappeared for what seemed an eternity to my sisters and me. And when she returned, she floated silently about the house like a ghost, always in her quilted blue housecoat and with a blank look on her face. Sometimes Dad would brighten the mood by taking us places on the weekends, like the zoo or the country club tennis courts. One time he was hired as the doctor for the Ringling Brothers Circus that was in town at the Astrodome. I got to accompany Dad when he made the rounds through the circus living quarters in the stadium parking lot. As always, the patients would remark how I looked just like Dad and how fortunate he was to have his "little helper" along. That made me beam with pride. And whenever I did the rounds with Dad, we conferred after the patient visits on the most probable medical diagnoses. The lion tamer did not have indigestion, he suspected, but heart disease, likely caused by work-related stress. A clown suffered from depression; his wife, also a clown, had diabetes and a drinking problem.

I agreed, noting that maybe being a clown was harder than it looked.

"Isn't that something!" Dad would exclaim, marveling at the irony that life can bring.

But the space between the happy times and Dad's upbeat stories became farther apart. There were no more cocktail parties. Mom stopped her lessons. And something crazy was always around the corner, like Dad slamming his fist against a cabinet of glasses. Things could change in an instant. One minute, Dad would be laughing and hugging us. The next minute, boom! My sisters and I were on our knees cleaning up broken glass.

In kindergarten, I made a storybook with a few words and big crayon pictures called "Dad's Trip to Mars." It was a simple tale that involved Dad building a space ship and going to Mars. When Dad arrived, he met a purple Martian and pulled out his belt. Since there was no gravity, the Martian's hair and shoelaces floated in the air, but weightlessness was no match for the belt. Dad spanked the Martian, made the Martian cry big, weightless tears that floated into the atmosphere, and then Dad went back to Earth.

Tension in our house was like smoke from a kitchen fire — sucking up air with no open windows to escape. But just as suddenly as it arrived, the smoke choking our family would clear and there would be no memory of the fire that caused it. My sisters and I went back to playing Barbies, Dad resumed reading his newspaper and drinking his martini, and Mom retreated to her dark bedroom with an ice pack on her head.

My other grandmother, who visited from Illinois when Mom was in the hospital, would often shake her head, bite her lower lip, and say Dad had a "bad Irish temper." I was told I also had a temper, and I frequently got in trouble at school for fighting. Between the ages of three and six, I often wet the bed. And I failed first grade because I could not read; I could not track the words from left to right.

At night, I had trouble falling asleep, especially when I could hear my parents yelling behind their closed bedroom door at the other end of the long hall. So I would sit in the dark in my rocking chair, going back and forth, finding comfort in the motion and creaking of the wood. I was worried that the boogeyman who lived in the mimosa tree in our backyard could be roaming about. I figured it was safer to stay awake because he might come into the house, and Laura was not there to protect me.

When my parents' shouting got louder, I rocked harder to make their voices go away. I could rock for hours. And if I rocked with the right kind of rhythm, the creaking sounded like a lullaby.

6

Child of Supai

The village of Supai that Billy Wescogame returned to in the 1980s was very different from the place he was removed from as a young child in the 1960s. Tourists passing through Supai annually to see Havasu Falls had increased from fewer than 1,000 in 1965 to 10,000 two decades later. The size of the tribe had also more than doubled in two decades to nearly 500 people crammed onto a seven-block area in the narrow canyon.[1]

Compared to the near-starvation that tribal members experienced in the early 20th century, some aspects of reservation life had improved significantly for the Havasupai. In 1975, President Gerald Ford signed into law the Grand Canyon Expansion Act, which increased the size of Grand Canyon National Park to 1.2 million acres. But most importantly for the Havasupai, it returned 185,000 acres of Coconino Plateau lands to the tribe.[2] It was the largest return of tribal lands in U.S. history.

The struggle to regain some of their lost plateau lands had been dragging on for six decades and the tribe's efforts to petition lawmakers in Washington D.C. were repeatedly thwarted by the National Park Service as well as environmental groups. Park officials and environmentalists argued the return of Havasupai lands could lead to development that would threaten the beauty and solitude of Grand Canyon. This battle only deepened the resentment the tribe held for the federal government and the Park Service.

In the early 1970s, a delegation of tribal members journeyed to Washington D.C. to lobby lawmakers to support Arizona Senator Barry Goldwater's proposal for increasing the size of the Havasupai reservation. One delegation member was Ethel Jack, then in her 60s, who was the granddaughter of Billy Burro. Jack talked of how she remembered visiting her grandfather's longtime summer home at Indian Garden before he was evicted. Havasupai tribal chairman Lee Marshall was also on hand to counter what the Park Service and environmental groups like the Sierra Club were telling Congress.

"The Park says they want to save the environment and archaeological places," stated Marshall during a 1973 hearing before Congress.[3] "They're not talking right. We have homes and burial grounds on the [plateau] lands. If the Park Service chases us off they will destroy everything that was ours and wipe out all trace of our people. If you think we lie ask the Park Service what they did to our old homes at Grand Canyon in 1934...Ask them what they did to our burial ground below Havasu Falls. That's how they protect things." Marshall also pointed out the hypocrisy of the National Park Service's extensive plans for resort-scale developments on the South Rim in Grand Canyon Village while the agency was simultaneously raising concerns about how the Havasupai tribe might not be good environmental stewards of any land returned to them.

"The National Park Service has to learn to be like Indians about the land before they understand the secret of saving the earth. We will be glad to teach them," added Marshall defiantly.

Ultimately, the tribe prevailed. The National Park Service also relinquished management of the campground below Havasu Falls to the tribe with the condition that the area stayed open to visitors. This was part of the Indian Self Determination Act, which Ford also signed in 1975. The law was aimed at giving Native Americans control over their law enforcement, tribal court proceedings, social and educational services, as well as providing support for tribes to develop their own sources of economic development.

In the 1970s, the Havasupai established their own K-8 elementary school in Supai, eliminating the need to send young children away to boarding school. Indian Health Services improved and expanded the clinic in the village, and Bureau of Indian Affairs created a locally-run law enforcement operation that included a jail as well as a tribal court. In order to grow its tourism business, the tribe built the 25-room Havasupai Lodge, the Havasupai Tribal Café, the Havasupai General Store and the Havasupai Tourism Enterprise that provided guided trips and mule packing services to visitors. Unlike other Native American tribes, such as the neighboring Hualapai that contracted with Anglo-owned corporations to run their businesses, the Havasupai resolved they would do it themselves, their way.

Utilities infrastructure also came to Supai in the 1970s. Federal programs financed the construction of electrical lines and generators as well as water and sewage treatment facilities. Yet other aspects of village life did not change. The only access to the village was still by trail (or helicopter) and it remained isolated with no grocery stores (except for the over-priced general store), no outside phone service, no trash collection and no fire department. But by the late 1980s, satellite TV had arrived in Supai. While the infrastructure for cable television was impossible to install in the village, the new lightweight TV dishes were packed down by mule, affixed to rooftops and honed in on the satellites tracking high over Grand Canyon. Tribal members still could not buy fresh produce or have their children attend high school in the village, but they could access thousands of TV shows.

And so, the two streams flowing through Supai deepened in their channels while also feeding off each other. The increasing numbers of tourists who passed through the village dropped cash at the café, lodge and store, but then they continued on to the falls without penetrating the veil behind which tribal members lived. The Havasupai took the cash, as well as government subsidies, to escape the village and rent motel rooms in Kingman 100 miles away where they shopped for food and supplies. The cash was also used to buy alcohol and marijuana from village bootleggers, which, along with tourism and government jobs, had grown to be a thriving industry in Supai.

This modern lifestyle took a toll on health and by 1990 nearly half of the adults living in the village had Type 2 diabetes. They enlisted the help of anthropologist John Martin, a friend of the tribe, who had spent an extended period in Supai during the 1960s working on his doctoral thesis. He went on to become a professor at Arizona State University. Martin teamed up with a colleague at the University of Arizona, Therese Markow, who was nationally renowned for her ground-breaking research in genetics. In 1990, Martin and Markow told the tribe they wanted to research possible genetic causes for diabetes in the tribe and hopefully this would enable them to discover ways to stop the disease. Some 120 tribal members gladly agreed to participate in the study and from 1990 to 1994 they provided more than 400 blood samples to the researchers who ferried the specimens from the Supai Clinic to university labs in Phoenix and Tucson.[4]

While the expansion of the reservation and return of some of the tribe's ancestral plateau lands were huge moral victories for the Havasupai, on a practical level, these did not change their day-to-day living situation much. Most tribal members did not have the funds or the motivation to build a home on the vast, undeveloped plateau. Even though the village at the bottom of Grand Canyon was dark and cold in the winter and crowded with tourists in the summer, it had become what tribal members were used to. There was electricity, social services, employment and non-stop TV.

But Billy did not return to Supai to watch TV. He was there to connect with his traditional roots. He retaught himself the Havasupai language and started attending the tribal sweat lodge ceremonies by the creek. He took a job as the police officer for the village after completing training with the U.S. Indian Police Academy in Phoenix. Armed with a high school education, which many tribal members did not have, and a professional certification, Billy expected that he would not only better himself but also bring improvements to the village.

Billy took enforcing the laws in Supai very seriously, even though he was doing it all by himself. "Sometimes I'd go out on a gun call and I'd have to break up a big party," he said years later. "I would put 15 kids on one long chain and march them all the way back to the jail."[5]

In the late 1980s Billy hooked up with tribal member Carla Crook and soon they had three children. Randy was born in 1988; they gave him the middle name Redtail, which means friend in the Havasupai tradition.[6] In 1989 Ambrose, a boy, was born, and in 1991, Brianna, a girl, came along. In February 1993, Carla and Billy made their union official and got married in Havasupai Tribal Court.

After enduring much adversity in his life, it seemed that by the time he had reached his early 30s, Billy's luck was finally changing. He was back with his tribe and speaking Havasupai to his children. He had a stable family and job.

But then it all unraveled.

~~~

Later in 1993 when Randy was four, Carla suddenly left the family. "She just ran off with another guy," said Billy years later. "She was still breastfeeding Brianna, so I had to teach the baby real fast how to drink from a bottle."[7]

Billy filed for legal separation from Carla in September 1993, and then received a divorce that October. "She has decided to leave us without any reason and will not return. And she doesn't want anything to do with the children," wrote Billy in his petition to the Havasupai Tribal Court. "I am taking care of our children without the help of their mother."[8]

With the assistance of his new girlfriend, Leandra, also a tribal member, Billy parented Randy, Ambrose and Brianna for several months. But then it turned out that even he was not following the laws in Supai. In December 1993 Billy pleaded guilty to sexual assault of a 21-year-old female inmate who was being held inside the Supai jail. The investigation also revealed that three other female jail inmates and a female BIA employee had made sexual harassment complaints against Billy, which caused him to be fired from his job. By February 1994 when Randy was in first grade at Supai's school, Billy left home to serve a 30-month sentence.[9] While Billy was in prison, Carla returned to Supai and took over care of the three children.

"When Randy's dad went to prison for rape, he was teased a lot in school," said one of Randy's former teachers who worked for two decades at Havasupai School. "He started acting out."[10]

In June 1996 Billy returned from prison vowing he was a changed man. He moved in with Leandra and they got married. He swore off alcohol, attended substance abuse counseling (a condition of his parole) and joined the Native American Church. While Ambrose and Brianna remained with

Carla that summer, Randy wanted to live with Billy.[11] Of the three children, Randy had a special bond with his father, and Randy said he missed his dad when Billy was in prison.

However, in August 1996, Carla petitioned the court to keep all three children under her guardianship and demanded that Billy pay her child support. She believed she had a right to full custody because she cared for the children when Billy was in prison. But Billy insisted he had legal guardianship that was granted him with the October 1993 divorce decree before his incarceration. This began a bitter, decade-long dispute between Billy and Carla over custody and child support payments that publicly played out in the tribal court located in the middle of the village.

Since he was a felon, Billy could no longer work in law enforcement. And he and Leandra had children of their own. While Leandra worked a full-time job at the tribal office, Billy took care of their young children. He became the village tattoo artist and whittled wood carvings that he sold in the tribe's tourism office. He also liked to write songs, which he played on his five-string bass, and archived the lyrics in a three-ring binder. The tunes with titles like "Why Don't you Listen to Your Grandma?" and "Children With No Ears," were aimed at getting his children to behave.

Carla had moved in with her boyfriend Bryon just a few blocks away from Billy and Leandra's house. Carla kept the three children at her home while Billy filed repeated requests in 1996 with Havasupai Tribal Court to get his children, especially Randy, back under his care. He complained that Carla lived in a house without running water and that Randy had sores on his feet that needed to be treated. "I have seen neglect toward Randy by the mother," he wrote in a letter submitted to the court. "She will go out to town and buy clothes for Ambrose but not Randy. She will take Ambrose places and leave Randy...Randy has lived with us in the past and can get along with us well."[12] The substance abuse counselor with the U.S. Department of Health and Human Services at Supai Clinic also submitted a letter to the court on Billy's behalf. She noted how unusually concerned Billy was for his children's welfare compared to other men in her caseload. "Mr. Wescogame would make a conscientious and concerned father," she wrote.[13]

Meanwhile, Randy was getting into trouble at school. In September

1996 when he was in third grade, he was written up by his teacher for "constantly talking in assembly" and the complaint stated that he "refused to listen and follow directions."[14] The next month he was suspended for the day for hitting a younger student in the eye at recess. "He knew this was the wrong thing to do. But [he] chose to hit him anyway," wrote the teacher who witnessed the incident.[15]

In many respects, Randy was just a normal kid. He had the wide set eyes and square jaw of his father while he inherited a tall, linebacker build from the Crook side of the family. In fourth grade he earned As in art, reading and PE. In fifth grade he got an A in penmanship. He enjoyed swimming in the creek and working with horses. He dreamed of one day being a rodeo champion like his grandfather Bela Wescogame. But in some significant ways, Randy was different.

"Randy would be normal and then all of a sudden, he'd come out of left field and say something totally unrelated to what you were talking to him about," recalled one of Randy's elementary school teachers years later. "Some teachers were impatient with him but I was able to talk to him and he got along with me. Even teachers with the tribe would say negative things to him, like he wasn't trying, and talk down to him."[16] A school administrator also described how Randy would suddenly "start laughing his head off for no apparent reason."[17]

Both Carla and Billy recognized Randy had problems, but they blamed each other for his bad behavior as custody of Randy bounced back and forth between them over a five-year period of fighting. Numerous court documents filed during the decade-long custody and child support fight shed light on the feud between Billy and Carla. "[Carla] leaves the children alone at night to run through town and buy more booze from the bootleggers," wrote Billy in a petition to the tribal court.[18] "Billy brutally whips Randy and makes him eat soap," complained Carla.[19] Billy countered that Randy was his favorite child and he could reform him with strict discipline.

A former administrator at Havasupai School in the late 1990s recalled years later how challenging it was to deal with students who had behavior problems in Supai because teachers and principals received no parental support. "I would send the kids home, but the parents would not do anything about it," he said. "These were often parents who had been taken away from the tribe as children in the 1960s and sent to boarding schools. Then they came back to try and live in Supai. They weren't fully functional as parents."[20] In some cases this could translate to parents who were dismissive with authority figures when their children were getting into trouble. In other cases, it could cause the children to be neglected in the home or abandoned by their parents altogether.

But Billy was not this way. He spent most of his childhood raised by a foster mother in Tempe who enforced house rules that conformed to her strict brand of Catholicism. When Billy stepped out of line, he was punished, usually whipped. And he was punished often. "Billy always wanted to better himself but he had a problem with anger," recalled Billy's foster sister.[21] When it came to raising his own children, Billy still believed in the value of corporal punishment.

"The No. 1 rule in this house is to behave," summed up Billy of his parenting philosophy. "In school, after school, no matter where you go, you *do not* misbehave. My children know that." Billy said when Randy was at his house, word would get back to Carla about how Billy had whipped Randy when he got in trouble at school. "Every day the cops would come by and ask, 'Why did you punish your son?'" recalled Billy years later. "And I would tell them because my son was misbehaving in school. Randy was calling his teachers bitches and doing bad things. That doesn't go in this house. So then [Carla] would file a complaint against me in court. And that was the way it went the whole time I had Randy."[22]

Even as Randy got in trouble at school for doing things like telling a female student in Havasupai that "your vagina is full of lice,"[23] the teachers and principals thanked Billy for showing concern about Randy's behavior. They sent Billy notes when Randy was having good days. "Billy and Leandra," said one note, "Randy has been doing great. He finishes his work early and he is even doing extra credit. Good job with him."[24]

In September 1997 Carla became ill and spent nearly a year away from Supai while she was in the hospital in Flagstaff and then recovering in Peach Springs, Arizona on the Hualapai Reservation. She took Ambrose and Brianna with her but left Randy in Billy's care so he could stay in school. She sent a letter to Billy in an attempt to clarify the arrangement. "Let it be known that you only have temporary custody of Randy Wescogame whether you like it or not. Remember Randy didn't ask to be born! [He is] your big responsibility!"[25]

~~~

When Carla returned to Supai in May 1998, she took Randy back into her home with her boyfriend Bryon and Randy's siblings. The fight between Carla and Billy intensified and they filed restraining orders against each other. Carla began aggressively petitioning the court for what she said were missed child support payments from Billy. Meanwhile, Billy denied he owed child support and he also wrote to the court asking for custody of Randy. "I believe that Carla Crook is using her maternal powers to manipulate the court into favoring her in child custody issues," said Billy in a May 1998 letter. "For the past four and a half years, she has deceived the courts into believing that she is a good mother so she can obtain child support. She has been illegally awarded child support although she was never given legal custody." [26]

In November 1998, the Havasupai Tribal Court awarded joint custody of Randy, Ambrose and Brianna to Billy and Carla, mandating that the children spend six months of the year with each parent. The ruling did not include anything about child support. Carla appealed the decision on the grounds that Billy abused and neglected the children and also did not pay her child support.[27] In May 1999, Carla's appeal was dismissed and the Havasupai Tribal Court again ruled that joint custody of the three children would go to both parents. In addition, the court mandated that Carla and Billy "attend and successfully complete Anger Management Classes."[28]

When Randy was 10 and 11 in 1998 and 1999, his grades were dropping in school, and his behavior problems were escalating from mostly verbal infractions to physical violence against students and teachers. In September 1999 as he was beginning a repeat of fifth grade, Randy attacked the school principal Ronald Arias. "Student was caught by me writing on walls with a marker. I told him he would clean the walls [and have] two days suspension," stated the report from Arias. "He then for the next approximately seven minutes on the basketball court said the

F word numerous times, picked up a chair to hit me, picked up a log to hit me, threw rocks at me…Completely defiant with his eye to eye contact. No respect, no listening to me the principal. I finally got the boy off campus by corralling his re-entrance movements." [29]

Randy was in the care of Billy at the time and after consulting with the principal, Billy decided to withdraw Randy from Havasupai School. Billy wanted to send Randy to Keams Canyon Boarding School on the Hopi Reservation in northern Arizona where he believed the teachers were better equipped to deal with Randy's behavior problems. "I wanted to thank you for your support in attempting to address the social problems that Randy exhibited in school almost daily," wrote Principal Arias in an October 1999 letter to Billy. "He has been cited for improper behavior and has received almost the full extent of consequences in our student policy handbook…I know that you have completed every step necessary to enroll Randy at Keams Canyon Boarding School, and I don't understand fully why Randy is not in attendance at the school." [30]

As Billy was taking actions to transfer Randy to Keams Canyon without consulting Carla, she found out and submitted a letter to the Havasupai Tribal Court to stop it. "Randy Wescogame has been removed from school by *who?* I am not sure on that, and my response is *no!* I do not agree with Randy going to Keams." Carla successfully argued that it was coming up on her time to have custody of the children for six months and that she would try to address Randy's problems while keeping him in Supai. "I have set out time and made arrangements to home school [Randy] until I see improvements from [him]," she wrote.[31]

Randy eventually returned to Havasupai School and barely completed the fifth grade, making mostly Cs, Ds and a few Fs. In May 2000, at the end of that school year, a psychologist visiting Supai evaluated Randy with Carla's approval. The reason stated by the school for Randy's evaluation was "low achievement school scores."[32]

In June 2000 when Randy was 12, Billy wrote to the Havasupai Tribal Court again to voice his concerns. "[Carla] has been known to be very violent toward the children…The police in Supai had to go to their home to break up fights between her and her boyfriend. The children would tell us about times when the mother would kick them or whip them with whatever she could get her hands on…My oldest son Randy has been into too much trouble due to the neglect he receives at the mother's home." Billy went on to describe how Randy had been charged with theft and attempting to burn down a house. He was drinking alcohol and using marijuana. "Randy has been seen by community [members] in an intoxicated state, even to the point that he was passed out in a ditch at the west end of the village," Billy continued. "He has been so drunk that children had to take him home."[33]

Randy was on probation when Billy wrote the letter. And soon enough, Randy would be back in a juvenile correctional facility for more petty crimes. He would not become a rodeo champion. He would not even make it to the sixth grade.

7

Child of Conroe

When I was eight, my family moved from Houston to Conroe, a small town 40 miles north of the city. Within a decade Conroe would become a bedroom community of the Houston metro area, but when we first moved there in 1969, it was still very much a country town on the edge of the Big Thicket,[1] where Mom observed "people do not wear shoes" and some longtime residents still hunted possum for food.

The oil boom had turned Houston into a city that was too crowded for Dad's tastes. Traffic clogged the streets and smog from car exhausts and petroleum refineries choked the air. Life in Conroe could give our family a fresh start, Dad said. He would be a country doctor and had accepted a job with a new group medical practice called Sadler Clinic. My sisters and I could ride our bikes wherever we wanted. And Mom could breathe the clean country air, which would hopefully help with her debilitating migraines. After all, Neil Armstrong had just walked on the moon. Anything was possible.

Our home was in a new subdivision called River Plantation. In the late 1960s developers filled in swampland along the San Jacinto River to build the area's first planned community that included a golf course, tennis courts and a country club. The theme in this corner of east Texas was colonial style with a special nod to the Confederacy. River Plantation's large two-story homes had front porches and big columns meant to resemble southern plantations. Streets were named after Confederate heroes: Robert E. Lee

Drive, Stonewall Jackson Drive, Jeb Stewart Lane. The street we lived on was Beauregard Drive in honor of a Confederate general.

What Dad saw in this de facto Jim Crow upper middle class suburb was a place where he could build his medical practice and support his family without the social pressures he felt in Houston. Even though he was charming and articulate and well-educated, there was something about his upbringing as a poor Irish Catholic from Galveston that made him squirm when he was among Houston's elite.

What I saw in this new suburb was a wilderness where undeveloped land stretched in every direction and was waiting to be explored. Like Dad, I was ready to leave the city life behind and follow the example of "Green Acres," one of my favorite TV shows. But I was heartbroken about saying goodbye to our housekeeper Laura. On her last day of work in Houston, she gave my sisters and me each a gift. Mine was a wooden cheese cutting board, which was something I had never seen before since we only ate Kraft American Singles in our family. It was too special to ever use and I would treasure it for the rest of my childhood.

One of the first things loaded off the moving van at the Beauregard house was our banana seat bikes. "Go for a spin," Dad said as Maria and I grabbed our bikes. It would be the first time we had ever ridden somewhere besides the patio in Houston. We pedaled to the end of the street, and then onto a dirt road where there were no houses, and at the end of the road, we propped our bikes against trees and walked farther and farther into the forest. Back then the Big Thicket was still mostly intact. The dense forest of longleaf pine went on forever and it was pulsing with life—giant frogs croaked in the bogs, armadillos rustled through the duff and snakes slithered around the tree trunks. On that first foray into the forest and on many others during what became a decade of unsupervised roaming, Maria and I often stumbled upon the remnants of the subsistence communities where people had once scraped together a living before their homes and fields were paved over by River Plantation.

Grogan's Mill was one of those pockets from the past. The sawmill that was just a mile from our house included a village where the workers lived in company-provided shotgun shacks.[2] When Maria and I suddenly popped up on the fringe of this community, it was like going back 100 years. No one had a car. Laundry hung from clotheslines and people sat on front porches. The windows and doors were open because the houses had no air conditioning. I would soon learn that the mill workers, all African-Americans, were mostly paid in tokens, which they used to buy overpriced food and supplies from the company store. They did not have transportation to get to the more affordable supermarket in town where we shopped.

While the people living in Grogan's Mill never ventured into River Plantation, the dogs were a different story. Within days of getting settled in our new home, a black and white stray, some kind of Labrador mix, had moved into our yard. His ribs stuck out, his fur was patchy from mange, and he had bite mark scars on his head. A neighbor told us the dog was most likely from Grogan's Mill.

"Isn't that something!" Dad exclaimed at how this dog would not leave our yard even though I swore I was not feeding him. "He's lucky to have escaped."

And that was how my dog got his name. Lucky quickly became my new best friend.

In the beginning, Mom was upbeat about our new life in Conroe. Our house was even bigger than the one we had in Houston, and my sisters and I each had our own bedroom that Mom helped us decorate. She was also helping me with my schoolwork and doing special exercises with me to overcome dyslexia. With Mom's encouragement, I wrote stories with illustrations about things like a buck toothed bee that had to get braces, a hippopotamus that wanted to buy tennis shoes, and a fire-breathing dragon that worked as a cook at McDonald's. Mom would rewrite the tales in her neat cursive and correct my poor spelling to make a book that she photocopied and proudly distributed to my former teachers and friends back in Houston. Mom met with other mothers in River Plantation and looked into what activities my sisters and I could join. One of her new friends, Barbara Graham,[3] was an evangelical Christian. Soon we were hosting a children's Bible study at our house that Mrs. Graham was involved in called the Good News Club.

Since Dad was at work, he was never home when the Good News Club was in session and Mom and Mrs. Graham were leading us in songs and Bible study games. If he had been there, I suspected he probably would not have been happy about how we were reading the Bible instead of the Catholic Catechism book that we used in CCD classes. But the Good News Club made Mom happy.

Meanwhile, I came up with my own idea for a club that met in the tree house in our backyard. It was called the Red Bandit Club, after one of my favorite cartoon characters Snoopy,[4] who resembled my beloved dog Lucky with his black and white fur and floppy ears. The purpose of this club was mostly to wage war and spy on neighbors, bullies and unsuspecting adults. In addition to Maria and me, several neighborhood girls were members, along with Lucky and an ever-expanding pack of stray dogs, called our "loved dogs," that congregated in our yard. The boys in the tree house next door were our official enemies. We spied on them, engaged in ruthless dirt clod wars, and regularly went on expeditions to pull up survey stakes in the woods where new homes were to be built. In between battles we made more dirt clods for ammunition and buried them in holes in the yard that Lucky had dug. Sometimes we would sneak around Grogan's Mill or we would spy on Elizabeth, then a teenager, and her boyfriend.

Following the journalistic style of Walter Cronkite who reported on the evening news about the Vietnam War, I faithfully recorded Red Bandit activities in the official club book. "Dec. 22, 1970: Red Bandit Club had a war with enemies Kurt and Stan. The war started with Kurt and Stan throwing dirt balls at the clubhouse. In the middle it was a lot of stick and dirt throwing. It ended by Mr. Saunders yelling at us. Dec. 23: We are making more ammunition to prepare for war."

By the time I was nine, I had become a full-fledged tomboy. I voraciously read about outdoor survival; my favorite book was *My Side of the Mountain*,[5] which told the story of a boy who ran away from his home in the city and lived in a tree in the wilderness with his pet falcon Frightful. I was particularly focused on fighting bullies and seeing how much I could accomplish through sheer willpower. Rather than going to a special school for children with disabilities where I was in a class with all boys, as had been the case in second and third grade, I desperately wanted to attend regular public school so I could ride the bus. I used my newfound willpower to control my angry outbursts and follow the teacher's instructions. I saved my trouble making for outside of school. By the start of fifth grade I triumphantly stood at the bus stop with all the other neighborhood kids waiting to go to Armstrong Elementary. I had a new purse full of markers Mom had given me, but not wanting to blow my tomboy cover, I carried the purse in a shoebox.

I viewed Mom and Elizabeth as "sissies," the polar opposite of a tomboy. I felt they were too easily intimidated when threatened—especially by Dad. Also Elizabeth was starting to wear makeup. But me, I would take all comers. I wanted Maria to toughen up, too, for her own good. I was constantly thinking of new ways for Maria and me to measure our strength and bravery. We jumped 15 feet out of the tree house, carried heavy logs across the yard, and searched for snakes to kill. Bathing was for sissies, too, so we tried to avoid that as much as possible.

After memorizing countless Bible verses and songs for months, the Good News Club was approaching a kind of graduation. The time had come when each child was to meet one on one with the pastor from Mrs. Graham's church and say a prayer so that he or she could be "born again."

When it was my turn, I sat with the pastor in our den while the other kids ran around outside. He showed me a Bible he was going to give me and on the title page was a space where we would write the date when I "accepted the Lord Jesus Christ as my personal savior." Saying this prayer with the pastor and then recording the date would not only allow me to be born again but also ensure that I would go to heaven. This sounded like a better deal than having to go to confession every month to achieve salvation, but I had some reservations.

"Will Lucky be in heaven?" I asked. I was worried that he might not be born again since he was not a member of this particular club.

"Oh, animals don't go to heaven," the pastor said. "Heaven is only for humans."

"Well, I don't want to go to heaven then," I said. "I would rather be with Lucky."

The pastor took the Bible back. He did not have time for such nonsense. That was the end of the Good News Club. But the Red Bandit Club became more active than ever, even requiring meetings in the middle of the night to plot secret strategies against unseen enemies.

While Lucky and other dogs dozed under the tree house and our parents thought we were asleep in our beds, Maria and I reviewed a page in the club book called "Something a Club Member Should Do," which I had written. "Obey orders and mind the captain (that was me). Try to hurt your enemies. Defend yourself against enemies. Never be a friend with an enemy. Never let the enemies come in the clubhouse. Go over your club book every day and take good care of it. Be nice to your loved dogs. Always spy on your worst enemies. Guard the tree house when enemies are around."

Maria and I also added a new section to the club book called "Notes About Bad Things." This chronicle recorded when I was shot in the butt with a BB gun, Lucky's fight with a neighbor's dog, and the time Maria was struck in the eye by a dirt clod that had glass inside of it. But the truly bad things were happening inside our house and were so beyond our control, we never wrote them down or even dared discuss them.

~~~

The country air had not cured Mom. In fact, she believed that it made her illness worse. She stopped working as a psychologist and devoted herself to her increasing physical ailments. Mom said she wanted to help us with schoolwork and take us to extracurricular activities, but she was too often bedridden to be involved. She told us her migraines were caused by allergies. The list of things she was allergic to became longer each year: dogs (Lucky had to stay outside at all times), trees, mold, dust, spices, cigarette smoke, house paint, fabric dyes, freeway smog, perfume and flowers. Basically, Mom was allergic to everything outdoors and many things indoors that had been contaminated by the outdoors.

On most Saturdays my sisters and I would wake to find a note from Mom on the kitchen counter that told us she had stayed awake until 3 a.m. and was finally taking a sleeping pill. "DO NOT WAKE ME!!!" she wrote in all capital letters. Then in very small handwriting on both sides of the paper she listed chores we had to complete before we could go outside and play. My sisters and I spent much of our weekends cleaning endlessly to keep the house free of dust and mold. After Mom finally emerged from her bedroom in the early afternoon, she followed behind us with a white glove to inspect the quality of our work. Sometimes I would secretly jam the vacuum cleaner with pennies or cut the belt with a steak knife to sabotage Mom's plans for us.

Our friends, once we had cultivated them, rarely came inside our house because they always reeked of something — their parents' cigarette smoke, Herbal Essence shampoo, dog dander. Even Dad had to hang his suits in the garage because they smelled of his patients' cigarette smoke. Mom rarely left the house, but when she did, she wore a double filter Vietnam War-era gas mask.[6]

The gas mask took Mom's illness to a whole new level. Up until then, her phobia around air-borne toxins had been something of a family secret. But now, when we went out in public, especially if my sisters and I missed the bus and Mom had to drive us to school, the gas mask offered glaring proof of how odd our family really was. The mask was stored in a gallon-size Ziploc bag, and it waited like a loaded revolver on top of the microwave. Sometimes Mom would grab it on our way out the door and sometimes, much to my relief, she would not. When she brought it along, the gas mask sat next to Mom on the car seat until she detected that toxins had reached a level requiring she strap it on.

Dreading the devastatingly embarrassing power of the mask, I would pray as we drove to both the God of the Good News Club and the bleeding Catholic Jesus that the mask would stay in the bag. But by the time Mom pulled up to the front of the school where all our classmates were standing, she inevitably had the large mask across her face. And Maria and I were lying on the floor of our station wagon's back seat trying not to be seen.

"Have a nice day, girls," Mom would say cheerily in a metallic, muffled voice as our friends peered into the car windows and we reluctantly sat up.

"Man, your mom is weird!" they would say as she drove away.

"Tell me about it!" I'd reply with a laugh, using my increasing reserve of willpower to not cry.

Although the profusion of nature in the Big Thicket became Mom's worst enemy, she said the sea air in Galveston, which was free of mold and pollen, made her feel better. So even though Dad seemed to enjoy visiting his family less and less every year, we went to Galveston more often. During the summer and on some weekends, we rented houses at a new development called Pirate's Beach. While Mom walked along the Gulf Coast shoreline gas mask free, Dad took my sisters and me for the obligatory visits to Uncle John's and his mother's house.

Dad's father had died in 1969 of a heart attack. Then his mother suffered a series of strokes and was bedridden in her home for nearly a decade. During our visits Maria and I stood next to Grandmother's hospital bed and held her hand, which we observed had a suspicious brown substance under the fingernails.

"My namesake! My namesake!" Grandma McGivney said when she saw me, grasping for my hand.

"Junior, help me!" she cried out to Dad.

Often, Dad was in the other room arguing with Uncle John about their mother's care. Since Dad lived far away, Uncle John managed Grandma's deteriorating condition, but Dad was always critical of the decisions his brother was making.

"I don't want that old bat taking care of Mother!" Dad shouted within easy earshot of Grandma's nurse. It would not be long before he got worked up into a rage, grabbed us and stormed out to go back to the beach house.

Uncle John had other challenges, too. Bibby's mental illness was worse and she rarely left the house. And Aunt Beth had died suddenly of a brain hemorrhage. Dad told us it was because Bibby pushed her mother down the stairs.

Meanwhile, our move to Conroe was not turning out to be the salvation for Dad's medical career that he had hoped. He was often an hour or more late to his morning appointments and was told by the Sadler Clinic supervisor that he spent too much time talking to the patients. The medicine of the 1970s was run by HMOs that required doctors to see a lot of patients quickly. But what Dad liked most about being a doctor was hearing people's stories. He especially enjoyed talking to the poorest patients—the ones from Grogan's Mill who could not pay but had interesting life experiences to share.

In pursuit of real stories rather than a lucrative medical practice, Dad went on to become the doctor for the Montgomery County Jail and, later, for the Texas State Prison in Huntsville. There, he visited with death row inmates for as long as the conversation required. Because of this, Dad was my hero, my Atticus Finch. He had a big heart, a witty sense of humor and possessed a passion for life that was missing from other adults I knew, especially Mom. I saw Dad as a compassionate champion for the underdog and those on society's margins. I believed he could have been a great writer, which was his dream, but he sacrificed for his children, his sick wife, and the poor.

Yet, my hero also wrestled with a "bad Irish temper." Dad took out the day's frustrations by hitting a ball hard against the backboard at the tennis court. He also vented at home.

In the evenings, behind the closed curtains of the big Beauregard house, there were increasingly frequent and volatile explosions.

~~~

When I was in sixth grade, Elizabeth found a way to escape our crazy household. She had become pregnant at age 16 with her boyfriend Steve, who was 19, and they announced they were getting married. Elizabeth met Steve while attending Conroe High School. They continued to date after Steve graduated and went to college in the nearby town of Huntsville. Steve's lower middle class family followed a fundamentalist Pentecostal religion and lived in a rural part of Conroe that was a world away from the opulent River Plantation.

Dad did not receive this news well.

I remember Elizabeth's exodus from our family as a confusing flurry of shouting and door slamming. There was a freak ice storm that morning in December, and Mom and Dad were talking in the kitchen about Elizabeth, who in my view was almost never home. I sat in Elizabeth's room and read through her diary to get some clues; there was something about a pregnancy test. Then Elizabeth and Steve showed up in Steve's green pickup truck. They sat with Mom and Dad in our formal living room on the fancy gold embroidered couches where we girls were not supposed to sit. I moved to the top of the stairs to spy on them.

First there was measured whispering, followed by loud whispering. And, finally, Dad was yelling. As far as he was concerned the pregnancy was shameful and not befitting a doctor's daughter.

Elizabeth said she would not consider adoption. She and Steve were in love and determined to get married. They wanted this baby.

"Well, you're not going to wear a white dress!" Dad shouted. "I can promise you that much!"

Then the conversation was suddenly over. Steve and a tearful Elizabeth sped away in the green truck, peeling out of the circle drive in our front yard. Minutes later, Mrs. Graham pulled up in her station wagon and Mom quickly got in while Dad sat inside the house reading the newspaper.

The next day Mom returned and she uncharacteristically doted on Maria and me. She made us hot dogs for dinner and we were allowed to eat them in front of the TV while watching our favorite shows, *The Brady Bunch* and *The Partridge Family*.

"Would you girls like anything else?" she queried Maria and me after dinner, much to our amazement since she almost never waited on us.

"Can we have a Ding Dong?" I asked, requesting our favorite junk food, which we were only allowed to have in our school lunches. And Mom happily obliged.

Six weeks later there was a hastily arranged wedding at Sacred Heart Catholic Church in Conroe followed by a reception at our River Plantation home. Elizabeth wore a peach satin gown covered with beige lace. Mom wore a wig and a yellow velvet dress and, thankfully, left her gas mask on top of the microwave.

I was mad at Elizabeth for upsetting Dad and not being appreciative of the sacrifices he had made for us. So I decided to sweeten the send-off at the reception by throwing giant handfuls of rice as hard as I could at Steve's face when he and Elizabeth exited the house. He was taking away my big sister, after all.

Once Elizabeth moved out following the wedding, Dad forbade Mom or Maria and me from all future contact with Elizabeth and her new baby. "She has committed a mortal sin against our family and the [Catholic] church," Dad announced. I figured Elizabeth deserved this punishment because that was how Catholicism worked.

The unspoken tension between my parents went from simmering to a roiling boil. Mom became a near invalid, rarely leaving her bedroom. In addition to allergy-induced migraines, she suffered from chronic pain that she self-diagnosed as Fibromyalgia.[7] Dad thought this was absurd and said there was no such thing as Fibromyalgia. Mom started regularly visiting a doctor more than 100 miles away in Victoria, Texas whom Dad called a "quack." Maria and I did anything to keep Mom placated (bring her more ice for the ice pack, vacuum behind the dressers, do all the cooking, beg rides off friends to get ourselves to school, keep all problems to ourselves) so she would not stoke the fire in Dad. Also, Dad clamped down on me. Our strict household rules became even stricter. I had a curfew and could not attend parties. And a boyfriend in junior high or later in high school was absolutely out of the question.

I still liked hearing Dad's stories, but I was becoming more interested in making up my own. I sat with Lucky by the pond behind our house, stared at the stagnant water that flickered with mosquitoes, and wrote stories and poems. One poem was about how I thought "God is like a Mountain,"[8] even though I had never seen a mountain. I also wrote daily messages to myself in a journal: "I wish Momma would get normal and I would stop acting like a brat." "Momma is still going to the doctor. I wonder how sick she really is?" "I love Lucky." "Momma and Daddy are being nice to me and I need to shape up." "I must remember not to worry about little things in this world but focus on the next world which is 20 times better." After each day's entry I wrote a Bible verse.

By the time I started high school, the Red Bandit Club had faded and my favorite activity was going on long walks in the woods with Lucky. We wandered deep into the Big Thicket, beyond the survey stakes and Grogan's Mill, where the pines were so dense in some places I had to crawl on my hands and knees. Unlike my home life, the world was safe and wonderful there. Everything made sense. I smelled the red clay earth and the moist forest duff that was full of mold. My ears tuned to the wind and the crunch of my footsteps. I felt the warmth radiating from the tree trunks, as if the whole forest had gathered to embrace me.

8
Michael

Tomomi arrived at Wounded Knee late in the morning on Jan. 2, 2000 after spending another night at the Kings X in Rapid City. On the second attempt she knew the roads of Pine Ridge, and the directions she got from a different ranger at Mount Rushmore worked. She parked at the bottom of the hill next to a rusting metal sign that said Wounded Knee Memorial. Someone had affixed a metal plate with the word "Massacre" on top of "Memorial." Underneath the plate was the inscription: "The site of the last armed conflict between the Sioux Indians and United States Army." Over the word "armed," someone—maybe the same person—had scratched "lies."[1]

At the top of the hill was a chain link fence with a gate. Tomomi opened it and stepped toward a tall stone monument that marked the mass grave. She read the names, some of which she recognized from her study of Sioux history: "Chief Big Foot, Mr. High Hawk, Mr. Standing Bear, Long Bull, Sitting Bear, Afraid of Bear, Ghost Horse."

It was quiet and cold, with no wind. The big sky was slate gray. Tomomi looked down a grassy ravine holding Wounded Knee Creek and out onto an ocean of prairie that dropped into a sculpted rock maze called the Badlands. She imagined how the Lakota band rode their horses up the ravine and decided to make camp in a place where they would have a good view of strangers approaching. They laid down their buffalo rugs on the grass and started small fires to warm their hands. The dark, full clouds told of snow that was coming soon.

Nearby was another, smaller gravestone carved out of polished granite. "Chief Big Foot Massacre, Dec. 29 1890. Big Foot was a great chief of the Sioux Indians. He often said 'I will stand in peace till my last day comes.' He did many good and brave deeds for the White Man and the Red Man. Many innocent women and children who knew no wrong died here."

Tomomi felt the gravity of this dark hole in the Earth. The chaos and the fury of the murders. She knew it deep in her heart, as if she remembered it from experience. Maybe in another life, she thought, she had been here, witnessing the horror.

"Do you come here often?"

A young white man with a goatee and sun-bleached blond hair pulled back in a ponytail was standing next to her. Tomomi was startled since she thought she was at the grave alone, and she did not get his sarcasm.

"First time," she said, embarrassed by how he had sneaked up on her. She looked at the ground and noticed his muddy hiking boots. He also had on a knit cap with a brim, the kind she had seen skiers wearing at The Hostel in Jackson Hole. The average American might think this guy was short, but he was a whole head taller than Tomomi.

"Are you from California?" he asked. He had wondered about the California license plates on her mud-splattered car when he parked behind her. He also saw the teddy bear in the passenger seat but did not ask about that.

Tomomi broke into a broad smile at the idea that she could be from California. How funny!

"I rented at Los Angeles airport," she said. "I am visiting from Japan."

She giggled. There was something different about this guy compared to the many other friendly Americans she had met on her travels. She felt nervous.

He introduced himself as Michael, from San Francisco. He was staying nearby in Custer and was doing some woodworking jobs for his uncle who had a log home business. Michael asked Tomomi if she wanted to get some pizza.

They walked down the hill and got in their cars. Tomomi followed Michael into the one stop sign town of Wounded Knee. She had driven through here at least five times the day before, but the post office, convenience store and pizza place were all closed then because it was New Year's Day.

Several weeks before her trip to the United States, Tomomi had finally split for good with Mako. He wanted to get a steady job in Tokyo and start a family. His father expected it. But Tomomi wanted to travel, especially to America. Many of Tomomi's friends from high school were already married and raising young children. At 28, she knew she was starting to pass the age when most women in Japan during that era were expected to get married, but so what? She did not want to be a salary man's wife. Her father did not care either that Tomomi was single; maybe he even preferred it.

Tomomi was not looking for a boyfriend, especially when she was traveling. She was happy just to see Big Sky sunsets and buffalo and be able to drive 10 hours down the open highway with no one to order her around. And, yet, here was this guy, Michael, wearing his knit cap indoors, asking her lots of questions and staring into her eyes in a way that made Tomomi stumble over her English.

They talked for hours in the booth at the pizza restaurant. Tomomi could not believe her luck that day, to meet someone like him. Michael had beautiful blue eyes. And he liked everything she liked. Native American culture. Hiking. The mountains. The Red Hot Chili Peppers. Lenny Kravitz. He even shopped at thrift stores!

One thing led to another, and Tomomi found herself inside Michael's log cabin at a place called Gold Camp in the town of Custer. She stayed there all night.

The next day they hiked together on trails through rolling prairie in Custer State Park. Then they went their separate ways. Michael had work to do, and Tomomi planned to hike in Badlands National Park.

Jan. 3: We saw a lot of Buffaloes. I don't have any word to tell about Buffaloes. Great, cute..!! I said good-bye to Michael."

Jan. 4: I met two golden eagles in B.N.P. They came down close. They are so beautiful.

The Lakota and other Plains Indian tribes believe the eagle is a direct link to the Great Spirit. To be visited by an eagle is a powerful sign; it indicates one's ability to live within the realm of the spirit world while remaining connected and balanced within the realm of the Earth.[2]

But the 24 hours with Michael had thrown Tomomi a curve ball. She was in shock that she had slept with him, and also tantalized by the possibility that maybe it could turn into something more. She vowed to herself she would not call Michael *("he played with me; I know that")*, and not tell anyone what had happened between them.

Always sticking to her trip itinerary (except for the two days she got off track with Michael), Tomomi continued on with her plans to visit her friends Ana and Jorge Coronado who were living in Fort Worth, Texas. The brother and sister were from Venezuela, and Tomomi had met them at English school in Mississippi. They had all shared an apartment together in Hattiesburg and bonded over their constantly amusing experience of being foreigners in the Deep South. Tomomi had called Hattiesburg "the Land of Hamburgers."

On the way, Tomomi spent a day at Pipestone National Monument in western Minnesota. The ridges of quartzite that cut into the prairie at the monument contain stone quarries that are sacred to various Plains Indian tribes. For maybe the last 1,000 years, Native Americans had excavated this stone to carve into a variety of ceremonial pipes. As snow dusted the red cliffs surrounding the park's visitor center, Tomomi studied exhibits about Sioux history and their connection to this place. She bought materials to make her own pipe.

Jan. 7: I made pipe with white stone. I didn't finish yet. It wasn't easy. Good feelin'!!

Tomomi drove 13 hours the next day to get to Fort Worth and Ana's apartment. Ana wanted to show Tomomi all the classic Texas hot spots that she was sure would delight her friend.

Jan. 9: 6ᵗʰ Floor. Downtown Dallas. Who killed JFK?

Tomomi enjoyed being with Ana. Tomomi considered Ana her sister, and she missed her terribly when she was in Japan. But as they cruised through cowboy country, Tomomi's mind was elsewhere. In just six days, after staying for a week with Ana, she was scheduled to fly back to Tokyo.

Jan. 10: Fort Worth stockyard. I like this kind of place. I wanna see rodeo!! I miss Michael.

Tomomi's heart ached in a way it had never ached for anyone. She rebooked her ticket and extended her rental car lease to give herself a few more weeks in the United States.

Jan. 17: Called Michael. We're gonna see each other Feb. 3!

Tomomi had time to kill before Michael returned to San Francisco from South Dakota. She was interested in learning more about the Cherokee tribe and also wanted to see Great Smoky Mountains National Park, so she made a detour into Tennessee before heading west. She cruised through the Smoky Mountains, sent her Grand Canyon friends Tim and Luana Nelson a postcard about her travels, then drove through Arkansas and New Mexico. On Feb. 1 she called her father to wish him a happy birthday. She told him she had bought him a South Dakota t-shirt and a baseball cap with a buffalo on it. He wondered when she was coming home.

Feb. 3: Michael's house. I met his mom and step pa'. His ma' looks younger than she is! What am I doin' here!?

Hanging out in his apartment in San Francisco's Haight Ashbury neighborhood, Tomomi got to know more about Michael. She had never before stayed in the home of a born-and-raised American. *Sugoi!* (Cool!) Michael's favorite color was purple, just like Tomomi. He had a cat. His two-room apartment was full of Native American crafts—a painted Lakota drum with eagle feathers, Navajo sand paintings, dream catchers that dangled from the ceiling. As Tomomi watched, entranced, Michael closed his eyes and caressed his doumbek drum, pounding out steady Native rhythms. On his coffee table was a tall bong for smoking pot.

Michael decided they should go to Yosemite National Park. "You will not believe how beautiful it is," he promised.

The first night in Yosemite, Michael and Tomomi stayed in a cabin tent in Curry Village. The barracks style camp was in the middle of Yosemite Valley and surrounded by towering granite domes that radiated gold in the crisp winter light. Michael started a fire in the wood stove and they cuddled on a squeaky cot under Army issue wool blankets. Tomomi thought she might ask Michael about smoking marijuana, which she had never tried.

The next day they ventured into the Sierra to see waterfalls cascading over granite faces and snow-covered mountains in a heavenly spectacle that John Muir famously described as "the range of light."

Feb. 6: Hiked whole day. Mist Trail and John Muir Trail. Beautiful falls, snow, icecicles (sp?), deers. Marijuana doesn't work for me.

After another day of hiking, Tomomi returned to San Francisco with Michael where he showed her the city: Fisherman's Wharf, lunch at Bubba Gump Shrimp, the Ghirardelli Chocolate Factory, shopping at thrift stores in the Mission District. Tomomi took pictures of Michael in his apartment in bed, playing the drum, and a close-up of his outie belly button.

Feb. 12: Said good-bye to Michael. He wants to be alone. I really bothered him. But he said he'll miss me. I hope that's true. I miss him. I miss him. I miss Michael.

Tomomi spent her last few days in the United States by herself exploring Joshua Tree National Park. She hiked to the top of Mastodon Peak and looked down on the brown abyss of the Salton Sea. One morning she drove on a dirt road off the Twentynine Palms highway, wanting to see more of the Mojave Desert. A cold front from the Pacific brought in a milky fog that settled on the basin floor the way a heavy rock sinks to the bottom of a lake. The fog had moved in quickly and Tomomi could not see 10 feet in front of her on the ever-narrowing, bumpy dirt track.

Suddenly, her grandfather, Fumitomo, appeared right in front of her car. He was in his kimono with his arms crossed and was wearing his hand-knit wool socks and silk house slippers. His eyes were bright and sheltered by his long, bushy eyebrows. He grinned from ear to ear, the way he would right before he told a funny story or played a prank. Tomomi threw the car into park, got out, and ran around to the front bumper.

"Grandfather?" she shouted into the fog.

He had vanished, but once outside the car, Tomomi could see she had veered off the road and was just 10 feet away from driving into a steep ravine.[3] Shaken, she got in the car, turned around and drove through the fog back to the highway. Once at her hotel that afternoon, she called home. Her father told her Fumitomo had died that morning. He passed away in his sleep in the thatched-roof house outside Takarabe where he had lived most of his life.

Tomomi said she would be home the next day to drive with her father down south for the funeral and attend the Buddhist burial ceremony at the family grave next to the Hanamure homestead. They would pray that Fumitomo made it to Pure Land, a "western land of peace and bliss." According to Shin Buddhism, the most widely practiced Buddhist sect in Japan, those reborn into the Pure Land can finally escape the endless cycle of birth and death in a life characterized by suffering.[4]

Fumitomo had lived to be 80, well past both of his wives and two of his five children. He had survived famine, disease, war, and nuclear attack; and he had witnessed Japan go from a rural country, where people pushed their food in a cart from the fields, to a nation that was among the most technologically advanced in the world. "We can all only hope to be around for that long," said Tetsushi as Tomomi wept at the thought of losing her grandfather. And, also, she thought maybe he had told her goodbye and was looking out for her in his own *bokkemon* way.

~~~

Feb. 23, 2000: I'm thinkin' about Michael whole days. I wanna call him but know I should not do it.

Back in Japan, Tomomi lived for her next trip to the States. She got a new job as an hourly temp worker (called "casual employment" in Japan because it was low paying and had no security or benefits, but allowed schedule flexibility for traveling) doing data entry in a large appliance factory. She worked as many hours as possible to earn money for another U.S. adventure. She wore the clothes she bought in America like a badge of honor—the thrift shop t-shirts and Puma sneakers and Nike sweatpants from the California factory outlets. She hung in her bedroom two Native American plaques that she had bought in thrift shops in Rapid City—a picture of a Sioux chief in a full feathered headdress and another of a little Indian boy that said "Little Nonny." She had also bought an American flag, the kind that is draped over the coffin of U.S. veterans, and she tacked it up on the wall.

Before Tomomi split with Mako, they had been living together in a Tokyo apartment. But, now, to save money, Tomomi had moved back into her father's apartment in Yokohama. It was tense and cramped. Tomomi was sharing the 700 square foot home not only with her father, Tetsushi, but with his wife, Fukuyo, and her teenage son, Eito,[5] from a previous marriage. When Tomomi was a senior in high school, and after she and her father had been just a two-person family most of her life, Tetsushi remarried, bringing Fukuyo and Eito into their home. Tomomi didn't like Fukuyo; she was bossy. And Tomomi didn't want another woman trying to take the place of her real mother. But Tomomi figured her father needed companionship since she planned on moving away soon, hopefully to the United States.

Tomomi's relationship with her father was complicated and often strained. Deep down, she loved him very much, but the obligations she felt toward him often seemed more like a leash that was keeping her from fully pursuing her own dreams. Even at a young age, Tomomi knew she wanted more out of life than the crowded, lower-middle class existence she and her father had in Yokohama. In a sixth grade essay titled, "Dad," Tomomi wrote: *I really love my father. Every now and then he gets angry and he gets scary. But then I remember that I was the one who was wrong and I regret that. Dad, you are where I feel safe; you are where I go to rest. Please watch me from afar when I become an adult. I am going to spread my wings and fly into the big sky."*

Tetsushi hoped the fascination with America was a passing phase for Tomomi. He would jokingly say to her: "You cannot date a man with light eyes!" And she would just shrug. He did not object to her decorating their apartment with items she brought back from the States. There was a Monument Valley magnet on the refrigerator, an American flag bathmat, and then all the things in her bedroom. Tetsushi also wore the American t-shirts and ball caps she had bought him. "Carmel," "Grand Canyon," "Custer, S.D." It was all English gibberish to him but also amusing to his buddies at work.

Sitting on a futon in her tiny bedroom, Tomomi assembled the first of what would become many detailed photo albums that documented her trips from beginning to end. She titled her first album "Nature Traveler." In it she compiled a chronology of every day, beginning with her boarding pass, then photos of each place visited and every motel room along with entrance fee stubs to all the parks, business cards from people she met along the way, her annual National Parks Pass and dozens of photos that showed close encounters with buffalo, wolves, sunsets and mountains. There were no pictures of people in the album, only Teddy. She wrote the name of each place she visited on a piece of paper and put it on the corresponding pages.

She also wrote a note to herself and put it in the front of the album: "I always thought there's no word to tell about nature. Beautiful is not enough. Awesome is not enough either. So I decide to make a word!!! Nature + (drawing of rainbow)." *Daishizen.*

Tomomi did not put any of the pictures of Michael in the album because she did not want her father or anyone else to know about him. But while sitting at the computer at work and riding the train on the long commute to her job, she ached for Michael as she listened to her favorite American music on her Sony Walkman (especially Lenny Kravitz's "You're My Flavor" and Macy Gray's "I Try"). Everywhere she went Tomomi was surrounded by so many people and, yet, she felt utterly alone in Japan. And she was filled with a yearning like never before. There was the pull of the Grand Canyon, Yellowstone, the Black Hills, and, perhaps, a soul mate. She resisted the urge to call Michael. But she wrote to him almost daily in her diary.

March 29: Michael, I always think about you. I don't know what I can do with this feeling. I miss you.

Tomomi started researching what it would take to live in the United States full time. She wrote to Tim and Luana Nelson in Tucson asking for their advice on how to go about getting a Green Card. Maybe she could get a job waiting tables at Phantom Ranch or at some other national park? She also thought she should improve her appearance and fix her teeth to look more like people in the United States. She wrote to her cousin Konomi who was working as an assistant in a dentist's office down south in Kyushu.

"Do you know how to get silver fillings replaced with white ones? People in the States are like 'What is all that crap in your mouth!' They don't use silver fillings in America. Who knew?"

Other women at Tomomi's work who were also in their late 20s and unmarried stuck together. They went out after their shifts for dinner and karaoke, which Tomomi excelled at. Two of Tomomi's new best friends were Shinobu and Rena. They loved to hear Tomomi talk about her travels in America and asked if she would take them on a trip. They pressed Tomomi about whether she had met any cute men in the States. "But she did not want to talk about love," recalled Rena years later.

April 12: Michael, do you know I'm thinking to go to San Francisco on my birthday? Are you gonna celebrate my birthday with me?

April 25: Michael, why don't you write to me? Is it because you don't remember me? Or you don't care about me?

Even though she had not heard from Michael and her new job did not allow any vacation time, Tomomi was determined to keep the promise to herself that she would celebrate her birthday in America. Without knowing whether or not she would see Michael, she bought a plane ticket to San Francisco for a four-day trip, two days of which would be spent flying.

~~~

On May 6 Tomomi arrived in San Francisco, rented a car, and drove to Muir Beach to walk along the Pacific. *"Carmel is a really pretty town!"* She called Michael that night from her hotel, and he answered.

They spent the next two days together. Michael told Tomomi he had missed her and was glad to see her. They went to an Indian music concert at U.C. Berkeley and ate dinner at a Moroccan restaurant.

May 8: Michael celebrated my birthday!! Thanks.

To commemorate her 29th birthday with Michael, Tomomi got a tattoo, a tiny green heart, on her lower left abdomen. According to traditional Japanese custom, tattoos are frowned upon, along with any kind of body alteration such as piercing or hair dying. It would be Tomomi's secret. Her family and best friends would not find out about the tiny green heart until it was chronicled years later in the coroner's report.

Tomomi said goodbye to Michael on May 9 and flew back to the crowded apartment in Yokohama, hoping that her stay there was nearing an end. A life in the United States with an American boyfriend who shared her passions —this was more than she ever imagined was possible. It would be a dream come true. She would make it happen! But there was also a part of her that expected to be let down. She steeled herself, as always, for the possibility of winding up alone and needing to soothe her own wounded heart.

May 10: I just got home and feelin' hell. I've never had a home.

*July 8: Michael, I called you but you're not there. Where are you?
I Love You.*

PART III

9

Mountains and Canyons

Junction sits at the outer limits of the Texas Hill Country. It is far enough west that it is beyond the German vacation towns named for a "burg" or the towns that cater to college students who float the rivers in inner tubes towing coolers full of beer.

But if you were to drive west on I-10 beyond Junction, you would land in a brown flat expanse that is the domain of speeding truckers and dust devils. The rushing waters of the north and south forks of the Llano River, which converge in Junction, slow to a trickle in the desert just to the west. The gentle rolling hills, the giant live oak trees and babbling creeks lined with white limestone escarpments all come to a halt west of Junction. The known world—or at least the world of my family—stopped at this boundary between wet and dry, green and brown, blessed and godforsaken. And that is why the plan for our summer vacation in July 1977 was to visit Junction, but go no farther.

We arrived at the KOA campground along the banks of the south Llano River around 9 p.m., just after dark. My parents had rented a motorhome in an attempt to try camping. On past vacations, we had always rented beach houses in Galveston or stayed in rustic motels in the Hill Country. This time, we were roughing it—trying to get closer to nature, as Dad described it, but not so close that it would trigger Mom's allergy-induced migraines. The 25-foot long RV had two dining areas that converted into beds, a tiny kitchen with electric refrigerator, and a narrow shower stall that was also the location of the toilet.

Having driven 340 miles after getting a late start from our home in Conroe, Dad was already on a short fuse. Now, we had to go through the ordeal of parking the RV in the dark, and finding level ground on the narrow campsite so the refrigerator would run properly. It was a three-person job. Dad sat behind the wheel; Maria stood watch in front of the leveling device on the refrigerator; and I was outside directing the rig and watching for possible collisions with nearby cars and picnic tables. Mom was lying down in the back fighting off a headache. I was 15 and Maria was 13, and by then we had become experts at mitigating my parents' potential for embarrassing outbursts. We were the family's mechanics, cooks, cleaners, negotiators and ambassadors to the normal world.

"Stop!" I yelled as Dad accelerated to within inches of the campsite's picnic table.

He slammed on the brakes and I watched items in the RV get tossed forward. He was on the verge of losing it.

"Felix, please!" Mom yelled.

"It's still not level," Maria said.

This back and forth went on for about 30 minutes until the gauge was level. Maria and I were relieved that it happened without any kind of scene, which was often compounded by my parents seemingly competing with each other for the spotlight. If Dad had started yelling at the campground host, you could bank on Mom emerging from the RV donning her gas mask.

"I've had it," Dad proclaimed as he tossed the motorhome keys on the broad dash. He grabbed a flashlight, his *Conroe Courier* newspaper and a lawn chair. "You girls finish up."

Maria set about converting the dinette areas into beds and putting sheets on the cushions in the tiny bunk above the driving compartment. I picked up a flashlight and did the outdoor chores, taking the stinky sewage hose from the RV's side compartment and cramming it down into the campsite's waste outlet. Then I unwound the rig's long electrical cord and plugged it into the site's electrical box. I watched as the lights in the RV blinked on and then flickered when the refrigerator started to hum. Lingering in the hushed night before going back in the RV, I heard the waters of the Llano nearby as the river moved swiftly over rocks. The moon was full and the river canyon's sheer limestone bluffs glowed white amid the darkness.

So this was camping, I thought. As I took in the night sky, I wondered what would become of me. In four days I turned 16. How would I find my way in life as an adult and escape the hell of my parents' world?

~~~

After my sister Elizabeth got married and had her daughter April at age 17, a glacial period settled over our family, and the relationship between my parents transformed from fire to ice. Over a span of five years, Mom and Dad had created separate lives in separate bedrooms. Even though Elizabeth and her young family lived in Conroe, Dad would not speak to her and insisted that we all continue to uphold the rules of her banishment. Meanwhile, Mom would secretly take Maria and me to visit Elizabeth in her small, run-down house where she spent all day with April and infant son Alan while her husband Steve worked long hours nailing shingles on roofs and attending college classes. Mom instructed us to tell Dad only that we had gone shopping.

"That's a lie," I protested.

"It's the only way," she said. "It's a white lie."

But gradually Mom let it be known that she was ignoring the banishment policy. She left the Catholic Church and started going to the evangelical Conroe Bible Church that Elizabeth and Steve attended. I suspected Mrs. Graham from the Good News Club was there, too. Mom joined a Bible study group that met twice a week and spent most mornings sitting at our kitchen table poring over assigned scriptures, comparing minute word differences between the King James and the New American Standard versions of the Bible. The thick books were wrapped in lacey, quilted cloth covers sewn by other Bible study ladies and given to Mom as gifts.

It was like Mom was having an affair with the Protestants and there was nothing Dad could do about it. Except for trips to the grocery store, going to the Bible Church was about the only time Mom left the house.

Meanwhile, Maria and I went to church with Dad every Sunday. We had no choice. Going to Catholic Mass was a more serious affair than ever. Now Dad was almost running back to the pew to pray after receiving Communion before the spell wore off.

The sporadic affection that Mom and Dad once displayed in their marriage was gone. Most days they were doing well simply to tolerate each other and poured their energies into disparate interests: the Bible and medical ailments for Mom, and playing tennis and planning novels for Dad. But our parents were united in their support of Maria and me. Whatever it was that we wanted to pursue, Mom and Dad cheered us on, always encouraging us to dream big. Every Christmas Dad would give me a book, one of the classics, and pen a formal, grandiose message on the title page. In 1977, it was *A Tale of Two Cities* by Charles Dickens, with the note: "To Annette, with love and every good wish for success. From her Father and Mother."

I was terrified of falling into the same trap that Elizabeth had, becoming pregnant and unable to go to college, forever stuck in Conroe. Fortunately, because I had grown to 6 feet tall and was so skinny, I was often mistaken as anorexic, and no boys were interested in me. Except for editing the school newspaper, I hated high school and the rural football culture around which it revolved. I didn't fit in with the established cliques of popular people (football players and cheerleaders), cowboys or stoners. I had one good friend named Shannon, and we amused ourselves on weekend nights by driving around town in her red Camaro and playing pranks. A favorite stunt was to put suspect items in unsuspecting people's carts at the grocery store (such as a package of condoms in a nun's cart) and then watch them go through the checkout and get embarrassed. But what I still enjoyed doing most was walking for hours through the woods with Lucky by my side.

I wanted to believe that Mom and Dad were right, that I had the potential to accomplish great things in life. But how? I had no adult role models to show me the way. The fathers of many of my friends were rarely home and the River Plantation mothers I knew seemed to spend their days chain-smoking while drinking vodka to pass the time. Meanwhile, I became increasingly aware of how these people made fun of my parents. I witnessed the sneers as Mom pulled out her gas mask when leaving a store or as Dad walked into church wearing his blue polyester plaid "Johnny Carson" suit with bright red socks.

So maybe my parents were eccentric, but at least they were sober, I thought to myself amid the snickering and pointing. In fact, after Elizabeth moved out, Dad had stopped drinking completely. No more vodka tonics at Uncle John's or martinis when he got home from work. I was thankful my parents encouraged me to dream bigger than Conroe, bigger than what constituted a good life in a rural east Texas town where most women hoped only to be housewives.

But it was as if my parents were cheering me on from a sinking ship. I was supposed to swim to shore, wherever that was, while they went under. I thought Mom was succumbing to a mysterious, fatal disease and that was why she had become religious. "Pray for me," she would whisper on the phone to Elizabeth or other Bible study friends whom I assumed must have known more about her condition than I did. Meanwhile, Dad was nearing retirement age and he seemed to have fewer and fewer patients. He had left the Sadler Clinic years ago and established his own private medical practice. Even though money was a problem, he treated increasing numbers of indigent patients who paid him only with pies and eggs. He would soon become the only doctor in Conroe who would agree to treat AIDS patients before it was fully understood how the disease was transmitted. And all the books he talked of writing never got past the idea stage.

Maybe it was because I was reading *The Diary of Anne Frank* for high school English class, but I had a recurring nightmare when I was 15 about the Holocaust. I could see Mom and Dad being herded onto a railroad cattle car with hundreds of others headed for the concentration camps. Mom took in the scene with an amused grin and Dad was smug in his sporty Johnny Carson suit. They were completely oblivious to what was happening. I kept trying to reach them, to save them, but I couldn't push through the dense crowd. I yelled and they couldn't hear me. The train started to move. A terrible death was waiting for them and they were clueless.

~~~

By the third day at the KOA campground, the four of us had settled into a rhythm. Mom stayed inside the shuttered RV reading the Bible and avoided anything that might aggravate her allergies. Dad sat reading in his lawn chair under a big mesquite tree, plotting out novels he wanted to write, and poring over a slightly tattered road atlas. Maria and I played foosball in the campground's rec room, but we also slipped between the barbed wire fence bordering nearby ranch land marked with "no trespassing" signs pocked with bullet holes. We ambled along the river's bank but always kept the campground within sight. I developed a crush on a teenage boy who worked at the campground and moved picnic tables along with other chores. Maria and I nicknamed him "Mr. Biceps," because of the way he could lift a heavy wooden picnic table above his head and put it in the bed of his truck. He was exotic, and not from Conroe. We were mesmerized as we sat on our site's picnic table for hours and watched Mr. Biceps move around the campground.

"You are going to see mountains for your 16th birthday," Dad announced from beneath his tree on the afternoon of the third day. "Real mountains."

"What?" I did not understand how that would be possible. And, I did not want to leave Mr. Biceps.

Dad had been studying the atlas and scoped out a place called the Davis Mountains that was west of Junction. Way west. It was 290 miles away on I-10 but still in Texas, which was a requirement for Dad. "There is no reason to ever leave Texas for a vacation," he always said. "Everything you could ever want is in this state." My parents had already decided they were going to rally and do something special for their daughter who loved the outdoors in ways they did not understand.

On July 4, 1977, my 16th birthday, we unplugged from the Junction KOA and drove west toward the setting sun, past the godforsaken desert towns of Sonora and Ozona, and the truckers' pit stop of Fort Stockton where the gas station restroom swarmed with horse flies. Giant tumbleweeds and truckers driving 95 miles an hour flew by our slow moving rig. By the time we got to Davis Mountains State Park, it was the middle of the night. I did not see mountains on my birthday. Instead, after going through the stressful RV leveling and hook-up, I stood outside in the night, looked up at the stars, and cried.

The next morning, everything was different. Maria and I stepped out of the RV and surveyed our surprising surroundings. We were a long way from the Big Thicket. The air was crisp and cool, and the sky was a bright blue. The campground was encircled by craggy summits that reached elevations of nearly 6,000 feet.

"I think we should climb that one," I said, pointing to the tallest peak.

"How?" Maria asked. She mentioned there was a swimming pool at the park's hotel we could visit instead.

"Well, we would just walk up," I said. We did not know there was such a thing as hiking trails then. We did not even know that there were stretches of public land so vast you could walk all day without running into barbed wire fences and their "no trespassing" signs.

We set out with no water, wearing denim overall shorts and our Rod Laver tennis shoes. Mom was already prostrate in the RV with a headache, and Dad had set up his reading post—this time under an oak tree. He was glad to see us wander off on some kind of adventure.

After walking through the rows of humming RVs, we followed a dirt road to the base of the peak and scouted the most direct line to the top, which was maybe a 1,000-foot climb. The mountain was a patchwork of oak, grass and rock at the bottom. It then shot straight up with bare igneous pillars reaching toward the sky. We traipsed up through the brush without trouble, but once we got to the steep rock, our progress slowed to a crawl. We slipped on the sharp rocks and brushed against cholla and prickly pear as we stumbled. Our shins bled, our shoes filled with cactus spines and we were thirsty in the beating afternoon sun.

"I don't know if this is such a good idea," said Maria.

She was right. Maybe it wasn't. But I was exhilarated in the raw desert landscape. I was drawn to the still-distant summit like a hooked fish reeled in by unseen forces. I needed to get up there and know what it was like to stand on top of a mountain.

The place where we scrambled had been the last stronghold of the Apache a century earlier. In the 1870s, as the Sioux waged war against the U.S. Army in the Dakotas, and the Havasupai resisted being corralled onto a reservation in Grand Canyon, Apache warriors led by a chief named

Victorio hid out in the Davis Mountains. The Tenth Cavalry, stationed at nearby Fort Davis, chased the Apache for 10 years and 1,500 miles from the Davis Mountains, across New Mexico, into Arizona and down to Mexico. It was perhaps the most violent and barbaric period in American military history. Apache warriors developed a feared reputation for routinely taking scalps from enemy soldiers as well as innocent homesteaders. But the U.S. Cavalry, Texas Rangers and independent bounty hunters also received government rewards for taking scalps from Native American women, children and the elderly as well as warriors.[1]

On Oct. 15, 1880, the exhausted Cavalry finally caught up with Victorio and his Apache clan. They were camped 60 miles inside the Mexican border in mountains called Tres Castillos. Victorio and all the Apache men were shot on the spot while the women and children were taken prisoner.[2] When Davis Mountains State Park was established in the 1930s, the federal Civilian Conservation Corps built a hotel called Indian Lodge to memorialize the region's history and it was furnished with blankets and rugs in colorful Apache designs. But the Apaches who had called the 5,000-foot high alpine environment of the Davis Mountains home were relocated to San Carlos Apache Reservation in the barren, southern Arizona desert, more than 500 miles away.

As a child, I was fascinated with stories of Apache warriors and the way they lived off the rugged western Texas landscape. A favorite game that Maria and I played was pretending we were Apache trackers while we hiked through the woods. But when I moved to Arizona two decades later and visited the 1.8-million-acre San Carlos Reservation, I learned the truth about what had become of the tribe. It was easy to see why Geronimo refused to settle there. San Carlos had no mountains, no streams, no trees and no job base. In the 21st century, nearly half of the residents on the San Carlos Apache reservation lived below the federal poverty level[3] and 50 percent of babies born on the reservation tested positive for alcohol or drugs.[4]

From the high perch where Maria and I hung onto rocks in the Davis Mountains, the adobe Indian Lodge had shrunk to a tiny white speck in the foothills, and the campground was swallowed by the deep canyon of Limpia Creek. We kept climbing and climbing. It must have been hours.

We pulled ourselves on top of a rock and then scouted the next 10 feet up. Our slick bottomed tennis shoes slipped on the scree.

Finally, I spotted the curved top of the mountain's summit. On the last 20 feet, the wind pushed back hard and we crawled atop the rounded summit, holding tight to rocks like handrails on a staircase.

Maria and I struggled to stand in the wind as we took in the view, which was like gazing out of an airplane window. Here was the birthday gift from my father. It was more spectacular than anything I had experienced in my 16 years. If there were signs of humans, we could not see them. The bright blue sky was both above and below us. To the east was a Texas tableland; to the south and west were rows and rows of distant mountains, jagged and purple. With that seemingly endless expanse all around me, I got down on my knees and took a picture with my Kodak Instamatic camera of a tiny red flower pushing up through the summit rocks. I would keep the blurry snapshot pinned to my bedroom wall in Conroe as a reminder of that moment when I first saw my future. It was in the West. It was in the wild.

~~~

In February 2001, nearly 24 years after climbing that first mountain, my friend Jane and I were huddled under a narrow overhang jutting from the Supai formation in Grand Canyon. Perched some 1,500 feet below the Grand Canyon's South Rim and 3,000 feet above the Colorado River, we were waiting out a surprise spring storm. Fat snowflakes and grape-size hail spiraled past our faces. A hulking gray cloud sailed in front of us like a schooner on the ocean. Thunder rumbled in the distance and then moved in close.

A few hours earlier, we had said goodbye to my husband Mike and my four-year old son Austin. Mike had driven us down a gut rattling 30-mile dirt road on the Havasupai reservation to get us to the remote South Bass trailhead in western Grand Canyon. He was not thrilled about the five-day, 48-mile backpacking trip that Jane and I were embarking on. But he also knew I was determined to do it, whether he approved or not. Over the last 10 years, while working as an editor for *Backpacker*, I had hiked all over the West, including many trails in Grand Canyon. But all those trips had been in the company of a group of experienced backpackers, and often with Mike. Jane had never hiked in Grand Canyon; she had never been backpacking at all.

"What are you doing?" Mike asked me the day before, perplexed at why I would hike into one of the most rugged and remote sections of Grand Canyon with a hiking partner who had zero experience.

And I could not explain why, exactly, except that I felt I wanted to know more about myself and about the Grand Canyon. To do this, I had to go in on my own, without a safety net. There would be no cellphone or satellite phone to call for help. No rangers or expert hikers to bail me out. I would rely completely on my wilderness skills, which I had methodically honed over the last two decades, motivated by a strong desire never to camp in a place with sewage and electrical hookups.

But on the second day of our trip, as Jane and I walked across the parched Tonto Plateau under a blistering sun, I wondered if I was in over my head. We did not make it as far as planned on the first day. We ended up camping on the lip of the plateau, some 2,000 feet above the Colorado River, at a site with no water. We packed up camp that morning and headed to Serpentine Canyon one mile away, expecting to refill our bottles there, but the tiny spring was dry.

With one liter of water between us, we hiked through the Tonto's black brush flats toward Ruby Canyon, just short of five miles away, where we hoped a spring would flow. Our boots crunched on a fine pavement of gray-green Bright Angel shale as we pushed east beneath the sun, too nervous about water to make any kind of small talk. The route we hiked was called "the Gems" for the side canyons, each named for precious gems harboring seasonal springs. The Gems offered spectacular views and adventure, but they were also potentially dangerous. Dozens of hikers had died of heatstroke over the years on this exposed, waterless stretch across the Tonto.[5]

We contoured around hulking, orange Havasupai Point, which jutted from the South Rim. We stopped to marvel at the bright pink blooms on prickly pear cacti that dotted the plateau. There was no clear trail so we searched for rock cairns here and there signaling the way. Navigating across the Tonto reminded me that I knew how to do this, to find my way.

Sometimes in the civilized world I felt lost, but whenever I ventured into wild places, my inner compass kicked in.

When we reached the top of Ruby, we anxiously peered 400 feet down into the sinuous canyon. At the barely visible bottom, a string of clear pools glinted in the sun. We heard the faintest trickle of water gently dripping onto rocks.

"Yes!" said Jane, fist pumping the sky.

We slid down steep scree to the canyon floor and sprawled on smooth, warm slick rock next to the pools. We had landed in a riparian oasis fed by an ancient aquifer that also nursed springs in Havasu Canyon and Indian Garden. These were all sacred, life-sustaining places for Grand Canyon's native peoples. Water seeped out of Ruby's walls and flowed in narrow channels over rock. It was soft and green, full of ferns and monkey flowers, fluttering with damselflies and canyon wrens. A trip that at first threatened to be lethal had turned out to be luscious.

"I think the Grand Canyon is a woman," said Jane.

I agreed, noting that she was tough on the outside but tender underneath. And we were definitely in one of her sweeter spots.

From Ruby, we connected the dots to other jewels, camping and lounging in canyons named Turquoise and Sapphire. Each canyon harbored its own unique oasis that pampered us and sang us to sleep with sounds of water.

On the last night of our trip, we camped on the Tonto where we could drink in the view. Just a few feet from our tent, the canyon dropped thousands of feet straight down into a tight corridor of black schist and green river. Some 20 miles distant, an archipelago of buttes and temples rose against the North Rim and turned every shade of pink and purple in the day's last light. In between was nothing, just a soul-stirring spaciousness.

That same day in South Dakota, a woman I did not yet know named Tomomi Hanamure hiked in the Badlands and also felt this space. She, too, was out there, seeking.

The next day, as Jane and I hiked up the South Rim on the Hermit Trail, I was recharged from my time in Grand Canyon and by the fact that I had completed a difficult wilderness journey. I missed my son Austin terribly and could not wait to get back to being his mother. At age 39, my life was better than anything I had imagined possible when I was 16. I had a child whom I loved deeply and was my reason for being. I was married to a man who shared my passion for the outdoors. We lived in a beautiful place. And I had a dream job.

But, despite all this, as I reached the Hermit Trail parking lot, I felt the familiar tug. Deep down, I knew something was wrong with me.

10
Blues

South Dakota in the dead of winter is not exactly a tourist hot spot. The daytime temperature rarely rises above freezing and at night it can sink to well below zero. But Tomomi arrived in Custer, South Dakota at Gold Camp Cabins on New Year's Eve 2001 with a plan to stay for at least a couple of weeks. "Who would come visit here in January? Not even hunters," mused Bob Jorgensen, who manages the cabins and a log home building business. "Tomomi was here, though. I don't remember much because she kept to herself, but I know my wife and I were just surprised that she had come back here in winter."[1]

To keep herself company and learn more about the Native American history of the area, Tomomi brought her favorite books: *Stories of the Sioux* and another Lakota traditional classic called *Black Elk Speaks*. She also brought her teddy bear. And she was planning to take classes about Lakota art and culture at Red Cloud Indian School on the Pine Ridge Reservation. But Michael, who she still hoped could become the love of her life, would not be joining her on this trip.

During the six months after her birthday visit to San Francisco, Tomomi had only received sporadic correspondence from Michael. She privately wrote to him almost daily in her journal, but she did not hear from him. In keeping with the Japanese custom of not being too forward, she was reluctant to contact him. But Tomomi worked long hours to earn money for a trip to the States while remaining optimistic that she would get lucky and see Michael, and their relationship would blossom. To this end, she also got her silver fillings replaced with white ones.

With her can-do attitude she bought a plane ticket to the States for her annual New Year's visit, and then she finally called Michael to tell him of her plans. She did not get the response she was hoping for. He told her he was going trekking in Nepal for three weeks in January and then visiting India. He would be gone for a month, maybe more.

"But keep in touch," Michael told Tomomi in a feeble attempt to cheer her up.

Tomomi spent Dec. 23, 2000, the Emperor's Birthday, in Venezuela attending the wedding of Ana, her best friend from the University of Southern Mississippi. "Ana was shining and very beautiful," Tomomi wrote in her journal about the wedding. "Of course she should be happy. I hope I'll be happy like her someday."

After the wedding, Tomomi flew from Caracas to Atlanta and then to Rapid City, making sure that she was where she wanted to be on New Year's.

Dec. 31: Michael, I'm back! I'm back in South Dakota! A year ago, I was here. A year ago, we were here!! But now, I'm alone as always.

On New Year's Day 2001, Tomomi drove around the Black Hills in Custer State Park looking for buffalo. Then she visited Crazy Horse Memorial, a privately-owned monument carved in a mountainside that is a tribute to the Oglala Lakota leader and also an attempt to right the wrong of nearby Mount Rushmore.[2] Back at the cabin, Tomomi finished making the Sioux ceremonial pipe she had started the previous year after visiting Pipestone National Monument. It would have seemed completely out of place to finish this pipe in Japan, so she carried the project and supplies in her luggage to work on it in South Dakota, close to the people who believed in the sacredness of such an item.

There was little that Tomomi did during her travels in the United States that was without intention. Either for reasons of significance to American history or her own experience, she only visited places that were meaningful. And she especially returned to places that were meaningful, almost in ritualistic fashion, timing her travels so she would be in a specific place on the anniversary of something that was important to her. On Jan. 2, 2001, she returned to Wounded Knee.

Jan. 2: Michael, I went to where we met. I went to Wounded Knee. Then I ate pizza, but not you. Doin' same as last year, but not you. My feet are cold at night but nobody can make them warm.

When given the choice, most people would avoid doing something that made them feel sad or lonely or otherwise uncomfortable. But not Tomomi. Sadness and loneliness were as familiar to her as her childhood teddy bear. Perhaps she even found comfort in seeking out the uncomfortable. Sigmund Freud, the father of psychoanalysis, described this kind of behavior as the repetition compulsion. "The patient cannot remember the whole of what is repressed in him, and what he cannot remember may be precisely the essential part of it... He is obliged to repeat the repressed material as a contemporary experience instead of remembering it as something in the past."[3]

Yet, Tomomi was not merely responding to a difficult and lonely childhood. Her compulsion to connect with the wild landscape and Native cultures of the West was also driven by a spiritual seeking, a desire to walk in beauty. She was determined to keep going down this path toward her true nature regardless of fear, sadness, isolation and other hardships that she encountered along the way. This conviction was more than *bokkemon;* it was *bushido.* While the Japanese term *bushido,* or "way of the warrior," is usually associated with the ancient samurai code, the concept is more about self-awareness and dedication than it is about fighting. The code held that samurai rank was attained through learning, self-discipline, and having the courage to face one's fears and weaknesses rather than running from them.[4] Staying the course despite all odds would ensure a "good death" for the samurai, a rebirth in Pure Land.

Despite her sadness about Michael, and the grief she felt at Wounded Knee, Tomomi pulled herself out of the pit of despair and hiked on Jan. 6 to the top of 7,242-foot high Harney Peak, the tallest mountain in the Black Hills as well as the highest U.S. summit east of the Rocky Mountains.

Named after U.S. Army General William S. Harney, who waged bloody battles against the Sioux in the 1870s, the mountain is, ironically, one of the most sacred places to the Lakota. It was the pinnacle of their world, where the stars lived, and a beacon on the Great Plains calling the tribe home each spring. From the craggy summit, they could see their entire homeland, what they called "the Sacred Hoop," and gaze at the stars, "the holy breath of the Great Spirit."[5] It was on top of this mountain that Black Elk, an Oglala Lakota medicine man, had a vision when he was nine years old. He recounted this vision along with the story of his life to American writer and poet John Neihardt for the 1932 book *Black Elk Speaks*.

"I was standing on the highest mountain of them all, and round about me was the whole hoop of the world," Black Elk told Neihardt of his vision as a boy. "And while I stood there I saw more than I can tell and I understood more than I saw; for I was seeing in a sacred manner the shapes of all things in the spirit, and the shape of all shapes as they must live together like one being."[6] Four years later, at age 13, Black Elk would fight in the Battle of Little Big Horn, and he later survived the Wounded Knee Massacre in 1890.

Having read *Black Elk Speaks*, Tomomi knew the significance of the mountain she had climbed. She took in the view from the summit and lingered as long as she could stand it in the biting cold. Then she hiked to the top of a granite sentinel called Little Devil's Tower, taking in more of the spectacular Black Hills landscape. And she also thought of Michael. *"What did you see in India?"*

Making the most of every day and fighting off the constant creep of loneliness, Tomomi shopped at thrift stores in Rapid City *(I bought fancy red cowboy boots!),* drove the scenic Iron Mountain Road, toured the Journey Museum with its exhibit on Sioux history, and visited the Wild West outlaw town of Deadwood. Thinking she might feel better around people, Tomomi left the Custer cabin for a few days to stay at The Hostel in Jackson Hole. She hiked around Jackson Lake, hung out with fellow travelers in the living room at the hostel, and even picked up a hitchhiker one day when she was driving. But no matter what she did, Tomomi still felt the blues. Her teddy bear was no substitute for what she imagined it could have been like with Michael. She decided she should return to the Black Hills.

Jan. 20: Michael, I'm always happy and never feel lonely in the U.S.A. But this time I feel completely lonely. Even when staying at hostel.

On her way back to Custer, Tomomi stopped in the town of Sturgis, which is near Bear Butte, a sacred mountain of the Lakota, and also home of America's biggest motorcycle rally. Tomomi went into a café and sat at the counter. A bubbly American woman named Sylvia who was visiting Sturgis with her husband could see Tomomi's sadness. Sylvia asked if she could buy Tomomi a slice of apple pie. She queried Tomomi about where she was from and what she was doing on her travels. Then Sylvia asked if they could pray together.

Tomomi agreed, thinking maybe this prayer would bring her good luck. Sylvia clasped Tomomi's hand in hers and closed her eyes.

"Dear heavenly father." Sylvia paused and took a deep breath, perhaps for emphasis or for divine inspiration. Tomomi wondered if the prayer was over.

"We pray today for your daughter in Christ, Tommy. We ask you, heavenly father, to look upon her and have mercy. We ask that you protect her on her journey and bring her peace and companionship and joy. May she feel the love that is shown all of God's children and look to you, heavenly father, for guidance. I thank you, Lord, for introducing me today to Tommy. In Jesus' name we pray. Amen."

Tomomi did not know she was supposed to say "amen." She just smiled, thanked Sylvia for the pie and asked for Sylvia's address to add to her treasured collection of American contacts. Then Tomomi went on her way, back to the prairie, where soon the prayer would be answered.

Tomomi spent the next two days alone in Badlands National Park, drifting through an undulating ocean of space with thumb-shaped buttes that sat like ships on a faraway shore and the vast blue sky that was a mirror reflection of the Earth. She hiked on the Medicine Root Trail and other places that were once the territory of the Lakota. These lands were at the heart of the Sacred Hoop and the place where the Great Spirit was summoned more than a century earlier with the Ghost Dance. Here, Tomomi knew she had been before, in another lifetime. She had a vision.

Jan. 24: Michael, I hiked Badlands Prairie. I felt long time ago I was something. I could be an animal. I could be an Indian.

~~~

In 1889, when many of the tribes in the West were starving, driven from their homelands onto reservations, suffering from smallpox and cholera epidemics, and desperate for any promise of returning to their life before Anglos arrived, Wovoka, the Paiute medicine man, seemed to have the only answer. His prophecy about how to drive the white man back across the ocean spread like wildfire through Indian country.

Contrary to what the U.S. Army thought he was preaching, Wovoka's message was one of promoting peace and nonviolent solutions, almost like a Native American version of Jesus. "Do not tell lies. Do right always. Live in peace. Do not harm anyone," he preached. Wovoka maintained that the tribes of the West must stop their longtime practices of waging war against one another and cease the traditional self-mutilation practices that had been part of the mourning for a deceased family member. [7]

Wovoka predicted that the restored Earth and disappearance of the white man would come in 1891, but to hasten this event and bring the return of lost relatives, all Indians should participate in circle dance ceremonies. During these events, which were to be conducted at specific intervals over a period of five days, men, women and children of a tribe should hold hands and dance in a circle, calling out to the Great Spirit and to the spirits of dead relatives. Dancers were instructed to place holy feathers in their hair and wear a colorfully painted "ghost shirt" that would protect them from the white man's bullets.

Ghost Dances were held with increasing frequency in 1889 and 1890 by tribes across the West — by the Havasupai at the bottom of Grand Canyon, by the Apache in Cibeque Creek, and by the Lakota in the Badlands, to name a few. Most often the circle dance was performed around a tree or pole, and the dancing lasted for hours on end. Participants would faint from fatigue, or, as if in some kind of delirious trance, yelling out incoherently as fellow dancers kept going. The goal was often to keep dancing without stopping until the dancer obtained some kind of vision or message from a deceased loved one.

Anthropologist James Mooney conducted interviews with Plains Indians who participated in the dances and published his observations in an 1894 Bureau of Ethnology article titled, "The Ghost Dance Religion and Sioux Outbreak of 1890." In the article, a Lakota tribal member, Mrs. Z.A. Parker, shared her memories of a Ghost Dance she attended at White Clay Creek on the Pine Ridge Reservation in June 1890.

"As the crowd gathered about the tree, the high priest, or master of ceremonies, began his address, giving them directions as to the chant and other matters," recalled Parker. "After he had spoken for about fifteen minutes they arose and formed in a circle. As nearly as I could count, there were between three hundred and four hundred persons. One stood directly behind another, each with his hands on his neighbor's shoulders. After walking a few times, chanting 'Father I come,' they stopped marching, but remained in the circle, and set up the most fearful, heart-piercing wails I ever heard—crying, moaning, groaning, and shrieking out their grief, and naming of their departed friends and relatives, at the same time taking up handfuls of dust at their feet, washing their hands in it and throwing it over their heads. Finally, they raised their eyes to heaven, their hands clasped high above their heads, and stood straight and perfectly still, invoking the power of the Great Spirit to allow them to see and talk with their people who had died."[8]

Parker reported that of the 300 to 400 Native Americans participating in the dance, at least 100 temporarily passed out during the ritual.

The Ghost Dance gatherings were not unlike Christian Pentecostal or other evangelical religious revivals during that time period. At these multiday events, Anglo participants were encouraged to basically go crazy, temporarily, in order to have a spiritual encounter. They would speak in tongues, collapse in a delirium, even pass rattlesnakes around, and the energized crowd would chant along with a preacher who was worked up into a sweaty lather.[9] The group frenzy was attributed to the healing power of Jesus. But leaders at Western outposts for the U.S. Army and Bureau of Indian Affairs administrators found the Ghost Dances intolerable and issued warnings to the tribes that they must stop. The Lakota did not heed the warning, certain that the Great Spirit would prevail if they kept up the dancing.

Oglala medicine man Black Elk was one of the few tribal members to survive the massacre at Wounded Knee in December 1890. But he felt that his tribe would never recover.

He would later tell author John Neihardt: "I did not know then how much was ended. When I look back now from this high hill of my old age, I can still see the butchered women and children lying heaped and scattered all along the crooked gulch as plain as when I saw them with eyes still young. And I can see that something else died there in the bloody mud, and was buried in the blizzard. A people's dream died there. It was a beautiful dream…The nation's hoop is broken and scattered."[10]

~~~

On the icy, wind-blasted winter nights in South Dakota, just as during her stay at the hogan in Arizona, Tomomi's thoughts inevitably turned toward the person she yearned for most: her mother. Tomomi's only thread to her mother was a single photograph that she kept on her dresser in her bedroom in Yokohama. This fading photograph was all the information she had on the person she desperately longed to know. Her mother was attractive, with short, curly hair and big, bright eyes. She was holding Tomomi, a bald baby in a frilly white dress, and standing next to a young Tetsushi. Everyone was smiling.

Except for having straight black hair, Tomomi had grown into a woman who looked just like her mother, with the same bright eyes, high cheekbones, and a big smile that lit up her face. What had separated her parents and what had become of her mother was a great mystery to Tomomi. Her father never spoke of his first wife.

After spending his teenage years working in a factory and living in a dormitory in Tokyo, far from his home in Takarabe, Tetsushi married a young woman who was also a factory worker and from a rural Japanese village. In 1972 they had their daughter Tomomi, which means "wisdom and beauty." But by the time Tomomi was four, Tetsushi said he "smelled another man" on his wife and kicked her out of the home.[11] Tomomi would never see her mother again. Rather than turn over custody of Tomomi to her mother, which was what most divorced Japanese men did at the time,

Tetsushi insisted he would raise his daughter alone. But he did not have family nearby or financial resources for child care. Eventually, Tomomi learned to take care of herself while her father worked 12-hour shifts at a factory.

Now, Tomomi hunkered down in South Dakota, where the days were gray and slick with freezing rain and snow. And the nights were covered in ice. She was determined to stay for at least several more weeks, and she was spending what was left of her savings on cheap motels in Rapid City and Gordon, a grim reservation town just inside the Nebraska border. The cabin in Custer had become too expensive. She signed up for a bead making class at Red Cloud Indian School taught by a man named White Buffalo. And she wanted to study Lakota in the place where the language was still spoken.

Jan. 30: Michael, the weather is pretty bad here now. Last night I slipped twice. I'm tryin' to learn Lakota myself. I got a dictionary. Will be good.

Feb. 1: Michael, it was second bead class. I also did loom work. I think I really like to do this kind of thing. I wanna do more.

Japan seemed a world away, and Tomomi did not miss it in the slightest, but she did think of her father. She called him on his birthday and sensed his frustration. He could not imagine what she was doing in South Dakota. When was she coming home, he asked. Soon, she said. But, actually, Tomomi did not know when she would return and intended to put it off as long as possible. She was looking for something and she had not yet found it.

On Feb. 3, Tomomi was driving on US 18 through the Pine Ridge Reservation after doing her laundry in Gordon. This desolate stretch of highway was lined with frozen 15-foot-high snowbanks that buried barbed wire fences. In the distance, smoke rose from government housing—either from woodstoves or perhaps tribal members who burned trash in their yards to stay warm because they had run out of money for propane. Black Elk described the scene in 1930 as his "people settling down in square gray houses, scattered here and there across this hungry land."[12] Not much had changed. And probably the only thing worse than being a person trying to live on Pine Ridge was the prospect of being a stray dog. There were hundreds, maybe thousands, roaming in hungry packs, searching for garbage or carrion to eat. Occasionally they ate other dogs.

Somewhere along this road, Tomomi came upon a pack of dogs that was in a furious fighting heap. As she stopped her car to get a closer look, she saw the dogs had ganged up on a puppy and were taking turns pouncing on it and biting it. She jumped out of her car and ran toward the pack, yelling sternly at the animals in Japanese. She was not afraid; this was a woman who had also approached buffalo and wolves without incident.[13] The dogs backed off and she looked down at the puppy. His snout was bleeding and half his fur was missing. The puppy flattened his ears as Tomomi neared, as if he expected to be kicked. Without thinking twice, Tomomi scooped up the puppy in her arms and ran back to the car.

Feb. 3: Michael, I found a blue eyed pretty puppy!! He's so cute!! But he has some kind of skin problem. I guess I'll take him to hospital. I just fallin' in love with him!!

The puppy was a shepherd-husky mix, a "rez dog" descended from a long line of mongrels that had lived with the Lakota before there was such a place as a reservation. Dogs were an important part of the tribe's tradition going back thousands of years; they were faithful companions, guarded the camps, and even pulled harnesses loaded with tipis and gear before the Spanish introduced horses to the Great Plains in the 1700s.

The stray found by Tomomi was about four months old. He was black with a brown star on his chest and brown markings on his front legs. He had one ear that perked up and one that flopped halfway over, Scooby-Doo style. And he had eyes that were as blue as the South Dakota sky on a cloudless winter day. Tomomi named him Blues, for his eyes and also for her love of American blues music. Because of the way Japanese pronunciation often turns English "l" sounds into "r" sounds, most Americans that Tomomi encountered with her puppy mistakenly thought his name was Bruce.

Tomomi took Blues to a vet in Gordon who told her that he was born with a form of skin fungus (commonly called mange) that made him lose his fur. She got medication to treat the fungus and also started investigating if it might be possible to take Blues back with her to live in Japan. She figured this would only be temporary because she intended to soon make a home for herself in the States, in someplace big and wild where a dog like Blues belonged. Blues romped after her on hikes in the Black Hills. He went with her to bead-making class and to a powwow on the Pine Ridge Reservation. He sat on a blanket in the car's passenger seat and watched attentively as Lakota dancers decked out in headdresses with eagle feathers and porcupine quills danced in a circle to chanting and drumbeats. The companionship of Blues gave Tomomi a new energy. She had rescued him, but he had also rescued her.

Feb. 6: Michael, I bought a lot of beads!! I want to make a Medicine Bag, Loop Tie, Buckle and so on. I'll make something for you. I hope you'll like it.

Feb. 13: Michael, I think Blues is pretty smart cause he understands me in like 3 days. But he is also too excited sometimes. It's so foggy now.

Teddy immediately took a back seat to Tomomi's new furry friend. With Blues riding shotgun, Tomomi drove 1,500 miles from Rapid City to Hattiesburg, Mississippi to visit her alma mater where she attended English school six years earlier. She went to her favorite stores and restaurants, the apartment where she used to live, and the University of Southern Mississippi campus. But many of the friends she had made at the college had moved on. She also took Blues to a vet who told her that the skin fungus might prevent him from passing Japanese animal inspection and being able to enter the country. Tomomi was disappointed at this news but determined to keep trying. She stalled for time, waiting for Blues to heal and continuing to travel until her savings were gone. She also hoped that maybe if she hung around in the States long enough, Michael would return home from India and she would get to see him.

From Hattiesburg, she drove back to Custer and stayed there with Blues for a few days. Then Tomomi flew with Blues to San Francisco. She drove past Michael's apartment, but he was not home. For the next two weeks she explored northern California with Blues, going to Yosemite,

Death Valley, Muir Beach and walking among the giant groves of the world's biggest trees in Sequoia National Forest.

March 7: Michael, Sequoia is something…something. I don't know. I saw what I can't explain. Nature makes me feel something that I am unable to find word.

Tomomi walked the streets of San Francisco with Blues and drew endless comments from passersby about how cute he was. She went to all the places she had visited with Michael, but this time, without Michael. She did find a vet in Carmel who gave Blues his rabies and other shots and issued the official papers for his transport to Japan. Tomomi was ecstatic. However, once in Japan, Blues would have to remain at the Tokyo Narita airport in quarantine for three months. Tomomi would visit Blues daily and, during these three months, he grew from a 25-pound puppy into a very large dog. Soon Blues would reach 95 pounds and when he stood on his hind legs to lick her face, he was nearly as tall as Tomomi.

Tomomi waited until she was in Yokohama to break the news to her father that they would soon have a rowdy rez dog from South Dakota joining them in their cramped 700-square-foot apartment. Her father said this was the "most outrageous American souvenir she could have ever dreamed up."[14] Her stepmother was not pleased either. Tomomi just wanted to be with Blues and, even though she was now completely out of money, she had to figure out a way to return to the States.

March 16: Michael, I'm in Japan. I don't feel that I'm home. I don't have a home. I'm looking for a home. Yes, I'm looking for my own home that makes me miss home. I've never had a home. Maybe when I was small. Blues is not here. I miss him.

~~~

On the other side of the world, at the bottom of the Grand Canyon, Randy Wescogame was also a boy without a home. That same year, in 2001, when Randy was 13, his mother realized she could not rehabilitate him on

her own as she had once hoped. She reached out for help, seeking to get
Randy psychological counseling and admittance to a boarding school for
troubled youth. It was her last ditch effort to keep him out of the juvenile
corrections system and from becoming a ward of the state.

She wrote to the Havasupai Tribal Court on April 28, 2001:

"As the mother of said Randy Wescogame I would like to submit this
statement to let the Havasupai Tribal Court be aware of the deep concern I
have for my son. During our marriage, his father very much favored Randy
from the time of his birth and after our divorce Randy was lost. I feel with
[Randy's] behavior being bad that's a part of his way of wanting attention!!
Randy does love both of us and it's very difficult for him to understand
the fact that he is away from his own father. I send Randy to go visit his
father and his father refuses to see him. The primary point here is that I
would like for Randy to get the professional help he deserves. I want him to
change and be a part of us. I will miss him but as I had mentioned he needs
HELP! Thank you. (Signed) Carla F. Crook" [15]

But in 2001 Randy remained in Supai until he was finally charged
for petty theft, public intoxication and assault of a tribal member. He was
also starting to use methamphetamine.[16] Without getting the psychiatric
counseling his mother had requested, Randy was sent to a juvenile
correctional facility near Phoenix that was filled with hardened urban gang
members.

Still fighting bitterly with Carla over child support, Billy asked that he
be released from responsibility for his children. He especially did not want
to be held liable for the actions of Randy.

Billy submitted a letter to the Havasupai Tribal Court on Nov. 7, 2001:

"I feel that the best thing for the children is to take away parental
rights from both of us parents, because the children have become so
incorrigible to the fact that the oldest boy Randy Wescogame is now in jail
and Ambrose Wescogame is in trouble at school and Brianna Wescogame
does not attend school. The children have become so out of control that no
one can do anything with them. I would very much like to see them placed
elsewhere, not here in Supai. I pray for a good solution to the problem with
the said children. Respectfully submitted, Billy Wescogame Sr."[17]

The Lakota word for children is *wakanyeja*, which means "sacred beings." The Havasupai tradition, like that of the Lakota, was to treat children with the greatest of reverence and care. But as Randy was falling into deeper trouble and crying out for help, there was no social safety net to catch him, and no one beyond his struggling parents seemed capable of hearing him.

11
Panic

Not long after returning from the Grand Canyon in February 2001, I started having heart palpitations. It felt like a fish was flopping inside my chest. Sometimes the sensation would also come with sharp pains. I was too busy working and taking care of my 4-year-old son Austin to do more than pause momentarily, wait for the flopping to stop and resume whatever I was doing. I was reluctant to tell anyone about it since it seemed ridiculous that someone who appeared as physically fit as myself could be experiencing heart trouble. But by that summer I found myself on a backpacking trip at the bottom of remote Chevelon Canyon in central Arizona with the palpitations so closely spaced I could barely breathe.

My husband, Mike, Austin and I had hiked down a steep trail that afternoon with Mike and me shouldering heavy packs while Austin hopped along, looking with wonderment at flowers and bugs. The relationship between Mike and me was at its best when we were in the wilderness away from the pressures of work and home. While I maintained the steady writing job with *Backpacker* that paid the rent, Mike bounced from one position to the next, working sometimes as a graphic designer and other times as a Grand Canyon hiking guide. What he really wanted to do was pursue being an artist and paint full time, but so far there was absolutely no money in that. And I needed him to hold down the home front when I traveled for story assignments.

Mike and I had met a decade earlier when we were both living in Austin, Texas. After graduating with a journalism degree from the University of Texas, I had worked my way up to being the editor of *Austin Magazine*. Mike was the art director. Even though I was 28 at the time, I could count on one hand the number of men I had dated in my life. I still carried with me the childhood fears about getting pregnant and how I didn't want to go down the same path as Elizabeth. Men seemed threatening, and Mike was especially dangerous. He was handsome, charismatic, a talented artist, full of stories about his checkered past, possessed a deep knowledge of cutting edge literature, and was an avid hiker. Mike loaned me his copy of William Faulkner's *Light in August*. By about page 100, I was head over heels in love.

Mike helped me find my way out of Texas and establish myself as an outdoor writer. In 1991 we moved to Pennsylvania together where I took a job as an assistant editor for *Backpacker,* and he worked in New York City as a graphic designer. Then we moved to Arizona as I continued to work for *Backpacker,* and he was the art director for the hip weekly *Phoenix New Times*. With our yellow lab Sierra and golden retriever Bunky in tow, we backpacked nearly every weekend in wilderness areas throughout the Southwest. During the week, we often hung out at bars with fellow hard working, hard drinking journalists.

But Mike also had his vices, with alcohol being No. 1. If I drank four beers in one night, he might drink 14. And he often went out drinking when I stayed home to meet my story deadlines. Yet, I found Mike far more interesting than other men I knew and the drinking just seemed to go with the territory. His passion for life, his art, and the wild mood swings that often drove him to drink were familiar to me — and in a twisted way, even endearing.

However, after Austin was born in 1997, the party was over as far as I was concerned. We could not go out to bars with an infant, and we also could not afford the myriad costs that came from Mike's binges: bounced checks, DUIs, lost jobs, pissed off friends and neighbors. After one particularly bad binge when Austin was a baby, Mike finally agreed with me. Surrounded by broken furniture he had thrown against the walls, he swore he would never drink again. He loved Austin and wanted to devote himself to being a good father. But the specter of alcohol was always there. It pulled on Mike from one end while I tugged from the other trying to hold our family together.

Mike said he needed my help to stay above water, to resist the deep dives into the dark spaces. By then, I had more willpower than I knew what to do with so I accepted the challenge.

Meanwhile, back in Texas, my parents were consumed with one catastrophe after another. And the crises were often exacerbated by Mom's increasing neuroses. The home where we grew up had become infested with termites. But because Mom said she could not tolerate the chemicals used in the pesticides to treat the termites, my parents just let the infestation get worse until the house was destroyed. With the insurance money they received, Mom and Dad moved into another home in River Plantation, which was inundated in 1994 by a 100-year flood. Mom said the moisture that seeped into the walls and floor filled the house with mold, so my parents moved again. Dad was well past retirement age but kept working at various low-paying medical staff positions with the county and state health departments because my parents' financial situation spiraled down with every crisis. Mom's chronic pain and headaches were worse than ever, which seemed to be matched in intensity by Dad's angry outbursts. Now with a child of my own to care for, I tried to keep my distance from their chaos. My greatest fear was that somehow I might be saddled with managing Mom, and my life would once again be held hostage by her long list of chores for me.

Despite our own financial struggles and Mike's battle with depression, I felt the life Mike, Austin and I had in Arizona was pretty good. It was free from Catholic rules, gas masks and no trespassing signs. I was proud of the way Mike had stopped drinking cold turkey and was grateful for the loving, compassionate father he had become. And we had successfully parlayed our mutual love for wilderness hiking into story assignments that allowed us to take Austin backpacking in Arizona's Sonoran Desert, Alaska's Kesugi Ridge and everywhere in between.

But that night in Chevelon Canyon, I thought the fairy tale was over. With all three of us zipped in a tent along Chevelon Creek, the fish was flopping inside my chest nonstop. "Mommy," Austin cooed. "Read the story."

I had paused for my heart rhythm to reset but it just sped up. The inside of the small tent started to spin and I pushed my way out of the mesh and into the fresh night air. Mike followed me.

"What is with you?" he asked.

"I don't know," I said, crying. "I think I'm having a heart attack."

Mike laughed and put his arms around me. I looked up at the stars and studied the Milky Way's arch across the blackness. Eventually, the stars calmed me and convinced me that I was not dying. At least not that night.

Once back in Flagstaff, I visited a cardiologist who did a full work up. Because I was a runner and a hiker, my cardio fitness level was beyond what his outdated treadmill machine could measure for a stress test. "You should go run an ultra-marathon," the doctor told me. He explained I was in excellent health and that the sensations I was feeling in my chest and the shortness of breath were the classic symptoms of a stress-induced panic attack.

So I was just stressed. With great relief and enthusiasm, I took on stress reduction as yet another challenge. Simply knowing that my heart was fine helped reduce my stress level for a time. I tried to be more relaxed about Mike's unpredictability and attempted to ease up on my own expectations about needing to be a Super Mom. I was determined to overcome the panic attacks. I was also determined to give Austin a happy childhood and be the kind of nurturing mother I didn't have. I added yoga to my exercise regimen and started getting a monthly massage. After enduring a panic attack on an airplane en route to a *Backpacker* staff meeting, I bought a self-help book at the airport bookstore called *Don't Panic*.[1]

But life continued to bear down on me.

~~~

By the time I was enrolling Austin in kindergarten in 2002, Maria and I were also moving my parents from Conroe to an assisted living facility in Austin, Texas for Alzheimer's patients. They had both been diagnosed several years earlier as having Alzheimer's disease. My sisters and I had tried to manage long distance a crew of caregivers in their home until the last one finally quit after Dad slit his wrists with a razor blade in a suicide attempt.

Maria was married and raising three daughters in Austin. Elizabeth had three children and lived in Arlington, Texas. And then I was in Arizona. As we tended to our young families, we knew that Mom and Dad were like a ticking time bomb and we hoped we could ignore it for just a little while longer. But then Maria got a call from the sheriff in Conroe. He said Mom and Dad had been found in a ditch on the side of the road in River Plantation. Dad was driving their big Lincoln Continental and Mom was in the passenger seat. Neither Mom nor Dad was injured, but they did not know who they were or where they lived. Eventually a neighbor came by and helped the sheriff's deputy get them home. Once inside, the neighbor found the house a den of dysfunction. Mom's little notes about her medical symptoms were everywhere, past due bills covered the tables, and there was hardly any food in the cupboards. Dad had finally retired and was just watching old movies all day. It took tough talk from the sheriff and the neighbor to finally convince my sisters and me that we had to step in.

"Well, they don't know how Mom and Dad have always been crazy," I told Maria when she called to tell me that the neighbor had taken our parents to see a doctor. "It's probably just them getting a bit senile on top of being crazy. Maybe they have a concussion from the car accident?"

"No," Maria said. "They have Alzheimer's. Both of them. And it's advanced."

A decade earlier, Elizabeth had been diagnosed with chronic kidney disease, for which no cause could be determined. She was in need of a second transplant and was struggling for her own life. And she had understandably never really reconnected with Dad after he banished her. So it was mostly up to Maria and me to deal with two parents whose lives were in a state of complete disarray. After Dad's suicide attempt, I gathered up Austin, stuck my *Don't Panic* book in a suitcase, and flew to Texas.

Being a physician, Dad was fully aware of the dire nature of the Alzheimer's diagnosis. But neither he nor Mom were willing to move from their home in River Plantation, even though Maria and I had explained to them there was no other option. So we decided to trick them, pulling off a kind of Red Bandit Club caper.

"We are going to take you to see a special doctor in Austin," I told Mom and Dad, explaining why I was visiting from Arizona. They were so happy to see me, Austin and Maria that they gladly agreed to the 250-mile road trip.

Maria and I packed the Lincoln with all the things Mom needed for the drive: the special foam pillows for her aching back, her gas mask, a cooler full of allergen-free foods, and her notebooks chronicling her symptoms that she wanted to share with the doctor. Mom and Austin sat in the back seat. Dad sat in the passenger seat with his *Conroe Courier* on his lap. He wore his tennis clothes in case we managed to travel back through time and land at a tennis match where his doubles partner might be waiting.

After we pulled out of the driveway, Maria and her husband Jose loaded their truck with Mom and Dad's clothes, their two recliners and pictures to decorate their rooms at an assisted living facility in Austin called Arden Courts. As I drove the lumbering Lincoln down the Interstate, Maria and Jose sped past without Mom and Dad noticing. My parents' recliners rocked wildly in the truck bed and Maria gave me a thumbs-up through the window. Maria and Jose were rushing to get Mom and Dad's rooms set up before we arrived.

In Austin, a welcoming party of people in white uniforms greeted us at the Arden Courts entrance.

"Hello Dr. McGivney!" said the facility director, taking Dad's hand.

Dad did not speak and gave a tense smile, the kind of smile I had seen many times before that showed he was angry. He knew what was up.

I ushered Dad to his room as my chest thundered with palpitations. He would live in a hall called Boat House Cove. Maria took Mom to her room located in Cottage Place, well away from Dad so hopefully she would not pester him with her persistent medical questions.

Fortunately, Mom and Dad were both far enough along in their disease that they adjusted fairly quickly to the structured environment at Arden Courts. Maria lived nearby and visited them weekly. I visited them several times a year from Arizona. We hired a Nigerian man named Gabriel, a graduate student at the University of Texas, to drive Dad around town and take him to get chocolate shakes at Dairy Queen. Gabriel would e-mail Maria and me reports on his outings.

One note from October 2004 read:

"Dear Annette, your dad is not just like a patient to me but like a dad to me. When we drive we talk about our past, our families and the great future ahead of us. I am so amazed at the way he remembers the stories I told him about my family still back in Nigeria. The truth of all this is your dad is very religious and God is taking good care of him. The few times I spent with your mum were so nice too."

Sometimes, Dad would be depressed and tell Gabriel he didn't feel like leaving his room. But Gabriel would not let Dad off that easy. "I won today," he wrote to Maria and me in November 2004. "He kept his promise of going out today. He was actually waiting for me as I walked in and asked where we were going. We had fun together. He drank all of his chocolate shake. I am so happy we could get back on our outing routine."

Once they got settled into the communal lifestyle at Arden Courts, my parents even went through a kind of Alzheimer's-induced romance. They went to dances together in the recreation room, held hands, played Bingo, and socialized with fellow residents in a way I that never witnessed in Conroe.

During this time, Maria and I also embarked on the daunting dismantling of my parents' five-bedroom home in River Plantation. We knew they would never return and the house was filled to the brim with all that Dad had worked for his entire adult life. What Maria, Elizabeth and I didn't want in our homes or couldn't fit in the rooms at Arden Courts was auctioned off or sent to Goodwill.

After staying as far away as possible from Conroe for two decades, I was now forced to return. Like an archaeologist sifting through the remains of a lost city, I spent weeks in the River Plantation house carefully examining and sorting through mountains of stuff while Austin played with my childhood toys and on exercise equipment my parents never used. There were all the books on writing I had given Dad that contained notes about his ideas for novels; there were the old 45 Glen Miller records that my parents used to dance to when we lived in Houston; there were tiny pieces of paper everywhere with manic scrawling by Mom about her bowel movements; Dad's tennis trophies; Mom's gas mask filters; Dad's medical magazines; my childhood writings that Mom had photocopied and saved; the cheese board our housekeeper Laura had given me that was still in the box.

And there was the bag that Dad carried around during his last months in Conroe containing a note with his name and address in case he forgot who he was. It was evidence of how much he was suffering when I didn't even know it. Also in the bag was a Bible verse scrawled on a piece of paper. Was Dad reading Mom's Bible, I wondered? I would have thought the note was from Mom except it was in Dad's shaky, almost illegible handwriting. "Psalm 102: A prayer in times of distress," it read. "Hear my prayer O Lord and let my cry come unto thee. Hide not thy face from me in the day when I am in trouble; incline thine ear unto me; in the day when I call answer me speedily. For my days are consumed like smoke and my bones are burned as an hearth. My heart is smitten and withered like grass, so that I forget to eat my bread... I am like a pelican of the wilderness; I am like an owl of the desert. I watch, and am as a sparrow alone upon the house top."[2]

Sitting there amid the relics of my childhood, I mourned my parents' fate, especially Dad's — all his dreams never realized. His belief in my potential and the joy of making him proud of me were always my biggest inspirations. But I also sensed an odd disconnect, like the person remembering these things — giving Dad the book, seeing my parents dance, treasuring the cheese board — was not me. I was like a robot. I could function all day long. But I could not feel.

~~~

After three-and-a-half years, the assisted living honeymoon at Arden Courts was over. As my parents' mental state declined, Mom became increasingly troublesome with her constant demands about physical ailments, medications and "Where is Dr. McGivney? I must see him!" She followed the caregivers around asking questions; she dug through the trash and other people's dresser drawers; she stayed up all night regardless of the sedatives the staff gave her. Even though Mom and Dad were in different halls and the caregivers were supposed to run interference, Mom would constantly seek out Dad and then he would blow up. It was an old dynamic that became magnified with their dementia.

"Marjory! God dammit! Leave me alone!" he would shout, clenching his fists.

As the caregivers came running into Dad's room, Mom would just walk closer and continue asking him questions, completely oblivious to his anger.

The staff at Arden Courts said they could no longer handle Mom. She was essentially getting booted from an assisted living facility for requiring too much assistance. The Arden Courts director suggested that Mom be transferred to a mental hospital in Austin that was legally allowed to use "soft restraints."

"What does that mean?" I asked Maria.

"Well, they would drug her and strap her to a bed," she said.

The other option was to move Mom to an assisted living facility near my home in Flagstaff called The Peaks. The staff there said they could handle Mom.

Dad liked Arden Courts and didn't want to leave, but Maria and I insisted. We didn't want Mom to die strapped to a bed in a hospital full of mental patients. And we also couldn't bear the thought of permanently separating Mom and Dad. We still held on to the dream that maybe our parents could somehow, someday be happy together.

Dad didn't like our reasons for uprooting him. He had never lived outside Texas and had no desire to leave the Lone Star State under any circumstances. "I'd rather live in a convent!" he shouted, throwing over a lamp in his room at Arden Courts.

But in August 2006, Maria and I were pushing Mom and Dad in wheelchairs onto a plane headed for Arizona, our pockets loaded with tranquilizers in case things got out of hand.

"You'll love the mountains," I promised Dad. "I can even take you to see the Grand Canyon."

12
Route 66

The life Tomomi returned to in Yokohama in spring 2001 had become like a prison. And she longed to escape. Following her three months of traveling in the United States, she got another temporary factory job and squeezed into the high-rise apartment with her father, stepmother, stepbrother and a puppy that had grown into a 95-pound dog.

Blues was Tomomi's primary focus, her only bright spot in Japan. The mongrel from the Pine Ridge reservation was the embodiment of the West and the Native American culture that she loved. However, for her father, Blues represented what Tetsushi believed were the despicable qualities of Americans—Blues was too big, messy, impolite and disrespectful of Japanese cultural norms. Blues was a lot like the drunk American soldiers he had crossed paths with years ago down south who were stationed on military bases in Kyushu after World War II.[1]

April 21: Michael, my father yells at me because Blues makes a mess. But Blues is still a baby. The people in this house are so stupid. I don't know how to explain this to them.

April 30: Michael, I do hate my step mom. I don't want to see her face again. I'll look for a job in the U.S.A.

Michael was still in India that spring, but Tomomi occasionally e-mailed him when she got up the nerve and continued to secretly write to him in her journal.

May 8: Michael, it's my birthday today. Do you remember? I know you don't. Well, a year ago I was with you and happy. But not this year. You're so far from me.

Although she had a tight group of girlfriends in Yokohama with whom she enjoyed socializing, Tomomi struggled with a feeling of loneliness and alienation that cut to her core. It was not just that she had been lonely the past few months since returning from the States, but that she had felt utterly alone her entire life. This despair was at times almost unbearable. She wrote once in her diary in 2001 that she wanted to kill herself. But Blues gave Tomomi something to live for — and there was also the prospect of her next trip to America and the hope of seeing Michael.

Sept. 30: Lately there's nothing special. No fun except playin' with Blues. He still thinks he's a king. I guess I wanna live with him. Find a possibility!!

Tomomi rallied. She kept working to earn money for more travel. She wrote again to Tim and Luana Nelson, the couple she met in Grand Canyon, asking for more information on how to get a Green Card. She received two e-mails from Michael over a period of four months that were the emotional equivalent of winning the lottery. By December 2001 Tomomi was flying to Atlanta for a month-long trip. Blues was in the cargo hold. Unlike the strict quarantine rules in Japan, the United States allowed dogs with all the required vaccinations to enter the country with no waiting period. Tomomi's plan was to drive all 2,200 miles of Route 66 from Chicago to Los Angeles with her best friend riding shotgun.

But the United States that Tomomi was returning to was a changed nation. A few months prior, on Sept. 11, terrorists had crashed planes into the Pentagon and the World Trade Center. Once hospitable Americans were suddenly afraid of foreigners, and no place was less welcoming than major airports like Hartsfield-Jackson Atlanta International. The new Department of Homeland Security's TSA guards found Tomomi suspicious and pulled her aside. Maybe it was the frequency with which she had visited the United States in the past few years that somehow raised a red flag, or that she told them she was looking for a job in the States, or that she was bringing a large mongrel into the country. The guards took Tomomi to an interrogation room and grilled her for several hours. *"I will never forget [the interrogator's] face. He was cold blooded and never smiled. Who can I trust?"* Eventually they let her go. It was the first time Tomomi had a bad experience in the United States.

The next day Tomomi called Michael. She had not heard from him in months, but she wanted to let him know she was Stateside. They made plans to see each other in three weeks in San Francisco. Tomomi was ecstatic.

Dec. 18: Michael, you are still nice to me. Thank you.

Before embarking on Route 66, Tomomi and Blues made a swing through the Deep South so she could visit her alma mater. It was part of her personal ritual to return to places where she had experienced joy, even if the place had lost its luster compared to how she remembered it from years past. She and Blues spent the Emperor's Birthday in her beloved Hattiesburg.

Dec. 23: I came back!! I love Mississippi! Hattiesburg has changed some but is still full of southern hospitality. Warm. Heartfelt. Fresh. Papa John's Pizza. New Orleans. I love the Southern Delta.

In Joliet, Illinois, 40 miles outside of Chicago, Tomomi and Blues began their long journey southwest on Christmas Day, although Tomomi was not sure exactly where historic Route 66 actually started. *"We couldn't find a 'Route 66 begins' sign."* Being a connoisseur of all things Americana, she was thrilled to learn that Chester Burnett, a.k.a. "Howlin' Wolf," one of her favorite Blues singers, was part of Route 66 history.[2] *"He traveled on this road with his harmonica and guitar. So cool!"*

Completed in the late 1920s, Route 66 was one of the first paved national highways in the United States.[3] It came of age with the horseless carriage and America's desire to embrace the new level of mobility that the automobile provided. Route 66 represented the mythic quality of the open road, especially as it transported poverty-stricken people west toward better opportunities during the Great Depression. The American highway was a central theme in John Steinbeck's 1939 classic *The Grapes of Wrath*, in which he famously wrote: "66 is the mother road, the road of flight."[4]

After World War II, as the United States became the wealthiest nation in the world, Route 66 ferried the burgeoning middle class on family vacations. Children of Depression-era parents were now driving new Chevy Impalas and Buick station wagons down the Mother Road in search of the West's natural beauty, native cultures and crown jewels that were promised in travel and automobile advertisements.

Two decades after writing *The Grapes of Wrath*, Steinbeck took a road trip across the United States with his dog, a standard poodle named Charley. The resulting 1962 book, *Travels with Charley: In Search of America*, was an instant best-seller and cemented a romanticized notion of the road trip, especially with a dog, in the American imagination. "I was born lost and take no pleasure in being found," wrote Steinbeck.[5]

However, the America Steinbeck encountered at age 58 was not exactly romantic. Compared to the hardscrabble days of the Depression, he observed that the new prosperity and automation of the post-World War II era had made Americans stressed, overly infatuated with technology, and out of touch with the natural landscape. "For it is my opinion that we enclose and celebrate the freaks of our nation and our civilization," Steinbeck wrote. "Yellowstone National Park is no more representative of America than Disneyland." Steinbeck's favorite state was Montana because he said people there were more laid back and it was a place "unaffected by television."[6]

As she and Blues followed Steinbeck and Charley, Tomomi also felt disillusioned, struggling to navigate the historic highway. She often could not even find it amid the spaghetti bowl freeway exchanges that had replaced the Mother Road.

Dec. 27: It's kinda hard to drive on Route 66 'cause sometimes there's no sign. It's easy to get lost. We were drivin' around St. Louis for five hours.

Route 66 was replaced in the 1960s and 1970s by a new interstate freeway system that bypassed towns in the interest of speed. Some dilapidated sections of the Mother Road were even closed completely in the late 1980s. Since then, the vast majority of motorists stick to the efficient interstates although Route 66 is still a draw for international travelers attracted to American kitsch.[7] Rather than access to wild lands and authentic Native American culture promised by the travel literature, Route 66 has always been more about freakish roadside attractions.

As Peter Dedek observes about the highway in his book *Hip to the Trip: A Cultural History of Route 66*, "…motorists experienced the West in the form of cafés shaped like giant sombreros, faux adobe motels designed to mimic ancient pueblos or haciendas and souvenirs sold at phony Indian trading posts and snake pits."[8]

This was not the authentic America that Tomomi was seeking. As she drove through the sprawling suburbs of Missouri, past the oil fields and industrial cattle feedlots of Oklahoma, and across the dusty flats of the Texas panhandle, Tomomi struggled to stay on the Mother Road instead of accidentally being funneled onto the interstate. One night in Oklahoma she discovered she had even been driving for hours in the wrong direction. And because the route through the Midwest was almost completely surrounded by private land, the only place for Tomomi to walk Blues was paved parking lots. *"This traveling is different. In almost two weeks we have only been to a state park or a national park once. I really miss nature. I want Blues to run in the forest."*

However, once she made it far enough into New Mexico and arrived in Santa Fe on New Year's Eve, everything changed. Tomomi was finally home.

Dec. 31: Yes, this is the EARTH! We really think so in the New Mexico desert. Hills. Bushes. River. Creek. This is my kind of travel!!!

Since Tomomi wasn't sure when Blues was born, she decided to make his birthday on New Year's Day. She celebrated Blues' first birthday on Jan. 1, 2002 with a hike in Red Rock State Park near Gallup, New Mexico on the Navajo Reservation. *"Red rock. Blue sky. I feel much better staying in town with Indian people."*

Every day for the next week, Tomomi wrote in her journal, *"Super Nature!!" Daishizen.* She took Blues hiking in the snow outside Flagstaff, and then she went to Grand Canyon. *"It was foggy but when we reached [the edge of] Grand Canyon, the sky was as blue as Blue's eyes!"* The next day she took a detour north from Route 66 and went to Zion National Park where she walked with Blues along the Virgin River between the towering red cliffs of Zion Canyon. *"Super Nature!! Next time, I'll hike more."*

The following week, Tomomi made it to the California coast where she completed Route 66 and reunited with Michael. She had not seen him since her birthday trip in May 2000, and she was worried that their time apart might have taken the spark out of what she still desperately hoped would be a budding romance.

Jan. 11: I love San Francisco! We went across the Golden Gate Bridge twice. Daytime and night time. Both are GREAT!! I'm so happy to see Michael.

It was as if time stopped during the two days Tomomi spent with Michael. She had been waiting and wishing for this for so long. Michael was now working for a charity that ran a thrift shop in San Francisco, so he and Tomomi went there and folded clothes together. They spent the night at his place; having sex was a central part of their relationship. Tomomi took more pictures of Michael in bed so when she was back in Yokohama, she could pull them to her chest the way a drowning person cradles a life preserver. They hiked in Muir Woods where Blues romped beneath the giant redwoods and came upon a banana slug. At Muir Beach, Michael took a picture of Tomomi and Blues. Tomomi was wearing a green thrift shop t-shirt, a choker with a Navajo turquoise pendant, and her Timberland hiking boots. Her broad smile was electric with joy. She was crouched in the sand with her arm around floppy-eared Blues, who appeared as if he was smiling, too.

Tomomi put off leaving California as long as possible, but she had to catch her flight back to Japan *(sucks!)* on Jan. 18. She said goodbye to Michael Jan. 14 and started driving east in a marathon push to reach the Atlanta airport in time.

Jan. 15: Casa Grande, AZ. You're so far away. No, we're so far away. I feel less and less.

On Jan. 17 Tomomi was in Texas and still 800 miles from Atlanta. She drove for 20 hours straight.

Jan. 18: We made it. Last day. Hard day. I'm so sorry Blues!

~~~

When Tomomi returned to the apartment in Yokohama, she could tell that her father had been sleeping in her bedroom while she was away. After 10 years of marriage, his relationship with his second wife apparently was falling apart.

Fukuyo was from the city. Tetsushi was from the country. The fact was that, lately, he didn't mind working long hours because it kept him away from home. And Tomomi was hardly ever there anyway. Rather than sitting in the apartment with his wife who watched silly TV game shows all day, he preferred the company of his buddies at the factory. Most of his work friends were also from Kyushu and spoke with his Kagoshima dialect. They would gather in an alley after their shifts and sip shochu, a strong barley brew popular in rural southern Japan. These were men who were born around the time of World War II and, like Tetsushi, had survived generations of unspeakable hardship.

After atomic bombs were dropped on Hiroshima and Nagasaki in 1945, an already impoverished Japan was devastated. Following Japan's surrender, Tetsushi's father Fumitomo returned to his rural farm village of Takarabe and tried to start his life. He worked as a tenant farmer with aspirations of buying a small plot of land. And he married a young woman with a beautiful smile named Itsko from Kagoshima City. A year later they had a daughter named Yuko.

But in post-WWII Japan, poverty and sickness had spread from the cities to the countryside. Food was scarce as was any kind of medical care.[9] Yuko died before reaching the age of 2. Fumitomo was nevertheless determined to have more children and run his own farm. In 1949, he and

Itsko had another daughter, Haruno, and in 1951, a son named Tetsushi. In 1953, another girl, Tsuyuko, was born and in 1955, Itsko, at age 32, gave birth to her last child, a girl named Fumiko. There were complications and no doctor. Fumiko died shortly after being born and Itsko died a few weeks later.

Fumitomo pulled together what little money he had to buy a gravesite for his family. It was a tomb in a new cemetery near Takarabe that would hold the ashes of his wife and daughter and future Hanamure descendants. Above the tomb was a stone marker with the Hanamure family crest: two cranes encircled in an embrace. Tetsushi, at age 4, along with his two sisters, watched as boxes containing ashes of their mother and baby sister were placed in the crypt. The Buddhist priest recited the Pure Land sutra, praying for rebirth in the "western land of peace and bliss."

Following his wife's sudden death, Fumitomo needed the help of a woman to manage the small farm and house he had built on five acres of forest at the edge of the village. He married a local woman named Emiko; she was 10 years his junior and wanted nothing to do with his children. So the Hanamure siblings were split apart. Tsuyuko was sent to live with her mother's sister in Kagoshima City, and Haruno was given to her grandfather Kanemori who lived in Takarabe. As the eldest son who would carry on the Hanamure family line, Tetsushi stayed with his father and stepmother to help on the farm.

Even as technology was changing life in Japan, the traditional culture and Confucian values in Takarabe and other rural Kyushu villages held fast. Every person was born into his or her role in society that was defined by economic class and gender, and the roles could not be changed. Women served their husbands and children served their parents. The individual put the needs of the community before his own and followed orders of government leaders without question.[10] A person who did not conform and "went against the grain" was an outcast and sometimes even considered to be insane.[11]

But resistance still happened in secret. When Tetsushi was small, his stepmother took out her frustrations on him. She often did not give him enough to eat, always feeding her own son first. With hunger burning in his belly, Tetsushi would sneak over to his grandparents' house and steal rice. His heart also ached for his real mother. Sometimes he would ramble through the cedar and pine forest in the mountain foothills above the village and fish in the river. Tetsushi found comfort in the wild river and steep canyon called Okawara Gorge above the village where water tumbled over basalt rocks and sheer cliffs. Nature held a power and beauty here that transcended the confines of village life.

Once the United States returned independence to Japan in 1952, the Japanese government set out to rebuild the nation's economy and infrastructure at a breakneck speed. In 1960 the Japanese prime minister announced a plan to double Japan's gross national production within 10 years.[12] Government officials said the future of the country was in manufacturing, and individuals were expected to sacrifice to help the nation reach its goals. Representatives from nascent Tokyo-area companies like Honda, Toyota, Fuji and Sony came to farm villages like Takarabe to recruit children for factory work.[13] When Tetsushi completed middle school in Takarabe, he was picked up by one of these recruiters for an assembly line job. Fumitomo and Emiko said this was the best way to earn money to support the family. Tetsushi would do what was expected of him. In 1964 at age 13 he left home to live in a factory dorm, hundreds of miles away in Yokohama. Meanwhile, at the Port of Yokohama, ships from the West were arriving almost daily to transport the many goods Japan was exporting. But the nation's growing wealth did not trickle down to the working class.

After Tetsushi split with Tomomi's mother in 1976, his prospects for supporting his four-year-old daughter in expensive Yokohama were grim. He only had a sixth grade education, but he had learned how to cut dies for machine parts that were in high demand and this gave him stable employment. Tetsushi worked as much overtime as he could get, often putting in 15-hour days. He earned enough money to buy modern conveniences that the cosmopolitan Japanese family of the 1980s was expected to have: a color television and air conditioning to cool the apartment.[14] Unable to afford the long train ride and time off from work, Tetsushi and Tomomi only visited Takarabe twice a year during New Year's and summer Obon, the festival of the dead when ancestors were honored at the family grave. Although he longed to return to the rural country down south, Tetsushi stayed in Yokohama for Tomomi. He wanted her to have a good education and the amenities of a cosmopolitan home that he did not have growing up.

But now that he was approaching retirement age, Tetsushi was counting the days until he could finally move back to Takarabe, and he resented the tense life in the cramped Yokohama apartment more than ever. He hated the way Fukuyo was cross with Tomomi and would take her food away before she was finished eating, just as Tetsushi's stepmother had done to him. He could easily imagine a future without Fukuyo but not without Tomomi.

Yet what was becoming of his beloved, precious daughter? When Tomomi got home from work or her travels, she rarely talked to him. She just sat in her room with Blues, listening to American music and poring over her photo albums.

"She would stare all day long at those landscapes," Tetsushi said years later. "And she had a faraway look in her eye."

~~~

In May 2002 Tomomi did it again. She gave herself a quick trip to San Francisco for her birthday and, with her fingers crossed, called Michael once she arrived at her motel. Only this time, he did not answer. And this time, she left Blues in Yokohama. Days went by. Holding true to her tradition, Tomomi methodically performed her rituals. On her 30th birthday, she visited all the places she had gone in previous years with Michael. She even got another secret tattoo; this time it was on the top of her left foot.

May 8: Sunny! Filmore Street! Haight Ashbury. Bubba Gump Shrimp. Thrift shoppin'!! Blues, are you OK?

On May 10, the day before she was scheduled to fly back to Japan, Tomomi finally heard from Michael. He said he had been busy. He did not have time to do much, but he agreed to meet her for lunch. *"Thai food with Michael. He gave me a picture taken in Muir Woods Beach."*

For reasons unknown, Tomomi would stop writing to Michael in her journal after that trip. The relationship—or the hope of a relationship—was over.

That next winter Tomomi returned to the United States with Blues. She flew into Los Angeles and drove straight to Las Vegas to visit a Yokohama friend named Akiko who had recently married an American and moved to the States. The band Red Hot Chili Peppers, another one of Tomomi's loves, was playing in Vegas but tickets were $200. Tomomi wrestled with spending so much for a concert. But she eventually gave in.

Dec. 30: I saw Red Hot Chili Peppers!! Great!! I wanted to get closer to see. But Americans are so tall!!

After staying with Akiko, Tomomi drove back to Los Angeles to take Blues to the beach for his second birthday. In her motel room on Jan. 1, 2003, she gave Blues a plate of gourmet dog biscuits that she had purchased at an upscale pet store along the boardwalk. She also gave Blues a birthday card with this message:

Dear Blues,
Do you know how much I love you? Do you know how much I appreciate you? I really don't know how many times I have to say I love you. I really don't know how many times I have to say thank you. Anyway, I love you and thank you Blues!
<3 Tomomi

From Los Angeles, Tomomi and Blues went straight to the Southwest for 10 days in *"great nature." Daishizen.*

She returned to Utah's Zion National Park and then drove north to Bryce Canyon National Park where she and Blues hiked through a labyrinth of sandstone pillars called hoodoos. From Bryce, they continued north on U.S. Highway 12, a National Scenic Byway, cresting over Boulder Mountain and landing in the kaleidoscopic cathedral of rock that is Capital Reef National Park. Then they began to loop back south and visited Moab where they scrambled up slickrock domes to view the 100-foot-tall span called Corona Arch.

South of Moab, Tomomi and Blues explored the sprawling backcountry of Canyonlands National Park. They followed a path along an intermittent stream that was lined with cottonwood trees and surrounded by ancient stone granaries tucked high into cliffs that were used more than 1,000 years ago by Ancestral Puebloan people. These Native Americans, ancestors of the Hopi and possibly the Havasupai, also adorned many cliff faces with pictographs of handprints, spirals, bighorn sheep and shaman figures. Here, amid the silence and the pictographs, in the heart of an ancient Native American culture's homeland, Tomomi felt the pulse of the Earth just as she had on top of Harney Peak and at the bottom of the Grand Canyon.

Jan. 15: Really good hiking in Canyonlands! No one was there. Sunny. Red land. Blue sky. Quiet. Off leash.

Tomomi kept driving south through Utah's canyon country and stopped at Natural Bridges National Monument to tour ancient Native American ruins. Then she arrived at the top of Utah 261, also called the Moki Dugway. This narrow dirt road is not for the faint of heart. Only one lane in places and with no guardrails, snaking switchbacks drop 1,300 feet in three miles. While the hundred-mile views from the road are spectacular, most tourists in two-wheel-drive sedans turn around and head for the safer highway. But not Tomomi.

Like an eagle riding thermals, she descended the switchbacks. Lenny Kravitz was cranked up. Blues stuck his head and chest out the car to soak in the smells. The sprawling views of the desert below were as if she was looking out an airplane window. Tomomi was suspended between heaven and earth. *Daishizen.* Eventually she landed in a vast, wild basin called Valley of the Gods.

By the time Tomomi got to Monument Valley, it was night. She decided not to stop at Agnes Gray's place because she thought it would be impolite to show up so late and unannounced. But Tomomi did pull over and look up at the sky. She said hello to the stars. She felt the *kami.*

Very, very beautiful night!

Throughout her trip, Tomomi took pictures of her beloved traveling companion with his head hanging out the rental car's passenger window. Her favorite shot was to get his reflection in the side mirror with his gums flapping in the wind and his black fur glistening against the red rocks.

At Grand Canyon National Park dogs were not allowed on trails below the rim, so Tomomi and Blues sat at an overlook and watched the sunset. She captured the moment with a close up of a contemplative Blues; his regal profile was outlined in gold in the late afternoon light, and his eyes were seemingly transfixed by the infinite panorama before him.

The day before her flight back to Japan, Tomomi's spirits were recharged after her walk in beauty.

Jan. 25: I always think my traveling will never last. But it will.

13
Randy

As he promised, Dad did not like Arizona. He was impressed, however, with the vast open canyon country that we passed through on the drive from the Phoenix airport to Flagstaff. And he was even more amazed when I explained to him that it was all public land, and you could roam across it for days or months without running into fence lines or being shot at.

"Isn't that something!" he said looking out the passenger car window at thousands of acres of jagged saguaro-covered hills where there was not a single human structure in sight.

But once we got to The Peaks assisted living facility, he immediately started going downhill.

Mom and Dad had separate rooms in separate halls as before, and the caregivers had strict instructions to keep Mom away from Dad. But The Peaks was smaller than Arden Courts and had only one dining room. Mom's anxiety and confusion were also exacerbated by the new surroundings. Mom was constantly knocking at Dad's locked door. "Felix!" she would cry. "You've got to help me!"

Before they arrived, I had decorated their rooms with 1970s-era second hand furniture in an attempt to replicate the look of the house in River Plantation. I thought this would help them with the adjustment and feel more at home. Mom was in what resembled my parents' master bedroom in the Beauregard House with a white lacquered dresser and nightstand.

She always said she loved mountains, and now she had a spectacular view of the 12,600-foot high San Francisco Peaks out her window. Dad was in the "den" with a walnut table and orange plaid chairs. I stocked a shelf with books and newspapers even though Dad no longer had the attention span to read. Framed school photos of my sisters and me, always grinning through gapped teeth and braces, were on every horizontal surface.

I wanted so badly for this last ditch, Hail Mary pass of a living situation to work for my parents. I had distanced myself from Mom and Dad my entire adult life in an effort to escape their screwed up world. But now they were living in my world. I hoped that maybe at the very tail end of their lives, they might experience some joy with me, Austin and Mike in scenic Arizona. Maybe Dad would finally realize that there were actually some beautiful places outside of Texas. In between story deadlines, maintaining a second job teaching journalism, completing my master's degree, and parenting Austin, I visited The Peaks every day to smooth the transition.

"I appreciate what you are trying to do, honey, but this is just not working," Dad told me one afternoon about two months after the move. I had sneaked into his room to avoid Mom seeing me. A plate of untouched food sat on the walnut table. He did not want to eat in the dining room because Mom would be there. He was losing weight rapidly and did not have the strength to make it to the bathroom and back. There was also the challenge of adjusting to Flagstaff's elevation of 7,000 feet.

I insisted the doctor examine Dad and come up with possible solutions. But it was hard to argue with the diagnosis: "failure to thrive."[1] There was also the very strange sense I got from Dad that he found my presence unsettling. Me. His favorite daughter—the one who was named after his mother and looked like him and did patient rounds with him when I was little and made him beam with pride over my journalistic accomplishments. And what's not to like about a daughter who was doing everything possible to improve her father's quality of life at the end stage of Alzheimer's? Yet, as Dad became increasingly incoherent, sometimes he would gasp and tremble when I stepped into his room. One time he even shrieked like I was a ghost when he saw me. I never observed him acting this way around the caregivers or anyone else, even Mom. There was something about me that scared him, and I had absolutely no idea what it was. I reasoned it was just another symptom of his mental decline.

Every time I visited him, Dad also asked me to call a priest to his room to hear his confession. It was the only thing he wanted and he was desperate for it. The priest came almost daily because Dad could not remember he had given his Confession the day before.

As the situation at The Peaks deteriorated, my marriage was falling apart, too. Mike helped move my parents to Flagstaff, but then he backed away from the daily grind of managing their care. And there was something about the act of me trying to single-handedly save my crazy parents that made Mike's moodiness and perpetual unemployment intolerable. I stopped helping Mike fight his depression. And since I broke our pact, he started drinking again.

"I'm depressed because you don't pay any attention to me," he said one day when I came home from The Peaks and was about to head out the door to pick up Austin from school. "You act like I'm invisible."

That was the last straw. "Move out! Move out right now!" I shouted as tears streamed down my face and my body trembled with rage. Mike and I rarely fought, and I had learned long ago how to keep my volatile temper under lock and key, but I felt such anger in that moment that I was on the verge of physically attacking him.

Mike knew I was totally spent. Maybe he even feared for his safety. We were done. By the time I returned with Austin from school, he was gone and he never came back.

~~~

In November 2006, Maria and I made arrangements for Dad to move back to Arden Courts. Dad was so weak he could no longer walk and he never left his room. But before he left Flagstaff, he agreed to share one last dinner with Mom in The Peaks dining room. I ate with them, fighting back tears. Dad was slumped over in his wheelchair looking down at his food while Mom was beaming at him like a schoolgirl. She was so happy, so in love with Dad, the dashing doctor who rescued her when she was a struggling single mother in Houston. Mom had no idea it would be the last time she would see Dad. And in her demented state, she thought that his sudden appearance was due to the fact that he had finally been found amid the confusing maze of halls and rooms.

The next morning, I dressed Dad in his burnt-orange University of Texas sweats and packed his last few belongings in his University of Texas duffel before we drove to the Phoenix airport. Even in the fog of advanced Alzheimer's, he knew what was happening.

"Thank you for doing this," he said as we headed down the mountain. He would get his wish to die in Texas. He would never see the Grand Canyon.

In the months that followed, Dad returned to his old room at Arden Courts and Maria looked in on him weekly. Sometimes Gabriel took him on a drive. But he was eating very little and rarely wanted to get out of bed. During Dad's death vigil, I continued to manage Mom's care at The Peaks, and I also now had to face the challenge of being a single parent to Austin. I was shell-shocked. Life was not going as I had planned. But what I kept coming back to, the thing that kept me grounded, was my desire to know more about Tomomi. And about Randy.

In February 2007 I dropped off Austin at Mike's apartment for the weekend so I could go to Florence, Arizona, a barren desert town where almost no one lived by choice. I was looking for Randy. Weeks of relentless phone calls to the Arizona state correctional system revealed that he was being held there in a vast complex of windowless one-story cinderblock buildings where it was more than 100 degrees at 10 a.m. on a late February morning.

After my visit to Supai a few weeks earlier, I became convinced that the next essential step in my reporting was to talk to Randy face-to-face. Coconino County Sheriff's Detective Larry Thomas, who investigated Tomomi's murder, had described Randy to me as "an animal." And then the Supai police officers I had interviewed called him a "black sheep" of the tribe. Even though I had never met Randy, I felt like I already knew him, or at least some part of him. And I had a hard time believing these labels, which seemed a convenient way for people to distance themselves from him and explain away what had happened.

If the officials who were prosecuting Randy's case knew I was trying to talk to him, they would surely stop me. As they prepared for a trial, the attorneys did not want their defendant saying anything to a reporter that might jeopardize what they expected to be a straightforward murder case. Still, one phone call after another finally produced Randy's inmate number, and then more calls provided the designated visitation days and hours for inmates in his group. It was like searching for an unmarked car in a full stadium parking lot.

I was honing in now, as I drove through a maze of roads comprising the industrial prison complex of the Central Arizona Detention Center. The numbered buildings rose from the seething creosote flats, each surrounded by a 20-foot high cyclone fence topped with coils of razor wire. Wavy heat rose from the ground, and except for the armed guards in towers, there were no humans anywhere.

Looking at this grim scene, I recalled a conversation I had with Randy's mother Carla when I was down in Supai on my most recent trip there. She was reluctant to talk to me but finally agreed to a brief visit at her workplace in the Havasupai tribal office. As she sat at her computer, she looked out the window at the helicopter landing pad. A chopper was getting ready to touch down with tribal members who were going to be tried that day in Havasupai Tribal Court. Two young Native American men wearing blaze orange jumpsuits and blue slippers stumbled out of the helicopter and ducked under the blades amid a tornado of sand. Their hands and legs were shackled; they were accompanied by an armed U.S. Marshall. Henry, the Supai police officer, was waiting in his quad to pick them up. A crowd of tribal members had gathered around to witness the homecoming.

"On these days when there's court, everybody watches the prisoners come in," said Carla, pointing with her chin toward the helicopter. "It's like they're movie stars. Randy used to watch them."[2]

Then she looked over her computer at a tribal member who was sitting on a bench with a cup of coffee and a stack of books. It was Damon. "That guy right there, he got Randy hooked on pot."

~~~

After numerous wrong turns, which drew the attention of the guards in the towers, I arrived at the right building in the detention center. Purely by coincidence, the designated visitation day for Randy that month was also his 19th birthday.

Inside, the lobby was filled with young women and children, all whom had come, as they probably did every month, to see their husbands, boyfriends, fathers. I filled out the form about whom I had come to visit and then sat in a plastic chair and waited. Even though I had made it this far, I fully expected that there would be some kind of block on Randy's name and I would be told to leave.

But after about 40 minutes, the phone at the visitor lobby desk rang and the armed receptionist picked it up. "Yep. OK." All the waiting women in the room stopped talking to hear what came next.

The receptionist looked at me. "You're up."

I passed through a series of dark corridors and vault-like metal doors that were opened electronically by unseen guards. Suddenly I was spit out in a noisy room filled with more plastic chairs, women and young children. I felt nauseous. Against the far wall was a row of some 15 windows where prisoners and their visitors could sit on opposite sides of glass and talk through telephone receivers.

About six feet tall and 200 pounds, Randy was a hulking presence in his blaze orange jumpsuit. He stood expectantly behind one of the windows, shoulders hunched with his wrists in handcuffs. And once he caught sight of me he was completely puzzled. When the guards told him he had a visitor, a crazy white woman was not who he expected.

I had promised Billy a few weeks earlier that I would check up on Randy, with whom Billy had had no contact since before the murder. But why was I there, really?

Now Randy was glaring at me, waiting for an explanation. I picked up the phone and he fumbled to pick up his receiver in his cuffed hands. We sat. I said I wanted to ask him some questions.

"What kind of questions?" His voice was soft and he looked down at the floor. It was hard to hear him over the echo of so many other voices bouncing off the cement floor and walls. Signs were posted on the windows stating that all conversations were being recorded.

I told him I was a journalist writing a story on Supai—about crime there—and I wanted to find out what it was like for him growing up on the reservation. I told him I did not want to talk about the murder or discuss anything that might interfere with his defense. Randy glanced up slightly to look at me without looking at me. He was not sure about this.

"You cannot take notes," he said.

"OK." I put my pen and pad in my pocket. I told him I had recently talked to his father Billy.

"My dad beat me sometimes when I was bad, but I don't hold nothing against him," Randy offered without pause. "I miss him. I've been thinking a lot about him in here."[3]

Now Randy looked at me, reading me, probably contemplating whether or not he should just end the conversation there. His eyes were deep black pools. His thick black hair stuck out an inch from his head in an uneven, overgrown crew cut. His cheeks were full and purple from acne scars. And compared to the expressionless mug shot that ran repeatedly in the newspaper, I was struck by his baby face. He was just a child. But, perhaps, he was also a killer.

I asked him what it was like to be a kid in Supai.

"It was very violent. And there was nothing to do. I didn't want to be down there, but it was like a vacuum always sucking me back," he replied.

Randy said he had been talking on the phone to his brother Ambrose who had been getting into trouble lately. "I tell him to stay in school. I don't want him to turn out like me."

At age 13, after being suspended the previous year for attacking the Havasupai School principal and being charged with petty crimes in the village, Randy became a ward of the state. He never returned to regular school and was sent to increasingly harsh juvenile reform facilities, mostly near Phoenix. Randy's peers at these facilities—juvenile delinquents from the city—became his family. In his teens he never had a normal life; he never played a team sport or went on a date. Randy was exposed to drugs and urban gang culture in these institutions, and he eventually built up a list that was six pages long of criminal acts he committed while in juvenile detention. When he periodically returned to Supai on probation, Randy would almost immediately get arrested for theft or assault of another tribal member and then be sent back to juvenile detention.[4]

Randy said when he turned 18 last year, he wanted to live on his own and get away from Supai because it was "so boring." But his mother kept trying to influence him to live with her and stay home.

"In the white world parents kick their kids out at 18, but not in Supai," he said. "My mom doesn't understand the way I am. She just wanted to keep me there, to protect me or something."

He said he liked reggae music and wished he had grown up in Phoenix where there was more to do. He liked to drink alcohol in Supai to pass the time. He didn't care for watching TV.

But Randy also wanted me to know he was not necessarily a nice guy. "I am just like my dad. I get mad," he said, locking eyes with me.

Randy said when he was in elementary school, kids were mean to him and he "became violent" to protect himself and his brother. "I would go off, take care of it," he said.

He still had a temper he added. "If I got mad enough, I might just come through this glass." Again, we locked eyes. My mind was suddenly flooded with thoughts of Tomomi and visions of what might have happened between them.

I tried to redirect our conversation, as it seemed to be slipping away.

I asked Randy how he felt about the tourists coming through Supai. "I don't want to talk about the tourists," he said, "except that they go down there to this beautiful place searching for something. And they are seeing things they are not supposed to see."

Randy said he was used to being in prison and he didn't miss Supai. No one in his family had visited him since he was charged last December.

"I don't mind it. I don't care," he said. "The only thing I miss is not being able to speak my language." He was resigned. He looked behind me, watching the soft drink machine getting re-stocked with hundreds of cans.

There was a lull in our conversation and the receiver started to fall away from his mouth. He was thinking about something. He put the phone back to his ear.

"Look, sure my dad beat me, but my mom didn't understand me. I love him," he said. "I have been thinking a lot now about what my dad told me, that you have to find your own way in life. You have to go inside of yourself to find the way."

This was not an animal talking. If I had come here looking for answers, I would leave only with more questions. And although I thought at the time that investigating the reasons behind Tomomi's murder was a distraction from my own problems, my reporting was actually reeling me into the darkest part of myself.

I did not know what to say in parting, so I blurted out something dumb.

"Well, happy birthday!"

Randy raised his chin and smiled. "Yeah, right."

14
Desperation

In May 2003, after saving up enough money by working long hours and living rent free with her father, Tomomi followed her tradition of honoring herself on her birthday with a quick trip to California. She visited her friend Akiko, went to Universal Studios in Los Angeles and walked down Hollywood Boulevard. In addition to loving nature, Tomomi loved to shop. She wanted to outfit herself head to toe in the most authentic American attire she could afford. At thrift shops in West Hollywood, she bought an Elvis belt buckle for cousin Konomi, a Red Hot Chili Peppers t-shirt for herself, and a rainbow colored collar for Blues, who was back in Yokohama. She also went to Venice Beach and the Lucky Jeans outlet store. She spent her birthday at the beach in Santa Monica.

May 8: I got a haircut!! It's too short but I was thinkin' it's OK. Hair is always growin'.

For the first time since she had begun traveling in the States, she was eager to fly home to Yokohama. Her heart ached for Blues.

May 9: Sad to leave but it's really better to have Blues around. I miss him so much.

Back in Yokohama, Tetsushi had divorced his second wife and he,

Tomomi and Blues moved into a different apartment. It was on the third floor of a high rise with two bedrooms, a small living room and a kitchen. Their home environment was less tense and Tetsushi was warming up to Blues. He often took the rowdy rez dog to his work so Blues would not be alone all day in the apartment. Blues would lie at his feet while he was cutting dies, and when Tetsushi went on break, he walked Blues up to the factory's roof where they would sit and look out over a sea of buildings along the Tsurumi River. After his father Fumitomo died, Tetsushi inherited the farmland in Takarabe and was now the eldest male descendent in the Hanamure family line. This position came with responsibilities.

As Tetsushi sat on the roof with Blues he liked to think about what he, Tomomi and Blues would do when they moved down south after he retired. He was fit and healthy, but with no spouse or other children to care for him, Japanese tradition dictated that Tomomi should look after her father as he aged and that they should return to the Hanamure homestead once he retired. Tetsushi imagined how in just a few years he, Tomomi and Blues could all go hiking in the forest where he roamed as a boy, fish in the river and peer over the edge of Okawara Gorge to look at the waterfalls. He knew he had not always been the best father. He had left Tomomi alone too much when she was little. He had lost his temper sometimes. But he could see on the horizon a time when he would be able to finally make it up to his daughter.

Tomomi was also glad to be living once again with only her father, and she was grateful for how he was helping take care of Blues. But she had other plans. While Tomomi gave up on the dream of a serious relationship with Michael, she was as committed as ever to moving as soon as possible to the United States. At her factory job where she attached price tags to Nike shoes and during drinks after work, Tomomi entertained her friends with tales of her adventures in the States and spoke of her desire to move there permanently.

"She had a very specific dream," recalled her best friend Mari years later.[1] "She wanted to manage an apartment complex somewhere in Arizona and that is how she would earn money. And on the first floor she would also have an outdoor café where people could bring their dogs. Next door she would also run a florist shop."

She told her friends Mari, Rena and Shinobu how she felt a strong connection to Native American cultures, and how much she loved buffalo, and how beautiful the Grand Canyon was.

"And what about cute American men?" they would always press.

Even with these women, who had been her closest friends for a decade, Tomomi never once whispered a word about Michael. Maybe it was because, deep down, she knew that Michael probably viewed their three-year relationship as just a casual hook up, a tentative friendship that also involved sex, and nothing more. In Japan, Tomomi was as straight as an arrow; there were no casual hookups. She did not even date.

"She always said she was either going to marry Brad Pitt or the lead singer for the Red Hot Chili Peppers," recalled Rena years later, laughing.[2]

When Tomomi and her father were preparing breakfast before work or making dinner after a long day, Tetsushi would sometimes bring up the land in Takarabe and how they should move. He said he needed to be down there to look after it.

"When you die, I'm going to sell the place and buy land in Arizona," Tomomi would jokingly respond.[3]

"Well, you will have to wait a long time because I am going to live to be very old," Tetsushi would shoot back.

Between 2003 and 2005 Tomomi continued to make two trips a year to the States but it had become too expensive and complicated to bring Blues. And the loneliness she felt after the split with Michael weighed on her. Rather than traveling solo, she brought friends and the daughters of friends. These Japanese women did not want to stay in a remote cabin in Custer, South Dakota in the dead of winter or sleep on the dirt floor of a Navajo hogan as Tomomi had done in the past. Tomomi took them instead to Universal Studios, California Adventure, Disneyland, and to see Red Hot Chili Peppers concerts in Las Vegas. They did a lot of shopping at American outlet stores and visited iconic national parks, but only for a brief stay en route to Las Vegas and Los Angeles.

In February 2004 Tomomi took Midori, the daughter of her former employer, on a trip that hit all the hot spots. Midori was 18 at the time and she viewed Tomomi, whom she called by the nickname "*Hanna ko*," as her older sister.[4] When Midori was little, Tomomi would pick her up after school at the bus stop. Tomomi had always been a role model for Midori, so when Tomomi offered to take Midori to the States, it was the best high school graduation present she could ever receive.

"We drove all over," recalled Midori years later. "It was *sugoi*. Everything *sugoi*."

They went to Disneyland and Universal Studios but also to Grand Canyon and Tomomi's beloved parks in southern Utah. Along the way, Tomomi did not just want to share the sights with Midori but also tried to teach her how to navigate in a foreign country, make decisions and plan an itinerary. She wanted to help prepare Midori for life as an adult. "*Hanna ko* wanted me to learn to take care of myself. She was strict but with heart," said Midori.

In the spring of 2005 Tomomi took a trip with her friend Rena and Remi, the 11-year-old daughter of her friend Mari. Since Mari could not get away from work and responsibilities at home, she thought the next best thing would be for Remi to go instead. Mari trusted Tomomi completely with her daughter.

Tomomi, Rena and Remi went to Disneyland, California Adventure, San Francisco, Grand Canyon and southern Utah. They also stopped in Las Vegas to visit Tomomi and Rena's mutual friend Akiko. One night, Rena and Akiko wanted to go out drinking on the Strip, but Tomomi refused. Tomomi said she was responsible for Remi, and partying was not on the itinerary during a trip with a fifth grader. At the time, Rena felt Tomomi was being too bossy and taking the fun out of her own experience. She was in the States to party and Tomomi was not.[5] The two longtime friends got into a bitter argument that was never resolved. After that trip, Tomomi was filled with regret. "*I have wandered so far from the way I was supposed to go,*" she wrote in her journal.

During her most recent travels, Tomomi had drifted away from the pure connection to the land that fed her soul. Plus, 9/11 made getting a Green Card even more difficult. And now that her father was single, she felt the tug of her obligation to him.

"There were three priorities in Tomomi's life," said her friend Akiko, "the States, Blues and her father."[6]

But one of those was at odds with the other two.

By 2006, Tomomi was no closer to fulfilling her goal of living in the United States than a decade earlier when she had stayed in Agnes Gray's hogan in Monument Valley. She started to feel desperate; she feared her days of traveling in the States might be coming to an end. Her dream, it seemed, was slipping away.

~~~

Meanwhile, life in Supai was becoming increasingly chaotic and crime-ridden. Although the dysfunction was largely invisible to tourists passing through the village, reservation life in the early 21st century was intoxicated with hard drugs and an ever-deepening resentment toward the outside world.

In March 2003 the tribe learned that the blood samples more than 100 members had donated a decade ago for the purposes of diabetes research had been used, instead, by academic researchers for other purposes, primarily for studies on the genetic origins of schizophrenia and the effects of inbreeding. The blood was also used to prove the Asian genetic origins of the Havasupai, which flew in the face of their traditional origin stories. It was the biggest betrayal by Anglos the tribe had experienced since their plateau lands were taken away a century earlier.

The tribe filed a lawsuit against Arizona State University and the lead researchers with whom they had placed their trust: anthropologist John Martin and geneticist Therese Markow. The legal discovery would find that when Markow and her staff were in Supai in the 1990s, presumably collecting information for diabetes research, they were secretly going through patient files at the Supai clinic looking for tribal members who had been diagnosed with schizophrenia or indicated symptoms of possible inbreeding. ASU had also shared the blood samples widely with other university laboratories for more than a decade. The Havasupai had absolutely no knowledge that they were specimens in the academic community where researchers were using the tribe's blood to advance their careers. Out of 23 academic papers and dissertations that were published and relied on Havasupai blood as a primary source material, 15 focused on schizophrenia, inbreeding and migration patterns, rather than diabetes.[7]

In the lawsuit the tribe demanded damages, but more than anything, they wanted their blood back.

Also in March 2003, Bob McNichols, the Bureau of Indian Affairs superintendent for the Havasupai tribe, sent an SOS e-mail to his superiors describing a law enforcement crisis in Supai and asking for more staff. While the federal government was investing heavily in the wars in Iraq and Afghanistan, the budget for law enforcement on Native American reservations had been slashed.[8] The police force in Supai was half the size it had been a few years earlier, and there was no one to watch the jail when officers responded to calls in the village.

"Crystal meth is prevalent throughout the community," wrote McNichols. "It is available, cheap, and is being distributed by Havasupai youth...Police officers in Supai were directed not to put anyone in jail because they don't have the staff to man the jail...Police officers in Supai are constantly threatened, cussed and told to get out of the village."[9]

On Christmas Eve 2004, police officer Henry Kaulity and his partner were on duty when a drunken tribal member shot another intoxicated tribal member. A mob formed outside the police station. Tribal members started throwing things against the building and firing guns.

"It sounded like a riot. They were pissed at us," recalled Kaulity. "We didn't take any calls that night. Me and my partner just slept in the station. It was real scary because we knew we could be ganged up on. Another time tribal members were coming at us with sticks and rocks when we were bringing a guy into custody.

"Things can escalate very fast down here," he added, "and backup is a long way away."[10]

McNichols and others in the law enforcement community warned that unless something was done, it was only a matter of time before drug-related crimes and lawlessness in the village escalated to violence against tourists.

Sarah Maurer was one of those tourists.

~~~

In early September 2005 Sarah was 22 years old and had been accepted into the doctoral program in chemistry at University of California Santa Cruz. She was driving from New Mexico where she had been conducting research at Los Alamos National Laboratory to California to begin her studies. Her hero was environmental writer Ed Abbey. Like Abbey, she was from Pennsylvania and was drawn to the beauty of Southwest deserts. And, like Abbey, she loved to hike alone in wild places. Sarah wanted to visit the Grand Canyon when she was passing through Arizona on her way to California, and a friend had suggested the trek to Havasu Falls. She made it to the remote Hualapai Hilltop trailhead by nightfall and slept on top of her minivan because the inside of the vehicle was packed with all of her stuff.[11]

Sarah woke up with the sun on a Wednesday morning and began the eight-mile hike down the canyon to Supai. She was 5 feet 9 inches, a muscular 150 pounds, often hiked 20 miles a day in New Mexico and was in the best shape of her life. She made it to Supai in just two hours. She observed that the village "was a normal reservation town," the kind she had often seen in New Mexico. "It looked friendly," she recalled a decade later.

It was still early, maybe 9 a.m., so few people were out and about. But there was a Native American woman in her 30s who was sitting on a bench near the store.

"Hey, you should be careful," the woman said. "There is a young man on the trail who slapped my ass with a horse lead."

"Oh! I'll pull my knife out then," Sarah said jokingly, unsure how to respond. She was not worried. The warning from the woman seemed more weird than threatening.

Once outside the village, Sarah knew it was two miles to the falls and she was eager to get there. She was traveling light, carrying only water, a snack and a book. She planned to eat her snack and read the book while lounging at the foot of the falls. Then after a nice long break, she would hike out of the canyon later that afternoon when the temperature had cooled.

About a half mile beyond the village, a teenage boy popped out of the bushes and asked Sarah if she had seen any horses. He was looking for them.

"He was just your typical Native American teenager," recalled Sarah years later. "He was tall, fit and looked healthy. He had short hair. He did not seem to be high on drugs or anything. And lost horses seemed plausible to me. But he was clearly agitated."

Sarah said she would keep an eye out for the horses. As the boy continued to walk alongside her, she asked him questions about living in Supai. How many horses did his family have? Did he like to go to the falls? He replied with one-word answers.

Sarah kept hiking, and the boy began popping in and out of the bushes, apparently following a different set of trails but still able to see Sarah's movements. She decided to let the teenager "cool off" and attempted to distance herself from him by taking a break. She sat on a rock next to the main trail, pulled out her snack and ate it while looking at the creek flowing beyond a thicket of oak and willow. A group of hikers passed on their way to the falls and Sarah thought for a moment about joining them but then decided against it. She did not see the teenage boy anymore. He must have moved on.

When Sarah was done eating, she turned around to grab her daypack before standing up. The teenager was leaning against the rock just inches from her. He had sneaked up without Sarah seeing him. It was Randy.

"I thought, 'What the fuck!'" Sarah recalled. "Now I was scared. All the rape prevention training I had learned suddenly kicked in."

Randy was 17 then and had recently been released from a behavioral health facility in Flagstaff. On that day, he was desperately horny.

Flustered, Sarah decided the safest thing to do was hike back toward the village. Randy followed her, walking inches from her, groping her breasts and butt. Sarah thought if she kept talking to him, she might be able to diffuse the situation, especially by speaking loudly in the hopes of attracting the attention of approaching hikers. But it was early on a weekday and the trail was deserted.

Randy grabbed her arm. He wanted to pull her into the bushes by the creek.

"What are you doing?" Sarah shouted, yanking her arm away.

"We are going into the woods to have sex," Randy said.

"Well, I don't want to have sex," she replied.

"That doesn't matter," he said.

"So you are going to RAPE me!" she shouted.

"And then are you going to murder me?" she shouted even louder.

Randy said he did not want to rape her or murder her but just have sex. Sarah explained that forcing someone to have sex was rape. Randy disagreed. The circular conversation continued for three or four minutes as Sarah was hiking faster and faster. And Randy was right next to her, groping her while trying to steer her off the trail into the brush.

"At this point, he realized I was going to get to town," recalled Sarah, her voice quivering. "We were about one quarter mile away. And he was clearly worried about getting caught."

Randy took his left arm and wrapped it around Sarah's neck as he tried to drag her into the bushes near Fifty Foot Falls. Sarah had grown up wrestling with her brother and knew how to get out of a headlock. She dropped all of her 150 pounds to the ground. Randy went down with her. His arm was so tight around her face that her glasses were crushed against her forehead and cut her eye. Sarah got away and took off running with her daypack still on her back. Randy disappeared down a side trail where the tribe had built a mud wikiup for sweat lodge ceremonies.

Once she reached the village, Sarah stumbled to the police station. She was "shaking like a leaf" and had blood dripping down her face.

As soon as she told the police officer on duty that she had been assaulted by a teenage boy, he immediately knew it was Randy. Just hours earlier, Randy had also attempted to rape a non-Havasupai Native American woman walking on the trail, the one who told Sarah about being hit on the ass with the horse lead. The police officer listened to Sarah's story, made a few notes and took pictures of her injuries. Then he said they should go look for Randy.

"Wait. You want *me* to help you find the guy who just tried to rape me?" Sarah asked, incredulous.

"Yeah," the officer said. "Let's go get on my four-wheeler."

So they did. They zipped down the trail on his quad, and Randy was nowhere in sight. Then the officer suggested that they go to Randy's mother's house to see if he was there.

"They had a corral next to the house," Sarah recalled. "And it held the saddest horses I had ever seen in my life. The horses were so emaciated and there were open sores on their backs. I looked at them and thought, there is nothing I can do. It was heartbreaking."

Carla came out of the house and talked to the officer in the Havasupai language while Sarah waited on the quad. Carla said she did not know where Randy was. She had not seen him since yesterday. Lately, he had been sleeping on a neighbor's trampoline.

The officer took Sarah back to the police station. He said since Randy was a minor he was not sure how he might be punished but that they would be following up with her. She was free to go.

"Well, can you give me some help getting out of here?" Sarah asked. She told him she did not want to see the falls anymore, and she did not feel safe hiking.

The officer said there was a helicopter arriving at 1 p.m. that could fly her out, but she would need to pay $300.

"I'm a grad student. I'm broke," she told the officer. "I can't afford that."

He said there was nothing the tribe could do to help her. Sarah was desperate to get out of Supai so she decided to hike back to her car. She started the arduous 8-mile trek at noon when it was 100 degrees. It took her almost five hours to get to the rim because she had to stop every 30 minutes to try and cool her body down. There was no shade. She had little water. And she had just been assaulted.

"That was the most dangerous thing I've ever done in my life," she recalled. "I thought I was going to die for sure."

Sarah made it to the deserted Hualapai Hilltop and then, still in a state of shock, drove another four hours to reach California. She only mentioned in passing to her college friends later that week that someone had tried to rape her during her journey from New Mexico. The Supai police never contacted Sarah to touch base as promised, and she decided not to investigate how to press charges on her own.

"I had no interest in following up," she said a decade later. "Honestly, after seeing Randy's home, I felt bad for him. He was just a kid. And his life was obviously already shitty enough."

Randy received a light sentence for the two sexual assaults he committed that day: five months at a behavioral health school for juvenile delinquents located east of Phoenix. Then, in February 2006, Randy turned 18, and he was released from the school. Since he was an adult, he was no longer a ward of Arizona's juvenile corrections system, and even though Carla sought to get government funding to continue residential behavioral treatment for her son, she was unsuccessful.[12] So Randy moved back to Supai, a place he did not want to be.

When not sleeping on trampolines, Randy was living in a flophouse with other meth addicts and in caves along the creek because his mother—still fighting with Billy over child support—was afraid to have Randy in her home. And McNichols' request for extra law enforcement had gone unanswered. The Supai police force was down to two officers who were afraid for their lives.

Carla insisted Randy not visit Billy, but one day in early May 2006 he sneaked over to Billy's house and had a father/son talk. They sat on milk crates in Billy's front yard. They joked around like they always had. Then Billy got serious. He was worried.

"I told Randy that he had to get out of here," Billy recalled.[13] "He had to get out now, or something very bad was going to happen. But he did not listen to me."

PART IV

15
Yokohama

My father died in June 2007. He had stopped eating and drinking, so the end came quickly. A Catholic priest visited his room at Arden Courts on the morning of his death and administered the ritual of Last Rites.[1] Dad was still conscious when Maria held the phone receiver to his ear. I was on the other end. I had not seen Dad since I put him on the plane to Austin seven months earlier.

"I love you, Daddy," I said, blurting out one syllable at a time in between sobs. "I love you."

Then silence. I listened. I held my breath to stop crying. I heard slow breathing into the receiver. There was a faint moan, an attempt, perhaps, to say something. But after about a minute the breathing stopped.

Austin and I traveled to Texas the next day, and two days later there was a funeral at the Catholic church Dad attended when he went to college at the University of Texas in Austin. That night my sisters and I, along with the few members of our extended McGivney family who were still alive, held a rowdy Irish wake at Maria's house. The priest came and drank whiskey with us.

Also that month, my story about Tomomi's murder was published in *Backpacker*.[2] The Havasupai tribal council was not happy about more publicity on the murder or with my accounts of the dysfunction in their village. However, numerous *Backpacker* readers responded to the article with letters describing their own bizarre experiences during hiking trips to Havasu Falls, including one woman who wrote that she had watched a tribal member push a horse off a cliff.[3]

Meanwhile, Randy was still sitting in jail in Florence. There had been no news about a trial or any other details of the investigation released to the press.

Once back in Flagstaff after the funeral, I felt a burden had lifted. A very difficult story assignment was behind me. My father was no longer suffering. And as Mike and I remained separated while divorce proceedings moved forward, I was no longer feeling responsible for Mike's happiness—or for Dad's. Mom was still very much a busybody at The Peaks, but the staff there was able to manage her and I continued to look in on her several times a week. The beautiful view of the mountain out her window calmed her. It was like she received a big hug every time she looked at it.

I completed my master's degree; I wrote a book; I taught classes at Northern Arizona University and took on more assignments for *Backpacker*. But, mainly, I was devoted to Austin and my yellow lab Sunny. I wanted to make life as perfect as possible for them. Our household was a kind of three-member version of the Red Bandit Club, only this time there were no enemies—at least not that I could see.

Austin and I went on hiking trips in Colorado, Utah, California and the Canadian Rockies. Money was tight, but I did not want Austin to feel it. When we were in Canada, we spent a few nights at the Fairmont Banff Springs Hotel because it resembled the Hogwarts castle from the Harry Potter books that Austin loved. Sunny had the run of the house, slept on my bed at night, and was honored on her birthday with her two favorite foods: lemon cake and Gouda cheese.

And, yet, as life hummed on, my thoughts often turned toward Tomomi. I would get a vision of her walking along some trail when I was out hiking alone in the woods with Sunny. Or I would think of her father and wonder how he was doing, even though I did not know him in the slightest. The Japanese Consulate in Los Angeles had not responded to several letters I sent asking for an introduction to the Hanamure family. But a voice in my head would periodically whisper: *You are not done yet.*

In April 2009 an FBI detective who worked on the murder case and whom I had gotten to know while investigating the *Backpacker* story invited me to a memorial event honoring Tomomi. The U.S. Attorney's office in Phoenix was holding the ceremony in connection with National Crime Victims' Rights Week. The detective said Tomomi's family would be there from Japan as well as the FBI's Japanese language interpreter who might be able to connect me with the family.

I attended the ceremony where Tomomi's father was presented with a plaque that contained a picture of his daughter smiling broadly on the rim of the Grand Canyon. It also was engraved with the English translation of a poem he had written in Japanese for the occasion.

> *Attracted to the vast open spaces of a faraway land*
> *Travelers who do not know the heart of evil*
> *Thinking back to your smile from days past*
> *You appear in my dreams*
> *I rise and put my hands together coming to see you now*
> *Her aspirations were cut short*
> *Cherry blossoms fall*
> *Oh prayer reach across the ocean*
> *May her soul rest in peace*

After the ceremony, I ran up to the FBI interpreter, Lisa,[4] as she waited at the elevator with the Japanese delegation. I introduced myself and gave her a letter that I hoped she might share with Tomomi's father who did not speak any English. The letter read, in part: "Dear Mr. Hanamure... Please forgive me for sounding forward, but I have felt a kinship with Tomomi since the report of her murder first appeared. I am attracted to the vast, open spaces of the West and have experienced some of the most wonderful moments of my life while hiking alone in Grand Canyon...I feel a strong bond with Tomomi and would very much like to write a book about her life...In order to write such a book, I would like to visit you in Japan...I know there is nothing that can come close to compensating for the horrible loss you have suffered, but I hope you will allow me to honor your daughter by telling her story in a way that she deserves."

It was a long shot at best. From what I observed at the memorial service, it seemed Tomomi's father clearly had already had his fill of

Americans. Plus, I did not speak Japanese and knew very little about the country or culture. The only time I had left North America was for a trip to Europe after graduating from college. In my world, roaming across the American West constituted international travel simply because it was outside of Texas. And I did not have the funds to pay for a trip to Japan. Also, I was deathly afraid of large crowds and big cities.

Two months after giving Lisa the letter, she e-mailed me. "They want you to come," she said, noting how unusual this was because the Hanamure family had shunned all journalists and did not want to have anything to do with the United States. "They believe Tomomi wants you to come." She shared a fax message intended for me that she received that morning from Tomomi's father.

"I am thinking I want to leave something for my daughter as well...I will be able to talk about what I know. I will get in touch with her friends and gather them around. Please come to Japan. I beg this of you."

"Congratulations, my dear woman," Lisa wrote. "You are blessed. This doesn't happen to just anyone. Good for you for persisting."

Next thing I knew I was emptying my savings account to finance a three-week trip to Japan for myself, Austin and Lisa, who lived in the United States but generously agreed to accompany me as an interpreter if I paid her travel expenses.

While my struggle with panic attacks had improved in the last few years, anxiety was always in the peanut gallery of my mind, heckling me endlessly. And there was much to be anxious about with such a big trip into the unknown. What if I had a panic attack on the very long flight? Or had a claustrophobia-induced panic attack in crowded Tokyo? What if something bad happened to Sunny while I was gone? What if something happened to Mom? What if I got anxiety-induced diarrhea? What if I could not get my book published after draining my savings?

However, as 12-year-old Austin, Lisa and I flew toward the rising sun, I felt an unfamiliar calm. It was like I had willingly stepped into a boat and was being carried by the river's current. Beneath all my superficial worries, there was a sense, deep down, that I was somehow following my destiny. Other forces were in control now. Tomomi's journey had become my journey.

~~~

Although I briefly glimpsed Tetsushi Hanamure at the Crime Victims' memorial service in Phoenix, my expectation about what he would be like once I arrived in Yokohama was still shaped by my own naive stereotypes of Japan. I imagined that he was probably an uptight business executive at a thriving Japanese corporation, had lots of money, and was a product of cosmopolitan Tokyo.

The man waiting to greet Lisa, Austin and me at the train station in Yokohama was not who I imagined at all. Tetsushi was a lean 5 feet 4 inches tall with sinewy muscles and appeared younger than his 58 years. He wore khaki pants, Nike tennis shoes and a t-shirt that said "California Adventure." His black hair was neatly combed to the side and his face glowed with a big, toothy smile.

Lisa had taught Austin and me some basic Japanese etiquette before the trip including how to bow. It was complicated—who should bow first, how low to bow, how often to bow, what situations definitely required bowing.[5] And since I was 6 feet tall, bowing lower than a Japanese person was especially difficult. But Austin and I practiced our bows for Tetsushi. We did it all wrong, which amused him greatly.

We put our luggage in the back of his black Toyota Landcruiser and piled in. Tetsushi told Lisa that Tomomi insisted he buy a car big enough for her dog. Now he used the vehicle mainly to go fishing, which was why there were fishing rods in the back. Once we got on the highway, Tetsushi looked back at me with a smile and turned on the car's CD player. The Red Hot Chili Peppers' *Californication* album filled the SUV with the band's distinctly funky American sound.

"Tomomi music!" Tetsushi managed in English, laughing.

Once inside Tetsushi's third floor apartment we were greeted by a very large and excited dog. Lisa told me earlier she thought Tomomi had a dog but, again, I had imagined only stereotypes and expected it to be a tidy, toy breed. Instead, the shepherd mix with bright blue eyes was as big as a goat. And he was growling and showing his large, sharp teeth. We would learn not to be alarmed; this was how he showed affection. Austin immediately knelt down and gave him a hug.

"Blues is my master," Tetsushi said, as the rowdy 95-pound South Dakota rez dog rubbed up against his legs, growling with happiness.

We took off our shoes at the entrance and put on terrycloth house slippers that Tetsushi had waiting for us. Because of my women's size 11 foot, only the front part of my toes could fit in the slippers. Again, we all laughed.

Tetsushi had been living alone during the two years since Tomomi's death. His life revolved around long days at work and taking care of Blues. And sometimes he went fishing. We were the first guests he had hosted in his home since the funeral reception.

Following Lisa's lead, I immediately went to the small Buddhist altar, called a butsudan, in the living room and bowed before it. The wooden cabinet containing a Buddha statue, a bowl of rice and cup of water is a shrine to deceased ancestors. We placed a gift for Tomomi, a framed picture of the Grand Canyon, next to the other gifts that friends had left when coming to pay their respects. There were stuffed hamburger dog toys that Tomomi used to like to buy for Blues and cards stacked in a pile. A large framed picture of Tomomi at the Grand Canyon sat next to a picture of Tetsushi's father Fumitomo. The plaque Tetsushi had received at the FBI ceremony in Phoenix was propped on a shelf next to the altar and still covered in bubble wrap. Lisa and I lit a stick of incense and put our hands together in prayer.

Everything in the apartment remained as Tomomi had wanted it. There was an American flag mat in the bathroom, magnets from various U.S. national parks on the refrigerator and in Tomomi's room hung the American flag she acquired somewhere in the States, along with the two plaques (one of a Native American chief in full headdress and the other of a boy, "Little Nonny," dancing in moccasins) she bought in a Rapid City thrift store. A Navajo sand painting hung above the futon where she once slept. In Tetsushi's room one suit hung in the closet, which I recognized from the FBI ceremony. He was not a salaryman. The apartment was tidy, with few furnishings and traditional straw tatami mats on the floors.

After isolating himself while he mourned his daughter's shocking and violent death, Tetsushi handled with grace the stressful switch of having three boisterous Americans staying in his small apartment. As we sat around the kitchen table and he served us iced green tea and snacks on the first afternoon of our visit, memories of life with Tomomi and her connection to the States came flooding back to him.

"I feel like she is going to walk through the door any minute," he said in Japanese, with Lisa interpreting. "She was gone so often but then, suddenly, she would be home again."

While we talked, Blues rubbed his back against the underside of the table, growling and panting. Before visiting Yokohama, the only information I had about Tomomi remained what I read in her autopsy report and a few random details from Lisa and law enforcement officers. Sitting at the kitchen table in her home, I realized I probably knew more about Tomomi's death than her father did, but I knew very little about her life and what mattered to her. Now that whole world was opening up to me.

I asked Tetsushi, via Lisa, what he thought it was about the United States that attracted Tomomi.

"I don't know," he replied in Japanese, shaking his head. Then he paused and said in English: "Big. Wide. Waaaaaahh." He outstretched his arms as far as they would go to demonstrate enormous size. Blues growled in agreement.

Even though Tetsushi kept Tomomi's decorations on the walls, he had stored most of her possessions and many keepsakes in blue plastic bins that were stacked in her bedroom. He said it was because he was getting ready to move to Kagoshima in a year or two. But maybe it was because he could not bear the sight of his daughter's treasures. He suggested we go in Tomomi's room and dig through the bins.

The first thing I pulled out was a shallow, lopsided basket. Judging from the familiar geometric design, I said it looked Navajo.

"She made that," Tetsushi said. "She wanted to be Native American."

There were birthday cards and pictures from the printing company where she worked. There was a photo of young Tomomi in her first kimono. Then Lisa pulled out an old, tattered photo of a bald baby in a white dress held by a young Japanese woman with curly hair. A young man, beaming, stood next to her.

"That is Tomomi with her mother," Tetsushi said. "Oh, I had forgotten about all this." He continued to dig through the bins. He pulled out an envelope of photos. "These are not for my eyes." He put the envelope back.

We came across lists of American music that Tomomi liked (Sheryl Crow, Lenny Kravitz, Counting Crows, Tom Petty) and books she wanted to read (Tony Hillerman, *Black Elk Speaks*, *Stories of the Sioux*). There was a newspaper clipping about the plight of Native Americans. We laughed at photos of Blues with a birthday hat on his head and sitting expectantly in front of a birthday cake Tomomi had baked for him. There were postcards from a Tim and Lonnie Morin in Montana and Tim and Luana Nelson in Arizona. I found the business card of Agnes Gray that would lead me to her hogan in Monument Valley that October. Other business cards were for a vet in Monterey, California, a log cabin business in Custer, South Dakota and an apartment manager in Hattiesburg, Mississippi. I frantically took notes as I began to collect puzzle pieces that I would try to assemble later.

Tetsushi explained that Tomomi attended English school in Hattiesburg, Mississippi.

"Mississippi?" Lisa asked, making sure she correctly understood this hard-to-believe fact.

"I guess going to school in Mississippi must have really changed her life," I added.

"No, *she* changed her life," Tetsushi said. "She decided what she wanted and made it happen."

Continuing to dig in the bins, I unearthed various notes that Tomomi wrote to herself. Many were about Blues, or how much she loved nature. But one read: *"Trust me. Trust. Trust."*

Tetsushi pulled out Tomomi's diary and handed it to me. "You take this with you," he said. "It's all in English."

He also insisted I take a photo of smiling Tomomi kneeling in the sand next to Blues. On the back, Tomomi had written, "Muir Beach, January 2002."

Tetsushi said he was going to take Blues on a walk. "Blues can only pee when he is in wide, open spaces," he explained. Austin went along. Austin and Tetsushi became fast friends during our visit. Tetsushi treated Austin like the son he never had. And Austin was, indeed, in need of a father.

As soon as Tetsushi left, Lisa and I fished out the envelope of secret photos. They were all prints of a young man with long blond hair. In one photo he was in an apartment playing a drum. In another photo he was bare chested and in bed.

"Those are condoms!" Lisa said, pointing at the shelf above the bed's headboard.

We put the photos back in the bin. I flipped through the English diary for clues. Did Tomomi have a secret lover? The answer immediately jumped off the pages: *Michael.*

When Tetsushi returned from the walk he pulled out Tomomi's photo albums. There were at least two dozen albums documenting every trip she took to the United States. Tomomi had given each album a title: "My School Days," "Nature Traveler," "Get Into the Navajo Nation," "Birthday Trip to Carmel and Monterey," "Get Your Kicks on Route 66." The albums included travel dates, park passes, business cards and ticket stubs along with endless photos of landscapes and wildlife. There were almost never people in the photos, but sometimes there was a teddy bear.

Even though Tomomi labeled the location of every photo in English, I did not need to read the captions. I instinctively recognized the places because I had visited every park that she also had hiked in. And in some cases I had been there at the same time as Tomomi. It was possible I even passed her on the trail. As I flipped through the albums compiled by a woman from the other side of the world, it was like tracing my own wilderness journeys during the past two decades. Lisa stopped interpreting and I translated for Tetsushi, pointing at the photos and naming the national parks.

"Badlands. Bryce. Grand Canyon. Monument Valley. Zion. Capitol Reef. Yosemite. Sequoia. This is the Mohave Desert. Joshua Tree. Saguaro. That is a Navajo hogan. Wow, it looks like she drove the Moki Dugway. Hey, I stayed at that motel once." And then we would laugh at the teddy bear in the motel rooms.

After dinner, Lisa and Austin were tired and went to bed. But Tetsushi and I stayed up and continued to sit at the kitchen table going through the photo albums while drinking Budweiser, his preferred beer.

"Black Hills," I said, pointing at a photo of undulating prairie that I knew well.

"Buffalo," I added.

"Buffalo," he repeated.

"Buffalo turd," I deduced from a photo of Tomomi's Timberland boot next to a very large pile of crap.

"Turd!" he exclaimed.

We both laughed.

Tetsushi popped open another beer. He sniffed and looked away, probably fighting back tears.

~~~

My fears about feeling trapped in dense urban gridlock were never realized. For starters, I was a giant in Japan, towering one to two heads above everyone else. Even in a sea of people on city sidewalks or commuter trains, I had a wide-open view all to myself.

During our Yokohama visit, Tetsushi would often come back to the question that so perplexed him about his daughter's murder. "How could this happen?" he kept asking. From his perspective, he imagined the United States would be one of the few places in the world that was even more wealthy and civilized than Japan. So shouldn't crime be low? And, on top of that, wouldn't the Grand Canyon, one of the most prized places in the richest country in the world, be one of the safest tourist destinations? It did not make sense to him at all.

Even though Yokohama was crowded and had poor, run-down neighborhoods as well as shiny rich ones, it was not plagued by the kinds of issues common in big cities in the United States—homelessness, theft, violent crime. In Japan, the homicide rate is less than one murder per 100,000 people, while in the United States it is more than triple that at 3.8 murders per 100,000 people.[6] On Southwest Native American reservations like the Navajo Nation, an average of 18.8 individuals are murdered per 100,000 people.[7] Crime, especially violent crime, is not something Japanese citizens worry about. Strangers do not pull guns on each other the way they do in the United States. Austin, Lisa and I walked the city streets, even late at night, without concerns for our safety. The only widespread violence in Japan comes from that directed toward oneself in the form of suicide.[8] In exquisitely manicured public gardens in Yokohama and Tokyo, Austin and I pondered signs that warned of stray caterpillars and other signs that begged people not to kill themselves in the park.

Every day during our stay with Tetsushi he wore a different U.S. national park t-shirt and ball cap that Tomomi had brought back for him after each trip. We walked Blues on a paved path along the Tsurumi River where many of the other dogs were toy breeds wearing outfits that resembled human clothes. Tetsushi said Blues refused to swim in the river but he liked hiking in the mountains. I responded that this was probably due to his Lakota roots. We also accompanied Tetsushi and Blues on their daily three-mile walk to the factory where we climbed up to the building's roof. Beyond a sea of concrete, we could barely make out the glimmering summit of a snowcapped Mount Fuji.

Tetsushi had also arranged for all the people who he thought were important in Tomomi's life to visit with me at his apartment. The first guest was Yaeko Ogata, who had been friends with Tetsushi for 37 years and helped look after Tomomi when she was little.

"Tomomi was very strong willed and quiet and held things in," said Mrs. Ogata. "But once when she was in middle school, she called me late at night and said, "Auntie, Dad isn't home yet and I am hungry. So I came over and took her to Denny's."

"Well, Tomomi always knew where the money was in the house. She could go buy herself lunch or dinner," Tetsushi chimed in. "Maybe the money had run out and that is why she called Auntie. She lived with that kind of freedom."

Tetsushi paused. The apartment fell silent as thoughts of Tomomi rushed in. The wall clock ticked. Blues panted from beneath the table.

"Maybe she had too much freedom," he said.

The interviews with Mrs. Ogata and others not only helped me with my research but also created a situation for Tetsushi that inadvertently caused him to reflect on the past three decades. As he listened intently to every interview, he learned things from Tomomi's friends he did not previously know. He reminisced about life with his daughter in a way that he was not able to do after her sudden death when news of her murder was immediately followed by a crime investigation.

Hiruta, Tomomi's boyfriend in middle school, noted how Tomomi seemed lonely but was also very considerate and liked to give him presents. He pondered how he and Tomomi had the same birthday, yet had very different fates. Tomomi's former employer, Keiko Saito, and her daughter Midori spoke of how Tomomi was "the most complete person" they ever knew. Midori said she had an older sister, but she viewed Tomomi as her true big sister.

"I would do anything for Tomomi," Mrs. Saito added. "She is almost more of a child than my real children."

Midori said that she had planned to accompany Tomomi on her last trip to the States in May 2006 but then backed out at the last minute because of work obligations. "If only I had not changed my plans," Midori said, sniffing back tears, "maybe *Hanna ko* would be here."

Tetsushi popped open another Budweiser. The clock ticked. Blues panted.

One evening Tomomi's longtime friends Rena and Shinobu visited. Rena spoke about how when she went on a trip to the States with Tomomi they got in a fight and never made up. "I was a heartless person when I was younger," said Rena. "But Tomomi's death taught me how foolish I was."

When Tetsushi stepped away to answer the phone, I whispered to Rena and asked if she knew anything about a guy named Michael.

"No, never. Was he American? Tomomi was very secretive," said Rena.

"And did she ever speak about her mother," I pressed, knowing this was also a subject Tetsushi did not want to discuss.

"She told me she always loved her real mother," said Rena. "And she was proud of her mother for how she was an outsider and was not afraid to be different."

In middle school Tomomi wanted to play basketball so she organized a girls' team because one did not exist at her school. The entire team came one afternoon to visit with me. "That's how Tomomi was," said Akiko, Tomomi's best friend in middle school. "She inspired people and made things happen." Akiko also said Tomomi liked judo and enjoyed writing stories and poems. Akiko brought copies of Tomomi's stories to our meeting and spread them out on the kitchen table.

All of Tomomi's friends also brought their sadness and regret, whatever it was they did not get to tell Tomomi before she died, and they set it at my feet.

"Do you know why she went on that last trip? What was she looking for?" I asked.

But they asked me almost the exact same question. While her friends and family gave me details on a superficial level about Tomomi's life in Japan, they did not have the answers I was seeking. Instead, I was handed more clues and riddles, like a Zen koan, that I would have to continue to contemplate and solve on my own.

And as it turned out, I was not in Japan just to get information, but also to give it. I was an ambassador for women who hiked alone in wild places. In this way, Tomomi and I were sisters.

"Why would she go there, to the bottom of the Grand Canyon, by herself?" asked the basketball team, weeping.

On our last day at Tetsushi's apartment, Tomomi's best friend, Mari, and her daughter, Remi, came to visit. Mari and Remi were the last people to speak with Tomomi before she left Japan for the States in May 2006.

"Tomomi told me that she finally had earned enough airline miles, and on the next trip to America in January 2007 she was going to try to convince you to come along with a free ticket," Mari said to Tetsushi.

This was news to Tetsushi. He said nothing and reached out to stroke Blues' back.

"We went drinking after work the night before she left," said a tearful Mari. "Tomomi spread a map of Arizona out on the table and she pointed to the Grand Canyon. She said she was going to this beautiful place where there are Native Americans and waterfalls that are really blue."

Mari paused. She could not talk while she was crying.

"If I could have one wish in my life, it would be to see Tomomi again."

16
The Land of Wa

The Kirishima Mountains on Japan's southern island of Kyushu rise thousands of feet from lush, forested valleys. The mountain summits in this semitropical region are often shrouded in fog. The foothills are blanketed with pink azaleas and other mountain flowers called *hana.* One of the tallest summits is Mount Takachiho. Here, according to ancient Japanese legend, the sky once touched the Earth. Although anthropologists say the first human inhabitants of Japan migrated from China, Korea and Polynesia, Japanese myth maintains that their origin place is on this mountain summit where a staircase made of clouds reached from the heavens, and the "people of the gods" climbed down.[1]

Another legend from Japan's *Kojiki*[2]—a collection of Japanese origin stories recorded in the eighth century—says the archipelago of Japan was created when the gods thrust a jeweled sword from the heavens into the vast ocean below. Pieces of Earth dripped off the sword's tip to make a series of islands that became Japan. The sun goddess Amaterasu was one of the deities who descended from the heavens; she traveled on a rainbow bridge and once on Earth gave birth to Japan's first emperor. The legend says the jeweled spear used by the gods remains on top of Mount Takachiho.

The *Kojiki* goes on to describe a period called the "Age of the Gods," when Japan, and the Kirishima Mountains region in particular, was home to an increasing number of spirit entities called *kami.* Eventually, more than 8 million kami[3] came to inhabit Japan, most often in nature but also sometimes in houses and possessions. According to this foundation of Shinto belief, nature is more than beautiful; it is pulsing with unseen spiritual essences that can hold sway over human life. Places in the natural world that inspire a sense of awe, such as a towering mountain or a deep canyon or a crashing waterfall, are full of kami. *Daishizen.*

While archaeologists have found Stone Age relics in Japan, including tools and pottery, dating back to 10,000 B.C., the first written accounts of Japanese culture come from the Chinese and were recorded during the first century B.C. The Chinese called Japan "the land of Wa"[4] and observed that the archipelago was comprised of hundreds of regional tribes. According to the Chinese texts, the first ruler of Wa was an empress named Himiko. During the late second and early third centuries A.D., Himiko helped unify the fractious tribes through her practice of shamanism. She was believed to have magical powers that allowed her to mediate between people and kami. Although the boundaries of Himiko's kingdom have long been debated, many historians contend she ruled in northern Kyushu, not far from where the gods allegedly descended.[5]

After Buddhism was introduced to Japan in the late sixth century, the country's spiritual epicenter moved north to Kyoto where numerous temples were built and the imperial family was located. However, Japan's connection to its most ancient traditions, to mysticism and the divine power of nature remains in the south. The Kirishima Mountains and surrounding region in Japan's Kagoshima and Miyazaki prefectures is alive with active volcanoes, hot springs and crater lakes. The Kirishima Mountains region was designated Japan's first national park in 1934, and the area is filled with Shinto shrines, attesting to a region rich in kami as well as cultural origin stories. In the shadow of these summits, along a spectacular canyon called Okawara Gorge, is the tiny village of Takarabe. Geographically speaking, the ancestral home of Tomomi Hanamure is in the middle of the Osumi Peninsula in northern Kagoshima. But spiritually, Tomomi's origin place is located in the heart of Japan.

Despite its heavenly location, Takarabe was not an easy place to live in the 19th and early 20th centuries. Tucked in rolling foothills next to the Okawara River, floods often washed out bridges and cut off access to the outside world, forcing the tight-knit farming village to be self-sufficient.

Even as the rest of Japan adopted Western influences in the 19th century, Takarabe remained isolated and the community held on to its own dialect, regional customs and spiritual traditions rooted in Shinto and Pure Land Buddhism. Subsistence living kept the community connected to the Earth but death was often close by. In the Hanamure family, the women seemed to have it the worst; generation after generation, the life of a mother, sister or daughter was cut short.

Tomomi Hanamure's great grandfather, Kanemori Hanamure, was born in Takarabe in 1897. According to the Confucian social order followed in rural Japan, Kanemori was expected like the many generations before him to be a farmer and raise his children to be farmers and farmers' wives.[6] Two decades earlier, the Meiji Restoration had begun opening Japan's long-closed borders to trade with the outside world. Ships carrying western goods were arriving weekly at the port of Yokohama near Tokyo, changing life in the country's urban centers.

However, while some western influences like coffee, chemical fertilizer, men's trousers and a non-feudal, bureaucratic form of local government had made their way to Takarabe, the village generally functioned in the early 20th century as it had for generations. Rice farming was a primary focus for most adults although some individuals had side businesses growing silkworms, making tofu, weaving baskets from bamboo, and harvesting shitake mushrooms. The calendar revolved around religious festivals, growing seasons, and cycles of the moon.[7] Adhering to Shinto rituals and maintaining harmony with the kami infused all aspects of village life. Sometimes when the gods were unhappy, nearby volcanoes on Mount Shinmedake or Mount Sakurajima would erupt, turning the sky black and covering the village fields with ash.

Although Buddhist ceremonies and rituals were practiced less often than Shinto—mainly for weddings and funerals—thoughts of the Pure Land were as pervasive as the morning fog. Unlike Zen Buddhism, which required hours of sitting meditation that was only practical for monks, Pure Land could be practiced while working in the fields simply by repeating the prayer: *Namu Amida Butsu* (I take refuge in the Buddha).

When Kanemori was 21 he married Yuko, who was 19 and also grew up in Takarabe. The next year, in 1921, they had a son named Fumitomo.

The family grew taro root, squash and beans in the garden next to their three-room wood frame house and rented a corner of a rice paddy below the village along the river flood plain. Yuko and Kanemori had two more sons, Shizuo, born in 1927, and Nobuo, born in 1928.

Even though Takarabe remained geographically isolated, there was mounting pressure on rural communities to increase food production to support the Japanese government's plans for economic growth and colonial expansion. There was also a sickness carried in the water that was infecting Takarabe and other rural areas. Hundreds of thousands of people across the Kyushu countryside were dying, and residents in poor farming communities like Takarabe could not afford to travel to the cities to get proper medical care. Some said it was dysentery and cholera brought from urban areas like Tokyo with poor sanitation. Others said it was poisoning from the mines in the Kirishima Mountains that caused a toxic cloud to settle over the foothills. The Toroku Mine in a province to the north was emitting arsenic into the air, and on some mornings, horses and cows were found dead in the fields.[8] During a six-month period in 1931, when Fumitomo was 10 years old, his mother and two brothers all died of the sickness.

At the Buddhist funeral ceremony, Fumitomo stood with his father and listened to the priest recite the Pure Land sutra, a prayer for rebirth in a transcendent realm, the "western land of peace and bliss." This land is "ultimate, like the open sky. Vast and boundless. It is born from great loving kindness and compassion on the right path. It is full of pure radiance." Those reborn in the Pure Land were promised "flowers of true enlightenment."[9]

Kanemori soon remarried a village woman named Hide whose husband had recently died. Their eldest son, Fumitomo, worked long hours in the rice paddy along with his father and stepmother. In the 1930s, the new regional agricultural office placed requirements on Takarabe and other farming communities to produce food for the cities and the military. In addition to rice, they would now plant wheat in the winter and raise chickens, hogs and cows. But there was little food left over for the Hanamure family and no time for rest in what used to be called the summer "slack season."

And Hide was mean to Fumitomo, whipping him with a bamboo switch and denying him food so that she and her children could have more to eat. But sometimes when his parents were working in the rice paddy, Fumitomo would slip away into the forests above the village and walk among towering cedar and pine trees, or he would scramble along the cliff edge of Okawara Gorge and watch waterfalls tumble. The biggest cascade was Kirihara Falls, where the river plunged over a sheer, 75-foot cliff. He knew the rocks, trees and wind were all alive with *kami*. And the unruly river, with its swift current and fog-shrouded banks, was the home of the *kappa*, one of the most mythical of Shinto spirits. Stories told of how this flesh-eating water imp could help produce bountiful crops, but if it was prone to evil, it might rape village women or pull young children into the river and drown them. "Be on your guard around the river," Kanemori warned Fumitomo. "The *kappa* cannot be trusted."

Another story told to Fumitomo and other village children was about the insatiable appetites of the "hungry ghosts" who had giant stomachs and tiny mouths. These were the spirits of restless ancestors who died young or violently; their spirits may be stranded between this life and the next. Given how many villagers had died young from disease or in childbirth, it seemed the hungry ghosts were everywhere in Takarabe. Living relatives tried to placate the ghosts by honoring them at the summer Obon festival and also making daily offerings of rice and water at the family butsudan altar in the home.

Like all healthy young men in the village, Fumitomo was drafted in the early 1940s to serve in the emperor's imperial army. Japan had bombed Pearl Harbor in 1941, and there was talk in Takarabe that the United States might invade Japan. People said U.S. battleships were heading toward the coast of Kyushu. The United States had dropped more than 22,000 tons of bombs on the Tokyo region, and refugees were streaming out of the cities into rural villages. Fumitomo became part of the infantry fighting for control of the Pacific Islands. During these WWII battles Fumitomo's comrades called him *bokkemon*. He had no fear.

Instead of a U.S. ground invasion, atomic bombs were dropped on Hiroshima and Nagasaki. After Japan surrendered in 1945, Fumitomo traveled through a wasteland of death and destruction to return to

Takarabe. He would never speak of the horrors he witnessed or what he had done to earn a medal for his service in battle. He just wanted to have his own family and farm in Takarabe. Soon he would become a father, and then a grandfather.

~~~

Even though Tetsushi had been living in Yokohama for more than 40 years, he did not consider it home. The place where he was from—and where Tomomi was from—was "down south." If I was going to write a book about Tomomi's life, he felt it was essential I spend time in Kagoshima and visit his true home in Takarabe. But he could not take time off from work to make the long journey, so his younger sister, Tsuyuko, who lived in Kagoshima, had graciously volunteered to be my guide.

After a six-hour train ride from Yokohama to Izumi City, Austin, Lisa and I arrived at the train station where Tsuyuko was waiting to greet us. She was the aunt who believed it was Tomomi's wish that I visit Japan. Tsuyuko was pulling out all the stops for her beloved niece. She used to work as a guide for a Kagoshima tour company and knew the region's many attractions well. Tsuyuko planned that we would get the three-day deluxe tour, hitting all the scenic and historic hot spots in the region, in addition to visiting Takarabe, which was far off the beaten path for most tourists.

Tsuyuko was about 5 feet tall, had short-cropped black hair framing her round face, and high, arched eyebrows that accentuated her exceptional perkiness. Throughout our three-day visit, she proudly wore her tour guide uniform: a short sleeve navy plaid blouse adorned with her name tag, a navy skirt, white hose and black walking shoes.

She and her husband Shinichi rented a van to comfortably accommodate our group. They both took off from work to ensure they could give us the kind of tour that would honor Tomomi and her ancestral home. We visited Kumamoto Castle that was built in the sixth century by a feudal lord. We drove to the top of Mount Aso, an active volcano, where steam rose from a cauldron of turquoise liquid, and then we toured tea farms and the tidy, traditional homes of 18th century samurai. We ate at a famous noodle restaurant where, no matter how hard I tried, I was unable to grasp the noodles with chopsticks. We also toured a museum dedicated to the memory of WWII kamikaze pilots and spent an afternoon at a spa where Lisa and I were buried up to our necks in warm black sand to help our skin.

As Shinichi drove between sites, Tsuyuko reflected on her family history. She said she grew up not knowing she had any siblings. After her mother died in childbirth when Tsuyuko was a toddler and she was sent away to live with her mother's sister in Kagoshima City, Tsuyuko was kept in the dark about her true parents, as was her older sister Haruno who was given to her grandparents in Takarabe. While Tetsushi stayed with his father Fumitomo and stepmother, he also was unaware that he had two sisters. "We would visit my father and stepmother's house during Obon, but I thought they were my aunt and uncle. And I thought my older brother was my cousin," she explained. Tsuyuko did not find out until she was in 5th grade that Tetsushi and Haruno were her brother and sister. But by then they had both left Takarabe to work in factories in the Tokyo area as part of Japan's "mass employment" movement during the 1960s.

"My stepmother was the reason me and my siblings were separated," said Tsuyuko. "When I look back now, I think 'how dare she do that.' She knew coming into the marriage with my father that there were three children and she should have accepted that responsibility."

The aunt who raised Tsuyuko in Kagoshima City never married and was a loving mother to her adopted daughter, making sure Tsuyuko went to high school instead of working in the factories. Tsuyuko looked out the van window at the passing green pastures and paddies of the Kagoshima countryside.

"My brother had a rough childhood," she added. "He did not get love growing up. I wonder, if my stepmother had not been allowed to do what she did, would my brother's destiny have turned out differently?"

On the third day we veered off the interstate and drove east toward Takarabe. The Shinmoedake volcano was erupting, sending a pillar of smoke and steam thousands of feet into the air. Tsuyuko said this was rare and attributed it to Tomomi wanting to show off the region to us. We wound our way up narrowing roads into lush, forested mountains. We crossed the basalt crevasse of Okawara Gorge where a shallow river rumbled over moss-covered rocks. Tsuyuko asked Shinichi to pull over so we could stick our hands in the fresh mountain water to purify ourselves according to Shinto ritual. Further upstream were Kirishima Falls, where a series of cascades hung side by side over a steep bluff like white bridal veils and dropped into black, glassy pools. There were a few tourist cabins nearby, but the area was mostly devoid of people and human development.

As the largest urban area in the world, the Tokyo region has a population of 37 million, with a population density of more than 8,000 people per square kilometer. But Takarabe and two other nearby villages only have a combined population of 39,000, with 99 people per square kilometer. And with older, longtime residents dying off, the region's population gets smaller every year. After WWII, the breakneck industrialization of Japan emptied out the rural areas as people moved to the cities — either by choice, to find better opportunities, or by force, as was the case for Tetsushi. In 1950, only 38 percent of Japan's population lived in cities. By 2011, that number had increased to 93 percent.[10]

Tsuyuko's and Tetsushi's older sister, Haruno, is one of the few rural holdouts. After working in a factory in Tokyo when she was a teenager, Haruno moved back to Takarabe at age 20 and got married to a man from a nearby village. She has been married to the same man and lived in the same house for 40 years.

We arrived at Haruno's home on the outskirts of Takarabe in the afternoon for lunch. The small wood frame house was at the end of a long dirt driveway and surrounded by small sheds and farm equipment. Haruno was out front waiting for us. She wore a plaid jumper with a t-shirt underneath. She had a farmer's tan and was dabbing sweat off her face with a hand towel. Haruno looked just like Tetsushi except she was thicker, with muscular arms and shoulders that probably came from decades of manual work outdoors.

Austin, Lisa and I made our bows, and I gave Haruno a framed picture of the Grand Canyon, which she placed next to the butsudan in her living room. We sat on cushions on the floor that were positioned around a low table filled with numerous dishes of food. Compared to the highly processed fare Austin, Lisa and I had been eating in Yokohama and on the road (sugar and butter sandwiches on white bread; hot dogs from vending machines; rice chips; Krispy Kreme donuts), the fresh fruit and vegetables Haruno served us was a home-cooked feast. Much of the food —watermelon, grapes, tomatoes, carrots, taro root, rice cakes—she and her husband grew themselves. Haruno was still living off the land the way her grandfather, Kanemori, had taught her.

Tsuyuko said that even though she was a "city girl," she had become close to her sister and brother once they were all adults and learned they were siblings. They and their families gathered in Takarabe at least twice a year for New Year's and Obon. When their father, Fumitomo, was alive, Tetsushi and Tomomi would stay at his house. After he died they stayed with Haruno.

"Tomomi slept right where we are sitting," said Haruno, laughing at the memories. "She was always bringing her pet marmots or birds. And then it was Blues."

Tomomi would offer to help tidy up the house, so Haruno showed her how to clean the straw tatami mats. "You wipe with the grain," explained Haruno, laughing hard as Tsuyuko began chuckling, too. "But Tomomi would not do it right. She always wiped against the grain."

Because of work demands, Tomomi and Tetsushi were often in a rush to return to Yokohama. Tomomi spent time with her grandfather, aunts, uncles and cousins, but she did not explore the surrounding region. She did not hike in the Kirishima Mountains or in Okawara Gorge. If she saw Kirihara Falls, it was from the window of a speeding car. There was simply no time. And she wanted to save her hiking for the States.

After lunch we said goodbye to Haruno and piled into the van for a short trip to the other side of Takarabe. In a clearing in the forest on the edge of town were about five acres that used to be the site of Fumitomo's homestead. After Fumitomo died in 2000, Tetsushi decided to tear down his thatched-roof house because it was falling apart.

"Brother will build a new home here after he retires," explained Tsuyuko. She pointed to a metal trailer on the edge of the property. "He is storing things in there in the meantime. It is mostly Tomomi's things."

On a hill above the Hanamure property was a small cemetery that held the Hanamure family grave. We drove up a gravel road to get there and parked beneath large power lines. The sprawling view from the hilltop looked out on emerald green farm fields below and a western horizon framed by the smoky, jagged outline of the Kirishima Mountains. Puffy gray clouds, heavy with rain, drifted like an armada of battleships across the blue sky. The Hanamure grave was marked by the family insignia, which Tsuyuko described as "two cranes hugging." The tombstone on the monument bore the names of 14 family members and the dates of their deaths. Only three—Kanemori, Kanemori's third wife Tsuru, and Fumitomo—had lived beyond the age of 55.

We each lit a stick of cedar incense and placed it in a holder atop the grave. There was no talking. The power lines hummed. Grasshoppers made a rattling noise. The summer afternoon air was sweet and thick like syrup.

"Do you want us to open it?" asked Tsuyuko gesturing toward the crypt.

I had requested to visit Tomomi's grave to pay my respects. But this was unexpected. Lisa would tell me later that opening the door of the grave was a gesture usually reserved only for Buddhist priests.

"Yes," I said.

I lit another stick of incense, wrapped Buddhist prayer beads around my hands and knelt before the grave. Shinichi pulled open the stone door at the base of the monument.

Inside were rows of dusty boxes and urns. I had traveled for three weeks and 6,400 miles to get here, but it felt more like several lifetimes. My eyes were blurry with tears. I waited for my vision to clear to get a better look. Even though I did not come to know Tomomi until after she died, she felt like my friend, my sister. And, somehow, I missed her terribly.

There it was. A white box in front of the others with no dust and wrapped in a shiny gold ribbon. It contained the remains of a family member who died far too young and whom Tetsushi and Tsuyuko had retrieved from the other side of the world, from the heart of the Havasupai origin place.

~~~

After our Kagoshima road trip, we joined Tsuyuko's two daughters Konomi and Sali, and Sali's husband Makoto, for a tour of the temples in Kyoto. Austin, Lisa and I said goodbye to Tsuyuko and Shinichi at the

Izumi City train station. Tsuyuko gave us rice balls to eat on the train and she made a pinkie promise with Austin. "This means that you swear you will come back and visit," she said.

Austin swore that he would.

I gave Tsuyuko a hug. I knew it was against Japanese etiquette to do so, but I couldn't help it.

Tomomi was like a big sister to Konomi and Sali and they had visited her often in Yokohama. They called her *Tomomi-neechan* a term of endearment meaning older sister. Although the three cousins had seen each other at family gatherings when they were little, it wasn't until a gathering at their grandfather's in 1996 that they really connected. The bond was especially strong for Konomi when she learned that not only was Tomomi interested in Native American culture like she was, but *Tomomi-neechan* had actually visited Native American reservations. *Sugoi!*

The way that Tomomi managed to learn English and travel regularly in the States also inspired Sali to learn English and spend six months living in Australia. "I was so impressed with Tomomi when I was in high school. More than anything, she just exuded this coolness in her manner," said Sali. "The feeling of living in Japan is narrow and stiff, especially for a young woman. There is a general lack of desire for adventure among the Japanese people. But Tomomi was not like that. She was *bokkemon*. She was free."

Tetsushi gave Konomi and Sali Tomomi's clothes after her death. As we walked around Kyoto, they wore Tomomi's thrift shop t-shirts, Native American jewelry, and floppy hiking hats with pride. We visited a temple called the Golden Pavilion and then the ancient Kiyiomizu-dera Temple. At Kiyiomizu-dera there was a woman who offered to tell fortunes.

"Please!" Austin pleaded.

I obliged and gave the woman a few yen. She rolled some dice for Austin. His fortune was very good, the best possible. Then it was my turn.

"Oh my god!" said Lisa when the woman showed her my fortune. Everyone standing around who could read kanji looked at me and laughed.

"Well, it's very bad," said Lisa.

"How bad?" I asked, alarmed.

"It just means that you are going to go through a very hard time," Lisa explained.

But I figured it couldn't be too awful because if Austin's fortune was good and I was now Austin's sole provider, then something really bad couldn't happen to me without it also being disastrous for Austin. And now that Mike and I had divorced, I thought my future seemed bright. What this "very hard time" could possibly be I couldn't begin to fathom.

On the train ride back to Yokohama, Konomi pulled out an envelope that contained dozens of letters from Tomomi written on colorful stationary and photos of her travels. There was a photo of Tomomi lying on snow-covered ground in Monument Valley making a snow angel with her arms and legs and a photo of Blues sitting on the rim of Grand Canyon. Konomi said the letters from Tomomi were *sugoi* for the stories of her adventures but also inspirational in terms of how she gave Konomi encouragement to think beyond strict Japanese cultural conventions.

Swaying in our seats as the bullet train shot across the tracks, Lisa read Tomomi's letters aloud.

There is more to being wise than just being old. You know what I mean? It's also about how much substance is in you and in your life. I think individuality is important, too. Tomomi went on to say in this letter written in 1999 that she wasn't sure, though, what she wanted to do for a job. *Maybe I could make clothes or purses out of leather or something like that. But no matter what, my No. 1 condition is to live in the States. I'm going to get a Green Card soon. I will get permanent residency in America! And you can come and visit me any time!*

After Lisa was finished reading the letters and I thought we had covered just about everything, Konomi decided there was something else she wanted me to know. It was about a dream she had the day before Tomomi was killed.

"I dreamt about her for the first time ever in my life," said Konomi. "Tomomi was far away and in a wedding gown. And next to her was her groom. He was a foreigner. And there was something strange in the background, a landscape I'd never seen before. Tomomi was looking at me, beaming. And I was looking at her and bawling my eyes out, begging her, 'Don't go, don't go!' I woke up totally freaked out. I thought I should try and call Tomomi. But I didn't. I guess I figured it was silly. It was just a dream, and she would already be out of reach."

Tears were streaming down Konomi's face, her voice muffled by the train as it passed through a dark tunnel.

"I mean," she said, sobbing, "how was I supposed to know Tomomi was going to die?"

17

Havasu Falls

In the spring of 2006 it seemed the universe was conspiring to keep Tomomi from going on her annual birthday trip to the States. She had put off completing the process for renewing her international driving permit and repeatedly failed the written test despite the fact she had passed the exam in previous years. Also, her friend Midori had decided at the last minute that because of work obligations, she could not accompany Tomomi as they had planned. And Tomomi was unable to firm up reservations for a stay at the lodge near Havasu Falls, the place she wanted to visit. Despite many calls and e-mails to the Havasupai Tribe, Tomomi could not get through to the Supai Tourism Office. The phone was always busy and there was no response to her e-mails.

As she rode her cruiser bicycle on the crowded streets of Yokohama to her boring factory job affixing price tags to Nike shoes, Tomomi thought of the photos of Havasu Falls, the way the water plunged over travertine cliffs into blue-green pools. She imagined what it would be like to hike there, a destination she had wanted to visit for years. Supai seemed almost too good to be true because it contained her two favorite things about America: the Grand Canyon and Indians. Tomomi felt the call of this place, just as she had when drawn to the hogan in Monument Valley and to the road on the Pine Ridge reservation where she found Blues. Following her instincts—as crazy as they often seemed to friends and family—had never failed her. It was her instincts, in fact, that sustained her, especially on her birthday.

Yes, she would go, she decided. And this time, she would go alone.

Tomomi bought a plane ticket to Los Angeles. And just days before her departure, she finally passed the driving test, got her international permit and reserved a rental car from Thrifty at the Los Angeles airport. It would be another quick trip. She would drive from L.A. and spend one night in Flagstaff, hopefully one night in Supai, a couple of nights at her friend Akiko's house in Las Vegas and a night or two near Santa Monica where she would visit the beach and her favorite outlet stores.

On this trip Tomomi was also going to implement a new strategy for alleviating her heartache over missing Blues who she would leave in Yokohama. She bought a laptop and a new cellphone and signed on with a cellular carrier that allowed her to receive images in text messages. Tetsushi promised he would take pictures of Blues every day and send them to Tomomi. In return, she said she would also be better about sending him updates on her travels.[1]

The day before Tomomi left for the States, she sent out a message to her friends notifying them of her new e-mail address: "NoBlues_NoLife." She said she would be back May 14. "I'll see you soon!" she promised.[2]

At 4 a.m. on May 8, Tomomi checked out of the Howard Johnson's Motel in Flagstaff. She wanted to get an early start to beat the heat on her hike down to Supai. She stopped at Walmart and bought some water and food and called her father before she ventured beyond cellphone range.[3] He wished her a happy 34th birthday. Tomomi thanked him for the photos he had sent of Blues sprawled on the floor of the Yokohama apartment.

Tomomi drove west on Route 66 and then I-40, getting off the highway at Peach Springs. From there it was 60 miles on the bumpy Indian Road 18 to get to Hualapai Hilltop Trailhead. Tomomi turned up the Red Hot Chili Peppers and watched the rising sun kiss the surrounding table lands with a golden light. There were few signs of human development on this vast stretch of the Coconino Plateau where the view stretched to the horizon in every direction. Somewhere out there amid the squat juniper trees were ruins of the Havasupai tribe's winter homes and hunting grounds. All abandoned now, these places lived on mostly in tribal stories and songs: Moqui Tank, Black Tank, and Sheep Tank, where the Havasupai held Ghost Dances in 1892.[4]

Tomomi made good time and arrived at Hualapai Hilltop around 9 a.m. when the temperature in the canyon was still mild. She parked her car in the dirt lot amid a sea of rental cars driven by tourists from all over who had also come to lay eyes on the legendary Havasu Falls. She loaded her daypack for a one-night stay in Supai and laced up her trusty Timberland hiking boots. Tomomi locked the rest of her belongings in the car and looked toward the sheer, multicolored cliffs of the Grand Canyon—a waterless, unforgiving landscape that might seem daunting to some but was inviting to her. This would be her third solo hike in the Grand Canyon and her 15th trip to the West.

But the scene at the trailhead was nothing like what Tomomi had witnessed on previous Grand Canyon hikes in the national park. There were skeletal horses tied to burned-out cars; graffiti on signs; teenage boys smoking a pipe in an abandoned trailer; litter snagged on brush and overflowing pit toilets teetering on the edge of a cliff.[5] The run-down setting did not faze Tomomi. It was not much different from what she had seen on the Pine Ridge Reservation when visiting Badlands National Park. She knew that the Havasupai, like the Lakota, were an oppressed people and poverty came with the territory.

Tomomi made one last attempt to call the Supai Tourism Office from the canyon rim, but there was no cellphone reception. She still did not have a reservation at the lodge.

She decided to hike down to the village anyway. She was feeling lucky.

As Tomomi stood near the top of the trail taking in the view, two couples from Kingman, Arizona approached.

"She was very friendly and seemed to know what she was doing," Dan Christian would later tell investigators. Dan and his wife Gracie were frequent Grand Canyon hikers and they were used to seeing Japanese tourists rushing off and on tour buses rather than running into them on the trails. "We wanted to talk to her more, to find out her plans," recalled Dan, "but she was eager to start hiking."[6]

Before descending the steep trail, Dan and Gracie posed at the top for a photo. Later, when they got their film back, they would spot Tomomi in the background. Her black hair was in pigtails, and she was smiling to herself as she headed down the trail, resuming her walk in beauty.

Tomomi had met with her friend Mari the day before leaving for the States and she talked about her plans. Tomomi said she "absolutely" wanted to go by herself and that she hoped to "remake herself" on this trek.[7] She wanted to figure out how to finally fulfill her dream of moving to the United States without betraying the bond with her father.

But Tomomi also had a suspicion that things might not work out. In the year prior to her Supai trip, Tomomi had secretly bought a modest catastrophic life insurance policy and named her father the beneficiary.[8] She told her friend Rena about the tattoo of the kanji character *hana* on her left foot and said she intended it to be an identifying mark if something happened to her.[9]

And when cousin Konomi was visiting Tomomi in Yokohama in 2005, she made a request: "If I die in the States, will you come get me?"

"Sure, no problem," Konomi replied, laughing, thinking at the time she was just joking.

Tomomi-neechan was always kidding around.[10]

~~~

As Tomomi hiked the 8-mile trail to Supai, Randy woke up hungover. He had been living at a tribal member's house, a distant cousin in his 30s by the name of Benji, and there was always a party going on. Benji's place had the reputation in the village of being something of a flophouse. Drunks and drug users were passed out for days inside. Benji had even been allowing an Irish homeless man named Neil Callaghan to stay there. Neil said he was a "goddess worshipper." He liked to do sweat lodge ceremonies and party hard with tribal members.[11]

When Randy first got out of juvenile detention that February after turning 18, he wanted to get his life on track. He tried to stop using meth and pot and smoked only cigarettes. He got a job at the café in Supai, and he took steps to obtain a Social Security card so he could secure real employment somewhere, anywhere, as long as it was Up There. But every day he spent living in Supai, the dream of escaping seemed more and more elusive. Randy was sick of his parents fighting. He both loved and hated his father. He was bored in the village because he was around the same people all the time. And the tourists coming through were a constant reminder of the life he didn't have. By early May, Randy quit his job at the café. Or maybe he was fired.

Lately, Randy just wanted to get high. That was an attainable goal. But on May 8 he was out of money to buy drugs. He went behind Benji's house and threw a butterfly knife against a large door, practicing one of his favorite pastimes. Randy loved to play with knives.

Randy mulled over his options that afternoon. He remembered he was supposed to cut wood to heat the tribal sweat lodge along the creek. He thought after that he might go swimming to cool off. He could float from a local swimming hole called "No Girls Allowed" down to Fifty Foot Falls. And then maybe he would rummage through unattended tents and packs in the campground to get some money. Randy had done this plenty of times before, along with other young men in the village who liked to party. But as the hangover wore off, Randy was also feeling horny, so he considered a different plan. Maybe he could instead rob an attractive woman who was hiking alone on the trail and she would agree to have sex with him.[12]

The Supai police were not the only people in the village worried about the increasing use of meth by Randy and others. Older tribal members were concerned, too. But they wanted to deal with the problem in their own way. They felt that drug use by young people in the village—and especially the outsider, Neil—was infecting the tribe with a dark spirit. A medicine man had been brought in that spring to exorcise the spirit, but the healer warned that it was going to take repeated ceremonies and rituals to get the darkness to leave the village.[13] One such cleansing event was planned for the evening of May 8. There would be a sweat for tribal elders at the sweat lodge by the creek and also a ceremony with a special Native American dance group that was visiting the reservation.

Supai was bursting at the seams the first week in May with some 1,000 tribal members and tourists. There were the dancers, drug users, tribal high school children home for the summer, backpackers occupying every square foot at the campground, a film crew scouting a show for the Travel Channel, an Asian tour group staying at the lodge, and Neil, who was wearing out his welcome. Maybe the only group that was lacking in numbers was law enforcement. Tension was rising with the summer heat. The campground toilets were overflowing. Tribal delinquents were smashing windows. Tourists were complaining at the café. It seemed the two streams that once quietly ran side by side through Supai—the world of Up There and the world of Down Here—were now both threatening to breach their banks.

~~~

Tomomi arrived in the village around 1 p.m. She went inside the café to buy a cold drink. Several tribal members would later report that they saw Neil visiting with Tomomi when she was sitting outside the café at a picnic table, sipping on her drink.[14]

With her fingers crossed, Tomomi then went to the lodge to see if there was a room available. Dan and Gracie, the couple she had met at the trailhead, were also at the Lodge waiting to check in. They were surprised Tomomi had hiked down without a reservation, given that the hotel was often booked solid months in advance and it would be a long, hot hike back out if there was no room available.

"I just need a room for one night," Tomomi explained with a smile.[15]

"Well, you are in luck," the desk clerk said. "We had a last-minute cancellation an hour ago."

Tomomi was assigned room 23, next door to Dan and Gracie.

"How did you manage to get a room when it is so busy down here?" Gracie asked Tomomi as they filled out paperwork and received their keys.

"I trust fate!" Tomomi exclaimed triumphantly.

Tomomi freshened up in her room with a hand towel, unloaded some belongings and packed her daypack for the two-mile hike to Havasu Falls. She would bring water, her camera, credit card, cash and cellphone. Around 3 p.m. she set out to see her 34th birthday gift.

Randy was walking on the network of tribal trails next to the tourist path when he spotted Tomomi. She was about one mile outside the village. She was hiking alone. She was beautiful. And she was nine inches shorter than Sarah Maurer.

Randy popped out onto the main trail about 20 feet in front of Tomomi. He was dripping wet from swimming in the creek. Tomomi could see right away that he was a member of the tribe she had come to learn more about. Randy was not visiting Grand Canyon; he was from it. This young man in basketball shorts and a Looney Tunes t-shirt was a descendent of the people of the blue green waters, the *Havsuw 'Baaja*.[16] He was an authentic American.

"Come this way," Randy offered politely, motioning to a side path in the brush. "I will show you a special place called Fifty Foot Falls."[17]

18
Flashback

I thought I might be killed—that this time, perhaps, the beating would go beyond what a small body could survive.[1] I did not cry. I did not flinch. I stood like stone. I was an eight-year-old girl being attacked by a 6-foot 3-inch, 220-pound man. My father. The right arm with the belt was coming down on me, over and over, wildly lashing at my back and legs. With every swing, he made a grunting sound, the same sound he made when hitting a tennis ball as hard as he could.

"I will not give you what you want," I thought. "I will not show you that I am scared." Not crying was all I had. I would rather die than cry.

My father only became more enraged and could barely hold on to the belt as he summoned all his might with every swing. His eyes were wild and unfocused, as if he was looking at something I could not see. He had become someone else.

"Aaagghh!" he grunted through gritted teeth, putting everything he had into hitting me again.

Now the buckle burned my skin. I felt the tickle of urine dripping down my legs. My mother was nearby. I did not look at her; I kept my gaze locked straight ahead. She was screaming, pleading for it to stop. But she would not intervene.

Dad did not stop; he ramped up. He was in a frenzy. This was the evening routine behind the closed curtains of the big Beauregard house.

Finally, when Dad was exhausted, I was sent to my room. I held a hand mirror up in the bathroom to survey the red, black and blue. I would keep the wounds hidden, out of sight and out of mind.

Sometimes after the beatings I would sneak into the backyard and sit in the dark with my arms around Lucky's chest, hugging him tight, smelling his fur, listening to the bullfrogs croaking in the woods. I slept with the curtains open on those nights so I could stare at the stars and slip into their mysterious vastness. Hour after hour, I lay there, eyes wide open, filled with adrenaline and confusion. Out there, somewhere, was God.

I knew the next day, or the day after, Dad would be cheerful again and say that he loved me. And I would try my hardest to believe him.

PART V

19
Search for the Killer

The first indication something was wrong came on the morning of May 9. A Supai Lodge employee entered Tomomi's room to clean and saw the bed had not been slept in and her belongings, including her passport, were still there. All that had been used in the room was one hand towel.[1]

Seeing that Tomomi was supposed to have checked out on May 9, the lodge staff contacted the Supai police. The officer on duty advised that Tomomi's things should be boxed up so the room could be rented to the next day's guests, and they would wait to see if she turned up to claim what was left behind. By May 10 the Coconino County Sheriff's Office was alerted to the situation and on May 11 a ground and air search began for what was at first presumed to be a lost or injured Grand Canyon hiker.

The Sheriff's Office, which managed search and rescue operations on most federal lands in northern Arizona, knew the drill and burst into action. Given the 100-degree heat during the day, cool nights and harsh canyon terrain, finding Tomomi quickly was imperative. More than 40 sheriff's officers and search and rescue volunteers descended on Supai and combed the Havasu Creek drainage around the falls and campground. An Arizona Department of Public Safety helicopter circled overhead looking for signs.

Tomomi's passport photo was used on a "missing" flyer that the search and rescue (SAR) crew posted around the village and campground. The sheriff's evidence technician searched the contents of Tomomi's rental car parked at the trailhead and sifted through her belongings for information. He noted bags of t-shirts from a Flagstaff thrift store in the trunk along with stuffed hamburger dog toys.[2] Tomomi's address book lead detectives to her father Tetsushi. They called him and left an urgent message in English to get in touch. There was no response. Then the Japanese Consulate in Los Angeles was able to make contact on May 12. The sheriff's officers wanted to notify Tetsushi that his daughter was missing and ask him if there were any physical or mental health issues they should know about. "Is there anyone who might want to hurt her?" they asked.

"Mr. Hanamure reports that she is in good shape," said a consulate representative in a voice mail to Coconino County Sheriff's Detective Larry Thomas. "She likes to travel and does travel alone. She has no mother and lives with her father and her dog. At this time the father has no intentions of coming to the United States."[3] What Tetsushi did not tell the consulate was that he was confident Tomomi knew how to get out of a jam. She was *bokkemon.*

Search crew members interviewed tourists along the trail to the falls and in the campground, asking if they had seen the "missing lady" in the flier. They went below the campground to comb the most likely places Tomomi might have explored on a day hike. Communication between the different search parties was difficult because their radios and even the satellite phones didn't work most of the time in the steep-walled canyon. Supai was at the peak of its busy season with hundreds of people staying in the campground and the lodge was booked to capacity. Dan and Gracie Christian said they had met Tomomi at the Hualapai Hilltop Trailhead on May 8. But none of the tourists interviewed reported any sighting of Tomomi at the falls or campground.

The only random clues extracted from the chaotic village scene was that Tomomi had been observed hiking back toward the trailhead on May 9 with a tall man who appeared to be Asian. And on May 8 tourists said Tomomi had also been seen visiting in the café with a heavily tattooed man who spoke with an Irish accent. Investigators would later identify this potential suspect as Neil Callaghan. Complicating matters was the fact that an Asian tour group of about 10 people was also down in Supai at the time, and other women were being mistaken for Tomomi.

"We thought maybe she went for a big hike," said Thomas, as he reflected on the search some five years later. "But the reality is it's hard to get lost in Supai. So we brought in a team of detectives in case something else was going on."[4]

The Supai police had given Thomas a list of seven individuals who lived in the village and were registered sex offenders or had some history of sexual assault. All the men were tribal members except for Neil. No. 1 on the list was Randy. The police told Thomas about Randy's two assaults on female hikers seven months earlier. No. 2 was Billy. No. 3 was a schizophrenic tribal member who had a habit of catcalling female tourists. No. 4 was a man named Goofy.[5]

"While the search was going on, we started interviewing these guys and getting them locked in stories," said Thomas. "We were not accusing anybody but just asking, 'Where were you on May 8? Did you see the missing lady?'"

Other tribal members who were not on the list were simply asked: "Do you know someone in the village who might want to hurt a lady?"

Almost everyone did. It was Neil Callaghan. Workers at the café reported seeing Neil talking to Tomomi and then walking away with her. Others said she was seen with Neil at the sweat lodge and also at a dance ceremony near the falls on May 9. One tribal member sought out detectives to tell them that he had seen Neil in the village saying he "wanted a woman."

Although Neil had been crashing for the past three weeks at Benji's place — the village flophouse where Randy also lived — the crazy Irishman was no longer in Supai when detectives showed up at Benji's door on May 12. Several nights earlier Neil had gotten drunk and ripped the clothes off a female tribal member who was also living at Benji's house. Neil said he wanted to "spank" her. Several male tribal members came to the woman's aid by punching Neil and kicking him repeatedly in the head.[6] A Supai police officer found Neil later that night sitting naked by the creek. He was howling at the moon and covered in blood.[7] With head injuries too severe to enable him to hike out, Neil was evacuated by helicopter May 11, the same day search and rescue crew members were coming in to look for Tomomi.

While many older Havasupai residents automatically assumed that if the "missing lady" had been the victim of foul play, it would be at Neil's hands, some village teens and young adults suspected otherwise. Word was secretly passing from one individual to another that Randy was talking about a dead body. According to one rumor, Randy had even pointed to a place in the creek where he said the body was located.[8]

On the afternoon of May 9 or 10 before Tomomi was publicly reported missing, an 18-year-old tribal member named Sage was walking on a private path along Havasu Creek when he encountered Randy. Sage would later tell detectives that Randy appeared "excited" and was talking fast. "There's a lady over here," Randy said pointing at the creek. "Got a lady over here. She's dead. Stabbed her. Don't tell nobody." Sage said he shrugged it off at the time because he thought Randy was high and just making up a crazy story.[9]

Also on May 9, Randy showed up at the basketball court in the middle of the village where tribal youth hang out. A 25-year-old Havasupai woman named Denise would tell investigators later that Randy was acting "jumpy and nervous" and had been smoking meth.

"He was always so calm and nice, but lately he was different," she said. Randy told her he had a gun and hammer in his pocket for protection. His clothes were covered in mud. "He was doing meth and was looking around, real paranoid," she said.[10]

Randy sat next to Denise and pulled out the hammer. "And look what else I've got," he said, as he took a shiny new cellphone out of his pocket. Then he pulled out a wad of cash. He also had a big bag of marijuana.

"Where did you get all that?" Denise asked.

Randy told her he "had been paid for something."

By May 12 the village was crawling with SAR volunteers, sheriff's detectives and the world of Up There. Tomomi's "missing" posters were everywhere. Detectives approached Randy that day in front of Benji's house and asked him where he was on May 8. He said he was working by himself packing pallets for horses at Hilltop and rode his horse back to the village in the afternoon. He was alone all day. He ate, showered and that night "some drunks came over." He had not seen the missing lady. The detectives asked if they could get a buccal swab from Randy's saliva for DNA testing and Randy agreed.

The night of May 12 Randy was more agitated as he hung out with other tribal teens at the basketball court. Denise noticed Randy looked like he had been crying. She asked him what was wrong. Randy told her that he had given the wad of money away. "He said he didn't want it," she told detectives several weeks later.

Randy was also approaching his peers in search of assistance. "I was playing basketball around sundown," Sage told investigators later. "Randy walks up to us and says he needed help moving a body."

Sage and others declined to help Randy, but Sage realized then that the boy he had known since they were young might have actually murdered someone. Sage was too afraid to say anything to the police at the time because he figured in a community where laws were so loosely enforced, what was to prevent Randy from murdering him?[11] And on that particular night Randy made it known he had his throwing knives with him, carrying one in each of his Shaq basketball shoes.

Joe Rommel, an experienced Grand Canyon hiker and SAR volunteer, recalled later that he felt there was something suspicious about how some of the young Havasupai men were acting during the first few days of the search. "I was asking all these guys hanging out by the creek 'Where is the spot where this woman could have gone?' And they'd point me to these obscure, treacherous trails," said Rommel. "It's weird how not one of them mentioned Fifty Foot Falls, a place so close to the lodge and where a lot of sketchy youth congregate."[12]

Feeling as if they weren't getting anywhere, sheriff's detectives brought in two trained bloodhounds and handlers on May 13 to sweep the area. They used some of Tomomi's clothing in her rental car to key the dogs on her scent. First the dogs moved through the village and then the handlers walked them along the tourist trail to the falls.

When they took the dogs to water's edge so the animals could cool off in the 100-plus degree heat, a group of tribal youth who were swimming in the creek came up to the handlers. The teens gathered around the dogs, asking if they could pet them. The handlers noticed one young man stayed in the creek and was hiding in the cattails. A photo taken by a handler would later show that the person attempting to not be seen was Randy.[13]

Meanwhile, Thomas was investigating an abandoned house in the village to which the dogs were drawn. Another detective was interviewing "person of interest" No. 2, Billy Wescogame. Even though Billy had not been charged with any felonies since the 1993 sexual assault, he knew the police would come looking for him because he was a registered sex offender. The officers took a buccal swab from Billy and asked him where he was on May 8. But they were interrupted by an urgent radio message that came in at 2:30 p.m.

"A group of tribal kids swimming in the creek say they have found a body. It's near Fifty Foot Falls."

Thomas and other detectives hopped on the Supai police officers' quad and rushed to the scene.

Billy went inside his house and started carving a cross from cottonwood branches that he would later place at the murder site when no one was around.

As the group of tribal teens looked on, several law enforcement officials who were first on the scene waded out to the spot where the youth were pointing. It was an eddy outside the main channel of the creek and covered with cattails. There were no visible signs of a body, but a mound of brownish fabric was barely poking up from the water. As the officers got closer, they could see it was a t-shirt. And there were letters on it.

The t-shirt read: "Hug Your Dog 24 Hours; I Wish These Happy Days Could Last Forever."[14]

~~~

Thomas had been working as a detective investigating violent crimes for 25 years, including a stint in Los Angeles in the 1980s during the peak of drug-fueled gang wars and carjackings. He had seen plenty of dead bodies in unlikely locations. But this one in Havasu Creek was making him do a double-take.

"The kids were pointing and screaming," he recalled later. "'There! She's right there!' But for the life of me I could not see anything."

Peering into the vegetation, being careful not to disturb a potential crime scene, Thomas noticed fly activity above the brown fabric. "Something was dead in that heavily vegetated pool, but there was absolutely no way to tell what it was. It could have been an animal. It could have been anything."[15]

Then detectives moved in closer and used a stick to move the solid brown mass. A white sock appeared and then a human hip surfaced. Then a head with long black hair. It was a female and there appeared to be multiple stab wounds. Officers pronounced the individual dead at 2:45 p.m. May 13, 2006.

Officially, no one could identify the person until an autopsy was performed. But law enforcement officers at the scene knew it was Tomomi. What had been a search for a missing hiker had suddenly turned into a murder investigation. Yellow crime scene tape was tied around the bushes along the trail and the creek. The body was left in the water until the sheriff's evidence technician could arrive the next day to process the scene. An FBI dive team would also come in and scour the pool for evidence. Three search and rescue volunteers were tasked with standing guard all night to make sure nothing was disturbed.

Thomas asked the group of teens who was the first person to discover the body. Three of the four individuals eagerly raised their hands. One of them was Randy. "They all wanted to be the hero," recalled Thomas later. Thomas immediately suspected Randy but also wondered if there might be others involved in the murder. "An unsophisticated criminal often thinks that if he is an informant he won't be considered a suspect," explained Thomas.[16]

The detectives split up and interviewed each of the four teens separately to get their stories. Thomas and Bruce Cornish took Randy. The detectives asked Randy questions as they walked up the trail toward the "No Girls Allowed" swimming hole where Randy said he left his shoes.

"Tell us what happened," said Thomas. "This is very serious stuff, so we just want to make sure we understand everything correctly."

Randy said he and his friends were floating down the creek from "No Girls Allowed" to Fifty Foot Falls like they always did. The mother of one of the boys had asked the group to look for the missing lady while they floated the creek. Randy said in the previous days he had been experiencing "very strong feelings" about the lady ever since he heard she had disappeared. "I thought, what if she is hurt and bleeding? What if her leg is broke and she is trying to get somebody's attention?"[17]

At some point near Fifty Foot Falls Randy said the group got out to drink water from a spring. This is when Randy started having "strong feelings" again and his buddy Shane started having feelings, too.

"Can you describe this feeling a little bit more? What do you mean?" pressed Cornish.

"It's hard for me to explain in your language," said Randy. "Us Natives, we believe that when something is real serious, you can feel it in your body."

Then Randy said he noticed drops of blood in the grass and he alerted Shane. The other swimmers were still at the spring. "Let's see where this takes us," Randy said to Shane. They walked about 10 feet to the pool by the creek and both saw the body at the same time. He said Shane got a stick and poked at the blob in the cattails.

"How did you know you were looking at a body?" asked Thomas.

"I just got that feeling, the feeling you get when somebody is hurt," said Randy. "My heart started pounding and I wanted to cry but I held it in."

After the detectives retrieved Randy's Shaq basketball shoes, Randy, Thomas and Cornish walked to the village to continue their recorded interview. All eyes were on them. News of the dead body had moved through the tribe like a wall of water during a flash flood. It engulfed every house and every family. The Havasupai were now awash in the darkness that elder tribal members feared. Surely this evil could not be from one of their own, they whispered. As the detectives sat on a bench talking to Randy, panicked tribal members came up to offer more information about Neil and also the tall Asian man.

While Cornish went inside the police station to make a phone call, Thomas sat outside with Randy. They found shade beneath a large cottonwood tree where the birds were singing overhead. The conversation became more relaxed, like two people just shooting the breeze. Thomas asked about all the tattoos on Randy's hands and arms. One said "brown pride"; another memorialized "4/20."

"I'm an artist," explained Randy. "I do my own tattoos."

Then Thomas asked about a round burn mark on Randy's hand.

"I did that a long time ago with a bong," explained Randy.

"By accident?" asked Thomas.

"No, it was on purpose," Randy replied. "When I was little my father used to beat me up a lot. But now I don't feel that pain no more."

"Do you like living down here?" asked Thomas, changing the subject to something lighter. "It's pretty."

"Well, if you have lived here since you were a baby, you get tired of it," said Randy. "The only thing I like down here is my family, the waterfalls and the dirt."

Thomas asked what he meant by dirt.

"The dirt here is very strong," said Randy. "The way my people see it is that when somebody dies, their spirit don't leave. They say this place is like heaven. All the spirits come down here to stay."

~~~

The next morning FBI Special Agent Doug Lintner arrived in Supai to work on the murder investigation. While the Bureau of Indian Affairs prosecuted non-violent offenses on Native American reservations, the FBI was tasked with handling major crimes. Lintner's specialty was counterintelligence, and he had spent the first part of his nearly 20-year FBI career investigating mob crimes in New York City. On his 40th birthday he decided he was done with the big city and asked to be transferred "anywhere." So he ended up working the FBI's Indian Country division covering Arizona and New Mexico. Lintner was not a coat and tie guy and preferred the wide open reservation country and BIA cops to Washington bureaucrats. But sometimes the bloody violence on the reservation got to him, especially when children were the victims. He said a mob hit was generally much cleaner than a drunken Navajo knife fight.

"When there are fights in other cultures, the guy goes down and the fight is over," said Lintner. "But in Native American cultures, there are a high number of beating deaths. In a lot of the [Indian Country] cases I've investigated, it's when the guy goes down that things pick up a notch. The other guy starts kicking him with steel toed boots and finishes him off."[18]

While two detectives searched for Neil who had disappeared after being evacuated to a hospital in Kingman, Lintner and Thomas focused on Randy. They went into the café where they had been told Randy was recently spotted crying. Yvette, the café manager, told the detectives that Randy was in the bathroom. She also had some information she wanted to share.

Yvette said that on the afternoon of May 11—three days prior—Randy came into the café acting strange and his arms had cuts on them. "He was extremely dirty," she said. "It was like he had taken refried beans and smeared them all over his upper body."

She then described how on the morning Lintner and Thomas were there, Randy had recently come in to use the bathroom, and he was distraught again. "He said he could taste the smell of her blood and that he didn't do it," Yvette recounted for the detectives.[19]

"That's my real dad out there," Randy also told her. "He's just really upset and angry. I just want to leave. I just want to leave."

When Randy came out of the bathroom and saw Thomas and Lintner waiting to talk to him, he started crying again. They asked him to step outside where they wanted to conduct an interrogation interview. Thomas was the good cop and Lintner was the bad cop. Both men had an intimidating physical presence, standing at over 6 feet tall, with deep voices to match.

As they talked to Randy, other officers were lifting Tomomi's body out of the cattails and placing her in a black plastic bag. After five days in the murky pool, the corpse was badly decomposed, but those working the scene were surprised at how there was no blood left in the body or lingering in the surrounding area. It had all washed down the creek, over the Mother of the Waters, and into the Colorado. The body bag was then carried by SAR members through a dense thicket of oak and willow and up the trail to the village where a helicopter waited.

"Randy, we'd like to ask you a few questions," said Thomas as he and Lintner followed Randy outside the café.[20]

This time Randy spoke in Havasupai. He said he did not know English well. A female tribal member nearby told the detectives that they should not be talking to Randy without his mother present.

"Well, he's an adult, ma'am," Lintner responded.

A few minutes later Carla showed up and asked what was going on.

Randy spoke to her in Havasupai.

"Randy says there are people with guns who are after him," Carla said, speaking almost in a whisper. "They are threatening him not to tell. He says the last person he saw with the lady was that Neil. He says Neil and these other guys threatened him and that is why he is crying."

Lintner then pointed out that there were holes in Randy's story. Lintner also noted that it was interesting how the body was found near the same spot on the trail where Randy had attacked the two female hikers last fall.

Randy responded with a war whoop kind of yell and banged his fists against the wall of a building. Both Lintner and Thomas assumed a fighting stance in case Randy came at them swinging.

"I am trying to tell you guys! What do you want?" Randy shouted.

"The truth," Lintner responded.

Randy then repeated the story about how he was swimming the previous day and he and Shane got a "bad feeling" right before Randy saw the blood and they discovered the body.

"What if I told you Shane said he didn't have any kind of feeling, and he also said you were the first one to point out the body," said Lintner. "Also, those drops of blood were miniscule. You could not see them unless you already knew something had happened there."

Again, Randy roared.

"I am trying hard to let it all out," he said. "But you guys have just showed your colors. You showed your colors and I can't trust you."

Lintner asked if they could look inside the place where Randy had been living. Randy said OK. Lintner, Thomas and Randy walked over to Benji's house and Randy pointed out a pile of clothes on the floor that were his. A Supai police officer accompanying them discovered there was also a Supai jail mattress in the house that Benji's teenage son had been sleeping on. Curious about how the mattress could have gotten there, the officer confiscated it and took it back to the jail. [21]

Lintner went through Randy's clothes and did not see any visible signs of blood. Randy pointed out that one pair of shorts in the pile was Neil's. After obtaining a search warrant, Lintner and Thomas confiscated the clothing heap, as well as a Shaq shoe in a trash can, various throwing knives and the white door in the backyard that had been used by Randy, Neil and others for target practice.

When Randy, Thomas and Lintner walked outside Benji's place near the middle of the village, the helicopter carrying Tomomi's body was lifting off.

"That's her, by the way," Lintner said to Randy over the roar of the chopper.

Arizona Department of Public Safety regulations prohibit transporting a dead body inside a helicopter, so the shrouded corpse was packed in a litter and suspended from a 30-foot cable. With the litter dangling beneath, the helicopter climbed 3,000 feet through the colorful layers of canyon — past the red Hermit shale, the green Toroweap Formation and the white Kaibab limestone. Far below, a stream of hikers made their way down the trail toward Supai, just as Tomomi had six days earlier. Search members also flying out then remember seeing a film crew for the Travel Channel headed down the steep switchbacks.[22] The show being filmed was part of the Discovery/Travel channel's "American Icons" series and called "Grand Canyon: Nature's Great Escape."

At the top of the canyon rim, the helicopter carrying Tomomi's body banked east as it headed toward the morgue in Flagstaff. It was May 14, the day Tomomi was originally scheduled to fly back to Yokohama after another amazing birthday trip.

~~~

That same day, Tetsushi and his sister Tsuyuko were both in shock as they sat on a plane headed for Arizona to retrieve Tomomi's body. Maybe it was because he was in denial or because he could not understand English, but Tetsushi had been slow to respond to the phone and fax messages left at his apartment in the previous days. He did not learn about his daughter's murder until Tsuyuko called and told him to turn on the television. There on all the TV news programs was Tomomi's passport photo with the headline: "Japanese citizen brutally stabbed to death in Grand Canyon."[23]

Law enforcement officials were calling, asking for Tomomi's dental records, which she had plenty of since she had recently replaced all her silver fillings to appear more American. The police were also inquiring about tattoos. This was news to Tetsushi and Tsuyuko, but her friend Rena and cousin Konomi confirmed that Tomomi did have an identifying tattoo on her left foot. No one knew anything about the heart on her abdomen.

As Tetsushi scrambled to get an expedited passport—something he never dreamed he would need—and pack his bags for a trip to the States, he stopped answering the phone in order to avoid the constant hounding from the media. Even when Tetsushi and Tsuyuko arrived at the coroner's office in Flagstaff on May 15, a Japanese TV crew was staked out in the parking lot.

Lintner advised Tetsushi and Tsuyuko that they should not witness the autopsy. "You don't want this to be your last memory of her," he said.

Tomomi would be identified with the dental records. Tetsushi and Tsuyuko waited silently in the lobby with a representative from the Japanese Consulate who was helping them navigate the maze of decisions regarding the criminal investigation and burial arrangements.

On top of the horrific nature of his daughter's murder, Tetsushi was also very upset about how strict Buddhist rules for death and burial were being violated every step of the way in the United States. In Japan, burial rituals are meticulously followed to ensure purity and heavenly transcendence. For the first seven days after a person dies, when the soul still remains in the world of the living, daily memorial services are to be held with prayers to help send the loved one on her way to the next realm, hopefully to the Pure Land. But Tomomi was alone in a creek at the bottom of the Grand Canyon. And now on the seventh day after her death, she was being cut open by a coroner, a world away from the family grave in Takarabe.

At the Christian mortuary in Flagstaff where Tomomi was cremated after the autopsy, Tetsushi asked that they save his daughter's "throat Buddha"—the tiny v-shaped hyoid bone in the neck—so he could give her a proper Buddhist burial when he took her back to Takarabe. One of the most important funeral rituals for the Japanese takes place at the crematorium when family members are allowed to retrieve bones from the burned body and put the bones—especially the hyoid—in a separate urn.[24] But the mortuary in Flagstaff had never heard of this practice and they misunderstood Tetsushi's request. They gave him Tomomi's lower jaw along with her ashes.

Before returning to Japan, Tetsushi and Tsuyuko drove to Grand Canyon National Park. Tsuyuko held the box containing Tomomi's ashes as they stood on the South Rim and looked upon the otherworldly rainbow of rock that Tomomi had told them so much about. "We wanted Tomomi to see the canyon one last time," Tsuyuko said later.[25] Then they flew back to Tokyo with Tomomi's warm ashes resting on Tsuyuko's lap.

When the media reported the gruesome details of Tomomi's autopsy that May, people from Flagstaff to Tokyo were outraged about the murder. And as the summer wore on with no one being charged for the crime, Arizona hikers and international tourists alike worried that a crazy, cold-blooded killer was still on the loose. Japanese media especially became obsessed with the Grand Canyon homicide and accused the U.S. government of not doing enough to solve the crime. Japanese television crews camped out in front of the Coconino County Sheriff's Office and at the Supai trailhead parking lot awaiting any news.[26]

Law enforcement officials had suggested to the Havasupai Tribal Council that the trail to the village be closed to non-tribal members until the killer was locked up. Instead, the council decided to ban the media from the reservation. A sign was posted at the trailhead stating no journalists would be allowed entry. Reporters who attempted to hike in anyway that summer were escorted out of the village and told next time their cameras and tape recorders would be seized.[27] This only further infuriated the Japanese press and fueled speculation that U.S. officials were not doing right by the Japanese victim.

Meanwhile, FBI agent Lintner was making Supai his second home as he worked the case throughout the hot-as-hell summer months. Wearing his polo shirt with "FBI" embroidered on it, his FBI cap, and his Glock 40 and handcuffs on his belt, Lintner became a familiar presence in Supai. Out of some 100 homes in the village, he visited dozens to interview tribal members and follow up on leads. Many of the homes he called on more than once because people kept changing their stories. The whole village was keeping track of which doors Lintner knocked on. So Lintner and sheriff's detectives started doing interviews at night in hopes they would be less conspicuous and people would feel more comfortable about talking. But since Supai had no streetlights or paved streets or sidewalks it was rough going.

"We were walking around without flashlights so no one would see us and I almost broke my ankle a couple of times stepping in gopher holes," Lintner recalled.[28]

"When I was down there, you could sense this hostility—not just toward law enforcement but toward all outsiders," added Lintner. "Or maybe it was just too hot and they were tired of people traipsing through their home. I don't know."

Violence in the community picked up during the murder investigation. And the meth problem continued as tribal members who were dealers did business with no fear of consequences. "There was retaliation against tribal members who talked to law enforcement," said Supai Police Chief Henry Kaulaity. "Some were verbally harassed, but others were beat up."[29]

Detectives tracked down Neil in Flagstaff and kept him in custody for a few days while they questioned him. He had a big black eye and stitches across his head. He said he had never seen a Japanese female hiker when he was in Supai. He was just down there to worship goddesses and do sweats. Detectives shared with Neil what tribal members had reported about his interactions with Tomomi.

"Well, they're lying!" he insisted repeatedly.

Officers obtained a buccal swab in case they needed it later. Neil also agreed to a polygraph test. He passed and was released. Also, the woman with the "tall Asian man" who was often mentioned by people in Supai during the search for Tomomi turned out to be a different female Japanese hiker.[30]

Thomas reached out to Sarah Maurer in June as he was compiling background information on Randy. Sarah was home from college when she got the call and she thought the police were finally following up on her own assault.[31]

"I can't give you the details because this is an active investigation," explained Thomas. "It is about another female hiker who may have been attacked by the same individual."[32]

Sarah described what happened to her in September 2005, how Randy grabbed her around the neck and tried to drag her off the trail. Thomas was dismayed to learn the severity of the assault compared to the cursory description of the incident that was in the Supai police report.[33]

Shortly before and after Tomomi's murder, Randy also committed various assaults on tribal members. He beat up a drunk, elderly man who was asleep on a mattress along the trail to the falls. Then he hit a middle-aged man in the head with a baseball bat. And one night, as on many nights, a drunken fight broke out between young, male tribal members. A man was badly beaten and he was lying in the dirt. He heard Randy call his name and he thought Randy was coming to help him. Instead, Randy cut him on the face and hand with a knife. Lintner was able to get the Supai Tribal Court to lock up Randy for the stabbing and keep him there while the murder investigation was being carried out.[34]

Ultimately, the investigation would involve following up on more than 100 leads and interviews. But it became increasingly focused on one individual. Lintner and Thomas suspected the murderer was Randy as soon as he had pointed out Tomomi's body in the dense thicket of cattails. But they had no hard physical evidence to link him to the crime except for a faint, partial shoe imprint at the murder site that resembled a Shaq tread. They had not found a murder weapon. And there were no eyewitnesses. The only people in Supai who decided to speak out against Randy were Yvette, Sage and Denise. Everyone else, including the group of teens who were with Randy when the body was discovered, denied having any knowledge that would help investigators solve the crime.

"What jury is going to convict a kid of murder only on circumstantial evidence and just because he said he found a dead body when he felt the juju?" pointed out Thomas. "We had nothing."[35]

As the murder investigation dragged on, Tetsushi sat alone with Tomomi's ashes in his Yokohama apartment. Buddhist tradition dictated that the remains were to be put in the grave in Takarabe by the 49th day, but Tsuyuko suspected her brother waited longer than that.

"He did not want to leave her side," she said.[36]

During the fall of 2006, while Tetsushi waited for news of who killed his daughter, he found life nearly unbearable. Suicide called to him, tempting him. But he fought it off.[37] He would stay alive if only because he knew Tomomi wanted him to take care of her beloved Blues.

20

Confession

During the summer of 2006 as detectives Thomas, Lintner and others visited Supai dozens of times searching for information that could move the murder investigation forward, Randy sat in the Coconino County jail in Flagstaff.

Eating three square meals a day and not using meth transformed him from a lanky teenager into a linebacker-sized adult. His cellmates were a rotating cast of violent offenders, mostly young men like himself who came from rough neighborhoods or the reservations. They often called each other by their gang names used on the "outside." Randy's name was Dub. His cellmate's name was Crunchy in honor of rapper Crunchy Black.[1]

The clock was ticking on how much longer Randy could be held in jail. The only charges against him were from the Supai Tribal Court for stabbing a Havasupai tribal member in May 2006. It was possible that if no additional evidence surfaced proving Randy's involvement in Tomomi's murder, he might receive a nominal sentence for the stabbing incident and then be released, allowing him to return to Supai.

Randy kept quiet for the first several months in jail. He had a public defender and invoked his Miranda Rights, which prevented detectives from being able to further interrogate him about the homicide. But by September Randy became consumed with what Thomas called "head noise."[2] Nightmares haunted Randy, and he found no escape from his thoughts during the day. And there were no drugs or alcohol to numb the pain. Sitting in his cell, awake all night, Randy passed the hours drawing pictures of the grim reaper.

"You should talk to somebody, man," advised Crunchy.

Randy submitted an Inmate Request Form asking for assistance with "a personal need."

Diana Fowles, the Coconino County inmate relations counselor, answered his call. Diana had sparkling green eyes and spiky red hair, and she competed in women's mixed martial arts. She was petite but tough and looked much younger than her 44-year-old age. As September wore on, Randy was requesting to meet with Diana on a near-daily basis. He submitted the Inmate Request Form sometimes multiple times a day, always writing the same thing: "I am requesting to meet with Fowles about a personal need ASAP. Thx."[3]

Diana had hundreds of other inmates to assist at the jail facility, but she always showed up for Randy. Every time he submitted a form, she responded, although on some days it would take four or five hours for her to get to him. When it seemed to Randy that Diana was taking too long, he would stop up the toilet and flood his cell in a form of protest.

Since Randy was not talking to anyone else in law enforcement and no one in Supai was helping the detectives, Randy's relationship with Diana became increasingly pivotal in the investigation. In the beginning Randy just wanted to make small talk. And he probably enjoyed getting attention from Diana, who was much easier on the eyes than Crunchy.

Randy told Diana dark, conspiratorial stories about his time in Supai the previous spring. He said an FBI agent was following him and one of his friends was going to pull a shotgun out of his pants and point it at the officer, but Randy told him not to.[4] "Wescogame went on to tell Fowles about a tunnel that was underneath his house," stated FBI agent Lintner in a report summarizing one of Diana's conversations with Randy. "Wescogame had told his brother to put his [pit bulls] in the tunnel while he was gone because his mother was scared of the dogs. Wescogame said he had $20,000 hidden under a mattress somewhere and that his younger brother knows about it." While Lintner was in Supai conducting interviews, he looked for the tunnels, the pit bulls and the money, but found nothing.

When they first started meeting, Diana followed jail protocols and kept Randy's arms and feet in shackles as they visited in his cell or in a conference room. "Everybody warned me," she said years later, "this guy hates female officers. He had broken the noses of some female officers when he was a juvenile."[5] But Randy did not like the shackles either, even if it was a condition that enabled him to visit with Diana. During one of their early meetings when they were locked alone in a conference room, Randy threw his arms apart and broke free of the restraints.

"So what are you going to do now? Choke me out?" Diana recalled saying to Randy. She was scared, but she was not going to show it, and she figured she could call his bluff.[6]

"Yeah, I might, if I wanted to," he said.

Instead of radioing the guards, Diana calmly waited for Randy to cool down. She thought that if she treated Randy "with respect" and kept him unshackled, they could have a normal conversation.

"I was doing it for her, [Tomomi,]" Diana explained later, acknowledging that she sometimes feared for her safety. "But I was also doing it for him." She was starting to care about the young man with surprising strength whose rap sheet included unprovoked attacks on jail staff.

As their friendship grew, Randy told Diana stories about his childhood. Diana always brought a pencil and pad to their sessions because Randy liked to draw pictures to illustrate the things he was thinking. He was a talented artist, and his detailed drawing style with delicate pen strokes strongly resembled that of his father Billy.[7] For Randy, drawing was easier than talking. Often he would start with just innocent doodles, but sometimes they would become sinister. First he would draw a smiley face, and then a smiley face with horns.

"His conversation often led towards the evil side versus the good side," wrote Diana in a report to detectives. "He kept talking about how he wanted to go to the good side but felt that he couldn't. I asked him what he would have to do to feel like he could. He stated 'I feel like I am missing a big piece of my puzzle.'"[8]

Diana would describe later how during their sessions Randy would talk about the bad things his best friend and cousin Robert had done. He described Supai to Diana, a place she had never been, and he drew a picture of Fifty Foot Falls where he said "it" happened, but he would not elaborate. Randy was often distraught over how when he attempted to draw a positive image, he said he felt "something evil" take over his hands and he could not control what he was drawing.[9] "Wescogame began to draw a cross," continued Diana in her report, "but then he switched to a man with horns coming out of his forehead and the bottom of the cross was pushing into the top of the man's head."[10]

"Randy would say to me, 'Who drew those horns?' "And I would tell him that he did," recalled Diana.

"No, I didn't," Randy insisted. "That was not me."

"Yes, you did," replied Diana. "I saw you do it."

On Sept. 26 Randy shared with Diana an exquisitely detailed drawing he had done the night before of a peacock standing in front of a brick wall and a clock that was cracked in half and stopped at 2 p.m. The peacock's long feathers became a flowing stream that ran down the page. There was also a genie's lamp with flowers coming out of it, an hourglass, a heart and a cross. The drawing was signed "Dub."[11]

Diana gave a copy of the drawing to FBI agent Lintner and she added a note about her interpretation. "Here is my story of the picture," she wrote. "The lines going down north and south under the peacock's feathers look like water in a waterfall. The waterfall is leading down to the river, which is running east and west…The clock could represent the time of death. The hourglass on its side where the sand will never run out could mean life inside the prison walls. The genie's lamp could represent that he is dreaming about being outside and seeing flowers…This picture is giving me the creeps, but I looked deep into it like I was him and this is what I came up with."[12]

Diana found through online research that a peacock symbolizes Kwan Yin in Japanese and Chinese Buddhist tradition, the revered female goddess of compassion and healing. The name translates from Chinese as "the one who hears the cries of the world." Kwan Yin is often portrayed in a long, flowing white gown with a peacock beside her. The legend of Kwan Yin is that she was immortal, but she wished to stay behind in the mortal world to aid humans in their spiritual evolution.[13] "Randy didn't have access to the internet in jail," Diana said years later. "He was just inspired to draw a peacock and he did not know why." She also said that she shared her interpretation of the drawing with Randy and he said she was correct.[14]

"I don't know what kind of crystal ball you are using but please keep it up," encouraged Lintner who felt he was making little progress in the investigation.

Although Diana assumed that the peacock drawing was essentially a confession, Randy did not want to take it to the next step. He and Diana continued to meet daily during the first three weeks in October. Randy sat quietly and without shackles, talking and drawing, sometimes for hours. He said he had been reading the Bible in his cell and thinking about God. Day after day, Diana hoped that Randy would finally tell her he was ready to confess. But he always wanted to talk about something else and then he would say in parting, "There is still one more thing I need to tell you but I am not ready yet."

On Oct. 27, the "head noise" had reached a fever pitch. Randy and Diana were in a conference room and Randy flipped through a magazine searching for some kind of positive image to draw. He came upon a boy kneeling in prayer with the words above his head: "Please Lord, forgive me for my sins." All Randy could write on his drawing pad was "my sins."[15]

Then Randy drew a picture of Havasu Creek and Fifty Foot Falls. He finally told Diana what happened there. He told her everything.

"At 1555 hours Wescogame said he was ready to talk to Agent Lintner," wrote Diana in a report to detectives. "He said he needed to get rid of all the bad stuff in him and find his spiritual self again. He also stated that he thought by releasing the bad things he had done is his life he could get the big piece of the puzzle he was searching for."

After Randy said he wanted to confess, Diana made an urgent call to Lintner. But Lintner was away that weekend taking his son to Disneyland. Diana asked Randy if he would be willing to talk to Detective Thomas instead. Randy agreed on the condition that Diana would be there with him.

"Of course," Diana said. "I am very proud of you for doing the right thing."

~~~

On Oct. 28 Diana ushered Randy in handcuffs to a jail conference room where detective Thomas waited with a tape recorder, candy bars, and soda. Trained in forensic psychology, Thomas felt the best way to deal with Randy was to be nonthreatening and go heavy on the sweets.

Randy brought his drawing of the peacock to the meeting.

"I hear you haven't been sleeping," Thomas said to Randy as they all sat down. "I am here to help you feel better."[16]

Thomas read Randy his Miranda Rights and then asked Randy if he still wanted to talk without an attorney present. Randy said he did.

Thomas offered Randy some candy and soda, treats the inmates were denied.

"Diet Pepsi or regular?" Thomas asked.

"It doesn't matter," Randy said.

"Hershey's chocolate or Reese's?" Thomas offered.

Randy took the Hershey's but said he wanted to save it for later. Randy told Thomas he was ready to talk about the bad things his cousin Robert had done.

"I don't like to see women hurt," he said. "Because I saw my dad beat my mom a lot when I was little and that really bothered me. But Robert, he is different."

Thomas played along. "So, tell me about this Robert," Thomas said.

On that day in May, Randy said he and Robert had been swimming at a spot popular with tribal members called "No Girls Allowed." Robert came up with the idea that they should "rob a female tourist." But Robert said they would also need to kill her so they would not get caught.

"I told Robert no," Randy said. "After all I've been through, in and out of treatment centers and group homes, I did not want to get in more trouble and I did not want to hurt somebody. It's like he was another person, like a devil."

But Robert did not listen. He told Randy to find a female tourist and bring her to Fifty Foot Falls where Robert would be waiting. Then Robert pulled out a rusty knife. It was like a steak knife with a four-inch blade but the handle was broken off.

"How can you make a handle for this knife?" Robert asked Randy.

"No!" said Randy. "I'm not going to help you. Killing somebody just to get money isn't right."

Robert had a blue bandanna tied around his leg and decided to wrap it around the knife for a handle. As Robert and Randy continued to argue, they saw a female walking by herself down the trail to the falls. Robert and Randy agreed with a handshake that Robert would be the one who would take responsibility for any trouble caused by his actions.

Randy followed Tomomi for a short distance and then appeared on the tourist trail. He told her about some falls on the other side of the bushes where tribal members went swimming. He offered to take her there.

When they got to the brushy area near Fifty Foot Falls, Tomomi took pictures of the falls while Robert hid in the bushes. Randy thought about warning Tomomi but he was afraid of what Robert might do to him. Then Robert came from behind Tomomi and put his left arm around her neck. He put the knife to her neck with his right arm. Randy was watching from about 30 feet away and speaking to Robert in Havasupai.

"Drop your pants!" demanded Robert.

Tomomi refused. She said she was on her period. This made Robert angry.

"Give me your money, bitch!" Robert said next.

"You know, like on [the TV show] 'CSI' and stuff," Randy explained to Thomas.

Tomomi started crying and screamed out to Randy for help but he did not respond. He was frozen with fear.

"She said, 'I respect you,'" Randy told Thomas. "You know, she meant, us Natives. I respect how you guys live and what you guys have."

Tomomi threw a wad of money on the ground and Robert picked it up. Randy estimated it was about $200.

"She was crying," recounted Randy. "She gave him every dollar out of her wallet."

Randy told Robert in Havasupai that he had to let her go. But Robert said if he did that she would tell. Then Randy walked away. But he could see from a distance what Robert was doing.

Robert wrestled with Tomomi as she pulled at his arm to try and get free. He cut her neck and then she dropped to the ground. Tomomi struggled to stand. Robert pushed her back down. With her face in the dirt,

Robert knelt over her and stabbed her back. Randy then walked closer. His whole body was shaking.

"I was trying to look to see where she was bleeding at. When Robert saw me he started stabbing her more," Randy explained. "She was bleeding a lot. The female was trying to hold her head up, and that's when I seen blood coming out of her. I had that strong feeling. I couldn't even move."

Then Robert said he was going to leave.

"No you're not!" Randy insisted. "You can't leave me here and make me be the one to take the blame."

So Robert dragged the body into the water and shoved it in a pool that was full of cattails. He cut some of the cattails with his knife and covered the body with vegetation. Robert then tossed the knife he used along with Tomomi's backpack and camera across the creek.

Randy did not want to talk to Robert after that. He went back to Benji's house, took a shower and listened to music in his room.

"I just felt like I wanted to cry, you know?" Randy said to Thomas.

Thomas asked Randy if after the murder he ever showed anyone else the body.

"No because the smell was nasty. It didn't want me to go back," said Randy. "I threw up for at least four or five days from the smell."

Thomas excused himself from the interview to use the restroom. He had drunk a lot of soda. He also wanted to confer with his colleagues who were listening in. They would decide it was time to turn up the heat.[17]

~~~

When Thomas came back he said he wanted to get some things cleared up about how Randy and his friends discovered Tomomi's body that day they were swimming.

"Now, to be honest, you already knew where she was, right?" said Thomas.

"Yeah," said Randy.

"Did any of those guys have anything to do with hurting the lady?" Thomas pressed.

"No, they were not involved at all." Randy was adamant that the only people who knew about what happened were himself and Robert.

And this led Thomas to the next thing he wanted to clarify.

"I realize this is very hard for you. I can't imagine many things being harder," said Thomas. "I think most people are good in their hearts because God made us that way. But sometimes problems with alcohol and drugs can make people do bad things. And sometimes it's easier to say someone else's name because it's hard for us to accept what we did ourselves.

"Now, I'm wondering if Randy is a good person and Randy made a mistake," Thomas continued. "And I'm wondering if you are saying Robert did it, but you know in your heart that it was you. Is it really Randy who did it? It hurts too much to say Randy, so you are saying Robert. Am I right?"

"No," replied Randy. "Because I was there when he did it. You are telling it wrong."

Randy felt anger rising up through his body. His ears got hot.

Thomas changed the subject but continued down the same path. He brought up how Denise in Supai had seen Randy with a big wad of money and a new cellphone.

Randy said he had stolen the phone from a guy in Peach Springs and that he had eventually taken some of Tomomi's money from Robert. That is why Denise saw him with the cash and also why he told her that he gave it away because he felt bad.

Thomas brought up how Sage said Randy was talking about wanting help with moving a dead body.

Randy said he didn't remember saying that. He said Sage was lying.

"It's hard for me to understand, excuse me," said Thomas as he burped from drinking more Pepsi. "It's hard for me to understand why Sage would lie about that. It doesn't do him any good. There was no reward money."

Randy changed his story and said he did remember talking to Sage about the body but that he was also high at the time. "I don't remember, you know," he told Thomas, "because every day I'm high or something."

"You know, Randy, telling us the truth about this stuff isn't going to get you in any more trouble. You've already been honest and said you were partially involved in her murder, right?" said Thomas.

But Randy stuck to his story. He said Robert grew up in Supai. He was not sure of Robert's age. Robert had stolen from the campground plenty of times, but he had never killed someone before. He liked to drink whiskey and used marijuana and meth.

Thomas pointed out that it was a pretty big leap to go from stealing items from unattended tents to murder.

"There's a bunch of people like that down there," Randy said. "If you were living down there, then you would know what I mean. Before, down there, it was all marijuana. But now it's just meth."

Thomas said he and his colleagues were going to need to interview Robert. "It will be interesting to see if he's going to be honest and straightforward like you're being. Do you think he will tell us the truth?"

"No," said Randy. "Because he's like me. He lies."

The interview had lasted for more than two hours. It did not seem like Randy was going to budge. Thomas said he needed to use the restroom again and excused himself.

"Do you want your candy bar?" Diana asked Randy when they were alone.

"No, not yet," he said.

"We need that piece of that puzzle, huh?" Diana whispered. "You know, like you said yesterday? One more piece."

"I think the whole piece is that it's truth, you know," said Randy. "It's time for me to tell him the truth."

Thomas came back into the room, this time with pizza. His colleagues listening in the other room had gotten hungry. It was well past dinnertime.

"Look what I found!" Thomas said as he placed the pizza box on the table and sat back down.

"I was the one who did it," Randy blurted out. "Everything I said about what happened is true, except the part about Robert."

"I didn't know if I wanted to laugh or cry," recalled Thomas years later. "That moment was very emotional for me. I had been working on the case for six months nonstop and I wanted so badly to get justice for the victim and her family."

Thomas pressed for exact details about the stabbing and the murder weapon, which would never be found. Randy said he held Tomomi in the crook of his left arm and stabbed her with his right arm. He could not remember how many times he stabbed her but insisted it could not have been more than five. He used a broken knife with a handle he improvised out of a blue bandanna. He was wearing Shaq basketball shoes, blue shorts and a white t-shirt that had a picture of the Looney Tunes character "Taz" (the Tasmanian Devil) on it. The shirt and shorts were in the pile of clothes that Detective Lintner had seized as evidence from Benji's house.

Randy said he acted alone. When Thomas pressed him about motive, Randy said when he saw Tomomi hiking down the trail, he decided he wanted to rape her and rob her.

"Why did you stab her the first time?" Thomas asked. "She gave you the money."

"Because I didn't want her to tell," Randy explained. He said he planned to kill Tomomi from the first moment he laid eyes on her. Confirming that the homicide was premeditated would lead to the first-degree murder charge filed against Randy six weeks after his confession.

"I was just swimming and I saw her," Randy told Thomas. "Then I got a flashback from the last [assault victim.]" Randy said he did not want Tomomi to escape and run to the police the way Sarah Maurer had done.

"Do you feel bad about what you did?" Thomas asked.

"Yeah, everything I've done," said Randy. "Everything ever since I was a juvenile."

Thomas excused himself from the room again. He wanted to check with his colleagues to see if there was anything else he should ask.

"I wanted to get out of there," Randy said to Diana when they were alone.

"Out of where?" Diana asked.

"Supai."

"Well, I think we're about done here," Thomas said as he came back into the room.

"Is the pizza OK?" he asked Randy.

Thomas undid the wrist restraints to allow Randy to more easily pick up the pizza and put it in his mouth.

"Mmmm," said Randy as he savored a giant bite from a slice of pepperoni.

Then Randy opened his Hershey's candy bar and ate it while he waited for the guards to come and take him back to his cell.

21
Punishment

Following the confession in October 2006, and nine months after he had been officially charged with Tomomi's murder in December 2006, Randy accepted a plea deal. There would be no trial.

"For Native Americans, there is a lot of shame involved with a public trial," explained Detective Larry Thomas. "Having to bring tribal members and family up on the witness stand is very hard. Randy did not want that."[1]

There was also conclusive evidence connecting Randy to the murder thanks to the admissions he made during his confession. After Randy pointed Thomas to the Tasmanian Devil t-shirt that he said he wore during the murder, detectives retrieved it out of evidence storage and sent it to the DNA lab for testing even though there were no visible blood stains on the white fabric.

"God is good," said Thomas. "Results came back showing Tomomi's DNA was on his shirt." That would make the case against Randy convincing in the eyes of a jury, which led Randy's public defender to encourage him to accept the plea agreement in order to avoid the possibility of receiving the death penalty. The plea deal reduced the first-degree murder charge to second-degree murder and the charges previously brought against Randy for robbery and kidnapping were dropped.

The agreement was also presented to Tetsushi Hanamure to make sure it was acceptable to him. Tetsushi did not want to have Randy put to death but asked for assurances that Randy would be in prison for life so he could never hurt anyone else.[2]

The rape kit taken from Tomomi's body came back negative.[3] And the DNA sample from the crazy Irishman Neil Callaghan did not link him to Tomomi. However, Neil's DNA showed up on some shorts. But they may simply have been Neil's shorts—as Randy pointed out when his clothes were confiscated—and wound up in Randy's pile in the flophouse.[4]

In reflecting years later on why Randy accepted the plea deal over seeing if he could somehow avoid conviction with a trial, FBI detective Doug Lintner said, "Randy simply preferred prison over the possibility of being in Supai."[5]

The nine-page agreement between the plaintiff, the United States of America, and the defendant, Randy Wescogame, stated: "The defendant killed the victim with malice aforethought…He stabbed her 4-5 times in the neck. After she died, he dragged her body to the river and covered her with reeds." Even though Tomomi's autopsy revealed 29 stab wounds, Randy insisted it was 4-5, so that is what was put in the agreement.[6] The agreement required Randy to plead guilty to "Second-Degree Murder" and accept a sentence of "life imprisonment without the possibility of release." He also waived all his rights for a trial or for an appeal. The agreement was signed Sept. 18, 2007 by Randy, who wrote in "Redtail" as his middle name, and by his attorney, a court-appointed public defender named Craig Orent.[7]

After several court-ordered psychological evaluations to ensure that Randy was fit to understand the plea deal, sentencing took place June 19, 2008 in the Phoenix, Arizona courtroom of U.S. District Judge Mary Murguia.

Rows of wooden pews lined both sides of a room that was cut down the middle by a red-carpeted aisle. People dressed in suits whispered to one another and waited expectantly for what was to come. The scene was eerily like a wedding.[8]

On the right side of the room was everyone attending on behalf of Tomomi. There were detectives Thomas and Lintner, Coconino County Sheriff Bill Pribil, the sheriff's evidence technician Tom Ross, Bureau of Indian Affairs police from Supai, jail counselor Diana Fowles, representatives from the U.S. Attorney's Office including U.S. Attorney for

Arizona Diane Humetewa and other law enforcement VIPs.

Sitting up front on the right side were Tomomi's family: Tetsushi, aunt Tsuyuko, cousin Konomi and friends Rena and Shinobu. They were accompanied by a representative from the U.S. Japanese Consulate and Lisa, the Japanese language interpreter working for the FBI, with whom I would travel to Yokohama the following summer. Tomomi's family wore headsets so they could hear Lisa translate the proceedings into Japanese.

The left side of the room was virtually empty. The only people attending on behalf of Randy were his mother Carla and Billy's wife Leandra along with three of Billy and Leandra's children. Billy was not there. Carla sat alone on the front pew wearing a red t-shirt and blue jeans. Her long black hair was pulled back in a ponytail and her bangs were neatly curled under. Leandra and the kids sat in the back.

At the front of the room, on the right side, a poster-sized picture of Tomomi sat on an easel. She was standing at the South Rim of Grand Canyon and smiling ear-to-ear.

From the left side, armed guards ushered in Randy, who wore a green prison uniform. His wrists were shackled to his waist and his feet were chained, causing him to shuffle to his seat at the front. Randy's hair was in a bowl cut, the kind you might give a three-year-old. He had gained weight and, compared to when I saw him in February 2007, he had lost his baby face. Randy looked out at the audience, caught his mother's eye and smiled. He also found Diana sitting among the dark-suited officers and, looking at her stone faced, he lifted his shackled hand to make a peace sign. Then he sat down and bowed his head. It was as if he wanted to put as much distance as possible between himself and the right side of the room.

Tetsushi was not going to let Randy off that easy. He leaned forward from the front pew, trying to get a better look at his daughter's killer. He stared long and hard, as if to shoot daggers out of his eyes. Tetsushi wanted to shout out to Randy and ask what his daughter's last words were, but he refrained.[9]

Randy had requested that he be allowed to speak Havasupai, his first language, and have an interpreter present. The Havasupai woman was a relative of Randy's and she wore a beaded headband as she sat quietly next to him.

Judge Murguia entered the room. With brown hair in a trimmed, puffed-up do, and wearing red lipstick and small gold hoop earrings, Murguia looked like she could be a soccer mom underneath her black robe. During her distinguished judicial career, she had risen through the ranks of Arizona's courts by presiding over the state's most violent criminal cases, many involving brutal Indian reservation assaults and domestic abuse.

Murguia asked Randy to approach the bench. As he stood, the waist of his pants sagged beneath the chains. He walked to the front of Murguia's elevated walnut desk, his head still bowed. The interpreter stood by his side.

"R stands for Redtail. Is that correct?" Murguia asked.

"Yes, ma'am," Randy mumbled.

"And you attended school until about the sixth grade?"

"Yes, ma'am."

"I have read the pre-sentencing report and it says you have pleaded guilty to a lesser charge of second-degree murder. The sentencing guideline for this charge is a minimum of 210 months in prison, but you have agreed to a sentence of life. And you have agreed to give up your appeal rights. Is that correct?"

Randy looked at the Havasupai interpreter and she whispered in his ear.

"Yes, ma'am," he said.

Randy's public defender, Thomas Haney, wore a brown suit and a toupee with blond highlights. Standing next to the interpreter, he told Murguia that he had been Randy's attorney since February 2008. He had visited with his client five times and reviewed the psychological evaluations. "Judge, I would like to ask that Randy be in a drug and alcohol treatment program, get more education when he is in prison, and learn how to develop self-control," he said.

Haney said he had no further requests but informed the judge that Randy's mother would like to make a statement.

Carla walked up to the front of the room holding a piece of paper and spoke into a microphone. "I cannot undo what my son has done," she said. "But I would like to ask the court to be just with him." She paused, crying; looking at Randy. He looked back at her, then he bowed his head.

"I'd like to apologize to the family of the victim. But I'd like to be here, too, to comfort my son."

A chilly silence filled the courtroom. Carla folded up the piece of paper, wiped tears from her face and walked back to her seat.

Judge Murguia asked Randy if he wanted to make a statement. He said he did.

Randy and the interpreter walked to the front, his shackles clanging. They stood at the microphone that was next to the picture of Tomomi smiling in the Grand Canyon. Randy spoke softly in Havasupai, the ancient Yuman language with ties to the earliest human inhabitants of North America. When Randy was done, the translator repeated his statement in English.

"My heart is very sad for what has happened. I think of the family every day. In my heart, I have discovered God, and I pray every day for the family. That is all I have to say for now."

~~~

After Randy and the interpreter sat down, it was Tetsushi's turn to make a statement. He walked to the microphone with a piece of paper and a blue handkerchief in his hand. Lisa, the Japanese interpreter, stood next to him. Tsuyuko also walked to the front and held a framed picture of Tomomi. She was there to support her brother. Tetsushi wore a freshly pressed gray suit, the same suit he would wear to the FBI Victims' memorial the following April and that I would later see hanging in his closet in Yokohama. It was his only suit and he had purchased it in order to be properly dressed at all the events surrounding his daughter's death.

Tetsushi made a deep bow to the judge and then bowed to the audience. Randy slumped forward so far that he almost had his head between his knees. Tetsushi read from the paper that he held in his trembling hand, speaking in Japanese and pausing several times as he wept and dabbed at his eyes with the handkerchief. Tsuyuko's face contorted with tears, but she did not take her hands off the photograph to wipe them away.

When Tetsushi was done, Lisa read an English translation of his statement for the court. She said Tetsushi expressed "sincere gratitude" to everyone involved in the investigation. "I am assuming that the ruling today will take a load off your shoulders as it settles the matter for the time being. As for my family and me, the ruling makes us feel as if we have just entered a tunnel with no end in sight." He said that he thinks of his daughter every day, and when he wakes in the morning, he places an offering of rice and water at the family altar in his home. Every night he burns incense at the altar for Tomomi.

Tetsushi said that he wished he could have been with Tomomi on that trip into Grand Canyon and taken her place in death. This thought left him with great bitterness. "Does the defendant think all he did was take my daughter's life?" Lisa said, as Tetsushi glared at Randy who was still slumped over. "He broke bonds with her friends and family, my hopes and expectations and everything. He terrified my daughter and even threw her into a river. Does he think all he has to do is just accept his punishment for the crime he committed? Does he realize what an enormous loss his insignificant materialist desire has caused?"

Tetsushi said that after Tomomi learned English, which is a universal language, she fell in love with the United States and made a trip to the States every year. "Every time she came home from her trip, she would tell me many stories about her journey," he said.

Tetsushi said the "best souvenir" Tomomi brought back was a dog from South Dakota. "He is as big as me when he stands on his feet, and he is very smart." Tetsushi said that last summer Blues started howling toward the eastern sky. "It seems to me he is howling toward the United States, hoping this howling would reach Arizona. I am not sure whether or not he knows that my daughter is not coming back, but he howls with a wistful voice."

Tetsushi said he would be retiring soon and he had planned to live with his daughter in his hometown. "But that also ended as an impossible dream," he added. "I plan to visit my daughter's grave to give her the news about the punishment the defendant shall receive."

Ultimately, Tetsushi was not only bitter and heartbroken, he was also in a state of disbelief. "How could this have happened?" he asked the judge, just as he would later ask me.

Judge Murguia could not adequately explain how it happened, but she attempted to sum up the situation in the interest of due process. After Tetsushi went to his seat, she turned toward Randy who had been ushered to the bench with his shackles rattling.

"You have a history of [childhood] abuse and neglect," she said. "Unfortunately it has transformed you into a very violent and troubled young man. You have been involved in substance abuse since a very young age. Interestingly, there is no evidence you were under the influence during the time of the crime." Randy kept his head down as Murguia continued. "This is the most serious criminal offense there is. It involves a tourist who was here to take in the beauty of the Grand Canyon, and what she encountered was the ugliest part of human society."

Murguia was not finished, but she had to pause because she was crying. Diana Fowles was also weeping and trying to hide her tears from the law enforcement officers sitting on either side of her. Staring into the depths of this tragedy, Diana and the judge could not help but get choked up.

"You coerced the victim to go to Fifty Foot Falls and once there you viciously attacked her, stabbing her 29 times," summed up Murguia as she regained her composure. "The victim's father questions how someone could commit such an attack. It's hard to explain to the victim's father why this happened," Murguia said. "The victim gave you her money and you still brutally killed her."

The cellphone of one of Leandra's daughters interrupted Murguia's statement with a disco ringtone. The judge waited for it to stop before she continued.

"This was an unprovoked murder," Murguia told Randy. "You are a risk to your community and to the United States."

The gavel came down. Randy Redtail Wescogame, age 20, the great-great-grandson of Billy Burro, was sentenced to spend the rest of his life in federal prison.

In closing, the judge turned to Tetsushi. "It appears your daughter was a very lovely young woman." Murguia paused again as her voice choked with tears. "You reflect the most noble of Japanese traditions. On behalf of the United States, I apologize."

Outside, on the blinding white stone plaza of the federal courthouse in

Phoenix, TV news crews gathered around Randy's prosecutors for a quote. "There are no winners here," said U.S. Attorney Humetewa, herself a Hopi whose ancestors shared homelands with the Havasupai. "The sentencing brings the criminal case to a close, but it does not end the heartbreak of a father who lost his only daughter to such a horrible act of violence."

As the reporters were focused on Humetewa, Carla Crook slipped out unnoticed and hurried away. Then the entourage from Japan exited. They rushed ahead but Tetsushi lingered alone for a moment, squinting up at the sky. He reached into his suit jacket and pulled out a ball cap as deliberately as if he was taking a samurai sword out of its scabbard. The green cap said "Custer" across the front and had a silhouette of a buffalo on it.

~~~

Two months after Randy was sentenced, a 100-year flood swept through Havasu Canyon. Although there was not heavy precipitation in Supai, six inches of rain fell in 48 hours on the Coconino Plateau above the village. Water rushing into dry channels and running into Cataract Canyon increased the flow of Havasu Creek from its normal 65 cubic feet per second to 6,000 cfs.[10]

During the day on Aug. 17, the creek began rising and Supai police received a warning from the National Weather Service about the potential for flooding. Water moving through the village and pouring over Havasu Falls started to run blood red like the earth instead of blue green. Some tribal members said the smell of a flood was in the air. Havasupai tribal rangers warned tourists in the campground that they should move their tents to higher sites. Some people followed this advice but many others figured they would just keep an eye on the creek. It was monsoon season, after all, and brief, heavy rainstorms were a near daily occurrence.

Around 10 p.m. on Aug. 17 a wall of water and debris came crashing down Cataract Canyon. It generally circumvented the village but headed straight for the campground and the mostly unprepared, slumbering campers. "The creek completed a jump from its channel over Navajo Falls," stated a Bureau of Indian Affairs report after the event, "sending its full volume toward Fifty Foot Falls and two unnamed gullies, poured down the channel over Havasu Falls and into the campground."[11]

Startled campers awoke to discover their tents filling with water. They scrambled to high cliffs and climbed trees to escape the torrent as the flood barreled through the canyon. After swallowing the campground, rising waters lapped at the Havasupai cemetery, a location where tribal members did the Ghost Dance some 110 years ago and prayed that their loved ones would return from the dead. The grave of Billy Burro was almost washed away.

"The water was rushing and raging," a woman who had been stranded in the campground told the *Arizona Republic*. "It sounded like a freight train."[12]

As several hundred stranded campers hung on for their lives, they watched Havasu Creek remake itself. "In the night, Fifty Foot Falls eroded," continued the BIA report, "and approximately two acres of 50-foot tall earth, rock and covering vegetation went down canyon." The evidence that detectives never found from Tomomi's murder—the knife and Tomomi's backpack—was presumably washed 11 miles downstream into the Colorado River. The trail to Havasu Falls was also washed away and the campground was buried in six feet of sediment once the water receded.

After the campers climbed down from their perches the next morning, they slogged through knee-deep mud to the village where they spent the next night on the basketball court until rescue helicopters could get to them. In the days after the flood, some 600 tribal members and tourists were plucked by helicopter from Havasu Canyon. No lives were lost but the Havasupai tourism business was devastated. The infrastructure to accommodate hikers and campers was gone — there was no campground, no porta-potties, no picnic tables, no trails, no bridges across the creek, no tourists. The tribe was forced to shut down its recreation enterprise and suddenly lost its primary source of income.

Arizona Governor Janet Napolitano declared the Havasupai reservation in a state of emergency. But for the Havasupai people, who had long told of stories of the power of water in Grand Canyon, the flood was not just a random natural disaster. It was a spiritual event. Floods of that magnitude had happened plenty of times before over the past thousand years when the Havasupai and their ancestors were living in Havasu

Canyon, but the deluges never happened by accident. The Mother of the Waters was speaking to the *Havsuw 'Baaja.*

22
Return to Supai

While Randy's sentencing brought some closure for Tetsushi, he believed there was still significant unfinished business around his daughter's death. Beyond the horrible circumstances of her murder, the way her body was mishandled and the absence of proper Buddhist rituals right after she was killed combined to make it a "bad death" in his mind.[1] The strict cremation procedures that help ensure a peaceful transition to the next life had been completely botched, as had the timeline for when the procedures were to be performed. Instead of her loved ones praying for her in the days after her death to help her spirit move peacefully to the next realm, Tomomi was abandoned and submerged in Havasu Creek.

According to Shin Buddhism, the best possible outcome is that people who attain enlightenment in their current life are reborn in the Pure Land when they die, thereby transcending the endless cycle of birth and death. However, for the majority of people who still have some learning to do, their spirits are reborn into another life on Earth, and this happens anywhere from three days, 21 days, 49 days, 100 days, or in rare cases seven years after death.[2] Consequently, adherence to proper rituals and prayer for the deceased during certain time periods are critical. But Tetsushi was not praying during those first three days. He did not even know his daughter was dead. Now Tetsushi worried that because of the terrible way things happened, Tomomi's spirit might be trapped at the bottom of Grand

Canyon. A Buddhist purification ceremony needed to be performed to set Tomomi's spirit free.

Tetsushi thought he would hike to Havasu Falls on the anniversary of his daughter's death and perform the ritual himself. But several years after her murder, he was still filled with too much bitterness to set foot on the Havasupai Reservation. When Tetsushi told me about his spiritual dilemma during my visit to Japan the previous summer, I told him I would perform the ritual on his behalf.

Now I was keeping my promise. On May 8, 2010, the four-year anniversary of Tomomi's death and what would have been her 38th birthday, I was hiking back to Supai. Accompanying me was Karen, an avid hiker who had worked on the law enforcement team investigating Tomomi's murder.[3] We got to know each other when I was reporting the story for *Backpacker* and had bonded over our love of Grand Canyon. Like the rest of the law enforcement and prosecution team who worked on the homicide investigation, Karen was deeply impacted by Tomomi's death, even though she had been involved in countless violent cases before.

After Randy was sentenced in 2008, FBI detective Doug Lintner retired. Tomomi's was the last murder case he ever wanted to handle. Coconino County Sheriff's Detective Larry Thomas said Tomomi's murder was the "most emotional case" he had ever worked on out of dozens of brutal homicides he had investigated during the past 25 years.[4] Inmate relations counselor Diana Fowles left her position at the Coconino County jail shortly after the sentencing. She decided she was too physically and emotional stressed by involvement in Tomomi's case to continue in that job.[5] And Lisa, the FBI language interpreter who accompanied me to Japan, was so moved by her contact with the Hanamure family that she had its family crest—the two cranes embracing—tattooed on her arm.

Karen hoped that accompanying me to perform this ceremony might bring her some healing. And I suspected it would bring me closure, too. All the sorrows and regrets that I received from Tomomi's friends and family the previous summer in Japan were a gift in terms of being able to tell her story, but they were also a burden that weighed on me. I thought that maybe doing this one last thing would help both Tetsushi and me to lighten our loads.

Karen and I started down the trail from the Hualapai Hilltop Trailhead around 9 a.m., about the same time Tomomi began her hike four years earlier. The air was still cool, and the canyon sprawled below us in the familiar multicolored layers of white, pink, brown, red, orange and green. Compared to the deeper part of Grand Canyon in the national park, which drops off in sheer cliffs, the canyon on the Havasupai reservation fans out in cascades of rock. From the rim it looks like it would be easier to hike, but once you begin descending the 2,000 feet of elevation on snaking switchbacks and slipping on the scree, there is nothing easy about it.

A Havasupai man driving a string of mules loaded with tourist backpacks passed us on the trail, nodding silently in thanks as we politely stepped aside. I had not hiked to Supai since January 2007 when I was working on the *Backpacker* story. Since tribal members were angry over the negative publicity my story generated when it was published in June 2007, I was worried now about being recognized. I wondered if I would be asked to hike out because I was unwelcome. Another reporter who wrote a story about Tomomi's murder had been officially "banished" from the reservation, but I had not received anything so severe, just angry letters directed to *Backpacker*.[6]

And just like my trip in January 2007, I was on a clandestine mission that I hoped would not be noticed by tribal officials. In my backpack I carried the items I had been advised were required for the purification ritual: cedar incense, the prayer beads I held at Tomomi's grave in Takarabe, and a statue of Amitabha, the Buddha who presides over the Pure Land. I also had the framed picture of Tomomi kneeling next to Blues at Muir Beach in California that was given to me by Tetsushi.

During the previous year, I had begun studying Buddhism and Zen in particular. At first it was just part of my journalistic research into Tomomi's life. But gradually the prayers and meditation practice struck a deep chord within me, and I was now regularly attending a weekly Zen service in Flagstaff. Compared to the Catholic religion of my childhood that seemed obsessed with how to get to heaven rather than how to live well in the present life, I liked the way Zen encouraged me to turn inward and focus on being at peace now. It offered the promise of a kind of heaven that was in the present and not in the future. And considering how prone I was toward anxious thinking, learning how to be at peace in the present would be a very good thing for me. If only I could control what Buddhists called "the monkey mind." I had not experienced a full-blown panic attack in years, but it seemed I had a whole zoo full of monkeys swinging around in my head most of the time.[7]

Yet, as Karen and I descended deeper into the canyon, I felt my worries drop away, just as they always did when I was in the wilderness. Once we hit the dry floor of the creek bottom, the canyon walls pressed against me, close and warm. The midday heat radiated from the orange sandstone cliffs that dripped with brown desert varnish, and the reflected light made the colors of the slickrock and our clothes fluorescent. The Havasupai call the bottom of Grand Canyon the womb of Mother Earth. It felt that way here—quiet, tender and nurturing. But Karen and I also saw signs of the flood when Havasu Canyon was writhing with foam and debris nearly two years earlier. We gawked at giant boulders and trees that were wedged on ledges 50 feet above the canyon floor, a testament to Mother Nature's not so tender mood Aug. 16-17, 2008.

We entered the village when the afternoon sun was high and hot, and not a human was in sight. I thought maybe it was the 100-degree temperature that was keeping everyone indoors. Only horses watched us as we walked the road into town. Even backyard trampolines were empty of children. The two rock pillars atop a cliff, called the "king" and "queen" by the Havasupai, stood guard over the village as always, and there was the familiar sound of reggae music being played somewhere. Turquoise water trickled through an irrigation ditch along the path. Giant cottonwood trees were adorned with new leaves of vibrant green. The only sounds besides the distant music were the wind in the leaves and the flowing water. Even in the middle of town, there was not a single village resident to be seen, just a few hikers sitting in the shade of a cottonwood tree eating their lunch.

After the 2008 flood, the Havasupai reservation was closed to visitors for nearly a year while the tourist infrastructure was rebuilt to repair $4 million in damages. The flood changed the landscape of the canyon, but it was the halt in cash flow that transformed the village drug trade and the violence that went with it. After August 2008, tribal assaults went down significantly. "There is just less fighting," noted a BIA police officer who said no one had been attacked recently with baseball bats or machetes — the village weapons of choice in 2006.[8] Several officers were added to the Supai police force in 2007, which also helped to keep the peace.

"The village *has* reopened hasn't it?" I asked Karen. She had been in touch with the BIA police before our visit.

"Yes," she assured me. "They started letting tourists back in last August."

Karen and I stepped into the Supai police station to say hello to her law enforcement friends, get a bit of air conditioning, and find out what was going on.

It just so happened that on that day, Tomomi's birthday, most of the tribe was on the South Rim at the sacred site of Red Butte. They were carrying out a ceremony to bury the blood of deceased family members. A few weeks earlier the tribe had won the seven-year legal fight against Arizona State University over the use of tribal members' blood for DNA research without their consent. The settlement with ASU would pay $700,000 to be divided among 41 tribal members. In addition, ASU promised to build a new health clinic in the village and agreed to return the blood samples taken 25 years ago from about 100 living and deceased Havasupai study participants. As soon as the decision was announced, a delegation of tribal members traveled to the ASU campus in Phoenix and retrieved 151 vials of blood from a university lab freezer while they sang traditional songs in Havasupai.[9]

Now the tribe was making things right, giving the blood back to Mother Earth and their ancestors. They were performing their own purification ritual.

~~~

Karen and I walked along the trail toward Havasu Falls, which had been completely rebuilt since the flood. New bridges had been constructed over the creek and embankments fortified with rocks. Below the trail was a jumble of still freshly churned earth and debris from the torrent that moved through the canyon like a liquid bulldozer.

It was around 3 p.m., about the same time that Tomomi had set out from the lodge on her hike to see her birthday gift. Karen and I were looking for the path to the murder site, the place where Randy beckoned Tomomi to follow him to see Fifty Foot Falls.

"It is so different now," said Karen. "I just don't recognize any of this from before."

She had not been on the trail since the day after Tomomi's body was recovered when she followed detectives Thomas and Lintner as they looked for blood in the grass. The crime scene tape that long marked the area had been swept away by the flood along with the bushes it was tied to.

"Here!" Karen said. The opening in the brush was a place we had passed twice, walking up and down, thankful there were no tribal members to ask us what we were doing.

We pushed through a tangle of brown flood debris and arrived at a shallow dry depression covered with dead leaves. This was where Tomomi had been killed, but now the creek was gone. The wall of water had picked up the earth in this one spot and moved it 100 yards to create a new channel for the creek on the opposite side of the canyon. The murder site that had been on the water's edge was now bone dry. Dead. Unlike the lush corridor along the new trail that was lined with willow and oak, the spot where we stood was gray and black, wrapped in thorns and swarming with ants.

"I guess we should just do it here," I said as I tried to keep the ants from crawling up my legs. Off in the distance frogs croaked in the creek, and a boy screamed with delight as he splashed in the water.

I placed the Buddha statue and the framed picture on a rock where the shallow pool that held Tomomi's body used to be. I lit incense and pulled out a copy of the Pure Land Sutra from my backpack, "The Stanzas of Wishing for Rebirth." I read the sutra aloud, holding the prayer beads around my hand.

"Like the sun, Buddha wisdom is bright and pure," said the last stanza. "And it dispels the darkness of the ignorance of the world. The pure multitudes who accompany that Tathagata are miraculously reborn from flowers of true enlightenment. *Namu Amida Butsu.*"[10]

Then we watched in silence as the incense stick burned down.

Suddenly, my entire body bristled with the white-hot knowledge of what Tomomi's final moments were like. How terrified she was that the person attacking her was completely out of control, and how there was no one around to stop him, and how she could not get away. Right then, she realized she was going to die. Right here.

"She must have been so shocked," I said to Karen, trying to bring myself back into the present.

"Yeah," said Karen. "Godspeed, Tomomi."

A warm wind washed over us and rattled the dead leaves. A chorus of frogs croaked in response.

Before packing things up, I took a picture of the temporary altar we had made so I could send it to Tetsushi to let him know of the ceremony. Then Karen and I made our way back up to the main trail and hiked toward Havasu Falls to see the creek running in its new channel.

Standing on a bluff and looking back up the canyon, we stared in disbelief at what the flood had done. Fifty Foot Falls was gone. No one would ever again lure a hiker off the trail with the promise of seeing this sight. The earth that had been picked up where Tomomi was killed and her body was stashed had not only cut a new channel, but the sheer force of its movement had made a new 75-foot tall waterfall. The multiple veiled cascades spilling over a sheer cliff looked eerily similar to Kirishima Falls outside Tomomi's hometown of Takarabe in Japan.

I thought of what Agnes Gray told me when I had visited her in Monument Valley the previous October: "In our culture, we say that when a person is killed, their spirit stays in the place where they were taken. Tomomi is now in the place she loved so much."

Maybe Tomomi's spirit wasn't trapped in Grand Canyon but had, instead, come home. And she was doing some serious remodeling.

"It looks like Tomomi already took care of things," said Karen, laughing in disbelief. "She purified the place."

Although the tribe would later call the new cascade Upper Navajo Falls, we named it Tomomi Falls. And Karen and I discovered something else. In a jumble of dirt on the edge of the creek, just above the new falls, was a wooden cross with Havasupai beads draped over it and a heart carved in the center. There were also flowers painted on it and "Tomomi" was engraved on the horizontal axis of the cross. A shelf had been constructed at the base of the memorial that held a clay pot containing the Grand

Canyon's red earth.

I suspected that this memorial blending Catholic and Havasupai traditions was made by Billy Wescogame. He had put a cross at the murder site the day after Tomomi's body was discovered in 2006, before he knew Randy would be accused of killing her. And now, even as other tribal members wanted to distance themselves from what happened, he felt the need to honor the woman who was murdered by his son.

Before hiking back to the village, Karen and I stood in silence staring at Tomomi Falls. Soon enough, some teenage tourists showed up and jumped off the top of the cascade into a deep blue-green pool. It seemed the two streams flowing through Supai —the world of Up There and the world of Down Here —were back in their respective channels, even though one had been completely purged and remade. This was where Tomomi's journey ended, with a burst of power that reshaped Havasu Canyon as well as the Havasupai tribe. And, yet, I was still searching for something. The need to figure out why the tragedy happened would not let go of me. I thought returning to Supai and performing the purification ritual at the murder site would bring me closure. Instead, it seemed to have the opposite effect.

~~~

Once back in Flagstaff, the monkeys were multiplying. There were plenty of surface level problems that kept my mind churning with worry. The book proposal my agent was circulating that seemed like a sure thing before I went to Japan had still not found a publisher. I was working two jobs and could barely make ends meet to support Austin and me. And my mom was in a steady decline at the assisted living facility in Flagstaff, losing both mental and physical functions, which required a stepped up level of involvement from me.

But, deep down, something else was going on. It was like I could sense pressure building behind a dam. With every passing day that June, the pressure increased. The inside of my head was vibrating, my vision started to get blurry, and my fingers trembled like a 90-year-old woman. Using my investigative reporting skills, I did extensive online research and diagnosed myself as suffering from the myriad symptoms of perimenopause. I was 48, after all, and if you Googled long enough, you could find proof that almost any symptom a middle-aged woman was experiencing could be attributed to the slow, torturous onset of "the change." Just to be safe, I went to the doctor and had my thyroid checked. It was normal. I was told I was in perfect health.

I figured whatever was eating away at me wasn't anything that my indomitable optimism, persistence and willpower couldn't overcome. I would work harder and meditate harder. I would tame the monkeys.

In addition to attending the Sunday morning meditations of my Zen group, I also started meditating at home. And I bought a book that one of the group's elders had recommended called *Zen Mind, Beginner's Mind*.[11] Unlike some other self-help books I had read, like *Don't Panic*, when I was plagued by panic attacks, the Zen book cut right to the chase. "In the zazen posture your mind and body have the great power to accept things as they are, whether agreeable or disagreeable."[12]

I did my best to meditate the way the book instructed. I sat cross-legged on a cushion alone in my house, closing my eyes and opening my mind to let the peacefulness blow in like breeze through a window. But as soon as my mind cleared, something else happened. Death came in dark flashes from the hazy corner of my subconscious. Whenever I drifted into a meditative state, an evil demon popped up from behind me, raising his right arm as he prepared to kill me. I was also stalked in my dreams by this ominous being. In these nightmares, I was trapped and I was convinced that I was about to be killed, or I was already dead. Just as in meditation, I would startle awake from the dreams, gasping for air with my heart pounding. The horrible feeling of death lingered long after the nightmare was over. Soon my body decided to stop sleeping in order to not have the dreams.

Despite my insomnia, I pressed on with the book research. Now that the homicide case was officially closed, FBI agent Doug Lintner, who had recently retired, was free to talk more openly about Randy and his thoughts on the murder. We met for a beer in Flagstaff the last week in June.

"I'm trying to figure out what kind of person Randy was," I explained. "What made him want to attack people?"

"Well, I know how Randy was, but I'm not sure how he got there," said

Lintner. He went on to describe how Randy beat up an elderly, drunken tribal member asleep outside on a mattress, and how he hit another tribal member in the head with a baseball bat, and how he cut a tribal member in the face when the man was collapsed on the ground. And then there were the two women he accosted on the trail before he went after Tomomi.

"Randy had a pattern of attacking defenseless people by direct ambush," observed Lintner, who pointed out that most other reservation assaults involved one-on-one fights. "Randy didn't want to rob these people. And he didn't have a grudge against them. His primary motivation was just to commit violence, to hurt somebody. And these people were easy targets."

"But could there have been other factors?" I pressed. "I mean, *why* would he do that?"

Lintner was patient with me as he finished his beer. For him, as with most law enforcement officials, the answer was simple. Randy was a sociopath.[13] That's all.

In addition to *Zen Mind*, I also began reading books about violent behavior to search out answers on my own. And on June 30, the three-year anniversary of my dad's death, I made an altar to him in my dining room that was bigger than in previous years. The robot in me was starting to short circuit and do weird things. I spent the entire day ruminating on how much I loved Dad and how grateful I was for the positive impact he had made in my life. And, yet, he had such big dreams of his own that were never realized, and his life ended alone in a near-empty room at Arden Courts. To honor him I cooked his favorite food, a grasshopper pie, which Austin and I ate amid numerous lit memorial candles.

On July 2, I had lunch with my friend Pam. She was 10 years my senior and I looked up to her as a mentor. She was the most accomplished Grand Canyon hiker I knew and we had done some rugged backpacking trips together over the years. Pam was also a revered professor at Northern Arizona University. She had inspired me to teach college students like she did. Her father had died of Alzheimer's three years before mine, and her mom was pretty nutty, too. Pam was level-headed and it seemed there was no challenge she couldn't tackle.

I told her about my insomnia, how I had been going night after night with no sleep. I expected her to respond with some kind of reassurance and tell me she had also experienced similar bouts of sleeplessness. Or she would tell me that as uncomfortable as insomnia was, it was just the normal manifestation of female hormones gone wild. But she didn't.

"Huh," she said. "I have had a night or two where I couldn't sleep, but it didn't last for that long."

Then she pondered my predicament for a minute. She looked me hard in the eye.

"I wonder what it is that you are afraid of?"

"I don't know," I said, fighting back tears. "Nothing is bothering me that much."

Pam's question sat like a rock in the pit of my stomach. The vibration in my head got louder. My vision got blurrier. I felt my whole body tremble. I thought about what the fortune teller had predicted at the temple in Kyoto the previous summer, how I was going to "go through a really hard time."

In the early morning of July 4, my birthday, I was lying awake in bed trying to read but I was too distraught to focus. The gray light of dawn was creeping through the curtains, the birds were singing and, once again, I had not slept. I wrote myself a birthday note on the title page of *Zen Mind* that looked like it had been scrawled by a drunk person: "Yesterday I fed my mother with a spoon. Her last tooth fell out. She is like a baby."

Then I turned to the chapter on "Emptiness" that started with this quote: "When you study Buddhism, you should have a general house cleaning of your mind."[14]

I was not cleaning my mind. I was losing it. I was finally, inevitably, going crazy like my mother. Yes, I was on the verge of a nervous breakdown. I was certain.

The pressure kept building. And I kept not sleeping. Not even a wink for seven more days.

And, finally, on July 12, 2010, the dam burst.

PART VI

23
Collapse

"Were you abused as a child?"

The psychiatrist had just stepped into the waiting room at the Guidance Center on July 12, 2010. His first question caught me off guard. I had been mulling over the many plausible reasons for why I was there with my friend Mary and requesting emergency assistance for an emotional crisis, what I thought was the beginning of a full-blown nervous breakdown. I was ready to tell the doctor about all the pressures I had been under. And how my hormones were causing perimenopause symptoms. And to top it off, I had been pouring myself into writing a book about a brutal murder. I recently read the transcription of the murderer's confession in which he described what he did, how he stabbed the victim repeatedly with a knife in his right hand. This, I was certain, was the source of my nightmares and why I had not slept for 10 days straight.

The psychiatrist's abrupt inquiry completely baffled me. It was as if his simple six-word question was in a language I didn't understand.

"Abused? What?" I responded.

Do I look like someone who was abused, I thought to myself. I'm not a criminal or a drug addict or any kind of social misanthrope obviously reeling from being horribly mistreated during her formative years. In my mind, it was people like Randy Wescogame, violent criminals and juvenile delinquents, who were predictably victims of child abuse. In fact, Randy had been in and out of this very facility in Flagstaff over the years, ordered by a judge to attend drug and alcohol addiction programs.

I had never before been asked this question. Sure, I had joked a lot with friends over the years about my crazy childhood and how my mom wore a gas mask. But I was a survivor. I was tough. I did not let anything get to me. How could someone as emotionally stable and as functional as myself (except for the last 10 days) have been abused as a child?

"Yes!" I cried, sobbing so hard I could barely breathe.

I didn't know who said that. It was someone else, someone who had been locked away for at least three decades. Now she had broken free and was wreaking havoc. She was a little girl who had failed first grade, who held emergency Red Bandit Club meetings in the middle of the night, who loved her dog Lucky more than anything, and who refused to cry. But she was crying now. A flood of tears was gushing forth.

"I don't really remember anything specific," I said. "But I'm pretty sure my dad beat me. He beat me a lot."

"Oh my god!" Mary said in disbelief as I sobbed and buried my head in her shoulder.

This revelation was a shock, especially to me. The part of me who experienced and remembered the frequent and brutal beatings by my father had been completely sealed off from my conscious mind for most of my life. I would later learn that psychologists call this feat, which is typical among child abuse and sexual assault victims, "dissociative amnesia."[1] It was not Randy's right arm, angry eyes and gritted teeth that I was seeing in my nightmares and while meditating. It was my father's.

As an adult, I always knew there was something off about how I had almost no memories of my parents during my childhood years—except those of Mom making me do endless housework and driving me to school wearing a gas mask. And the panic attacks and anxiety, not to mention the rocky marriage to Mike, who had the same wild mood swings as my father, should have signaled to me that I had big, unresolved issues from childhood. But I kept it all locked down, out of sight out of mind. The tipping point finally came with my connection to Tomomi.

In doggedly investigating Tomomi's life and death, I was acting out what Freud coined the "repetition compulsion," a subconscious desire to creep closer and closer to the ultimate horror that I was keeping secret from myself.[2] Freud noted that "repeating repressed material as a contemporary experience" allowed childhood trauma victims to sleepwalk through a dysfunctional adulthood without knowledge of what was really eating away at them. Sometimes they abused their children while remaining completely unaware that they were once abused by their parents.

I was not just championing Tomomi and what she stood for, but also the little girl in me who persevered in a cruel world that was filled with unspeakable fear and pain. On the surface, I was a tenacious adult journalist who was after a story that investigated the nuanced reasons behind Tomomi's murder. But the little girl who still wielded control from her realm in the subconscious, thought this way: If I could figure out why Randy killed Tomomi, then I could understand why my father beat me. And if I knew why Dad was constantly attacking me, then I could make it stop. That little girl inside the body of a 49-year-old woman and mother was still trying to survive her utterly confusing and violent childhood.

Author and psychiatrist Alice Miller describes the twisted inner logic of a traumatized child this way: "A child can experience her feelings only when there is somebody there who accepts her fully, understands her and supports her," writes Miller in the 1997 book, *The Drama of the Gifted Child*. "If that person is missing, if the child must risk losing the mother's love or the love of her substitute in order to feel, then she will repress her emotions. But they will nevertheless stay in her body, in her cells, stored up as information that can be triggered by a later event. Throughout their later life, these people will have to deal with situations in which these rudimentary feelings may awaken, but without the original connection ever becoming clear."[3]

The psychiatrist at the Guidance Center concluded that I had "delayed onset post-traumatic stress disorder,"[4] something he saw all the time in middle-aged women who, until they reached the tipping point, were highly functional and masterminds at hiding their abuse. He wrote me a prescription for a sedative and told me to find a good therapist.

I reached out for the prescription with a trembling hand. I had avoided taking psychiatric medications most of my adult life. Not only did I feel I didn't need these kinds of pharmaceuticals, but I believed I had lost my mother to Valium, so I resented that drug and anything like it immensely.

But now I was so broken and desperate to sleep that I agreed to take a modern version of the same thing, which was terrifying.

"This is just to get you through the next few weeks," the doctor said, noting that the medication was addictive. "You better get help or you're going to end up a blubbering idiot."

~~~

In the 1970s, Dutch psychiatrist Bessel van der Kolk helped bring awareness about the ravages of war with his pioneering research on Vietnam War veterans who suffered from Post-Traumatic Stress Disorder. But after decades of continued research, van der Kolk discovered that PTSD was especially toxic in families plagued by domestic abuse and could be even more devastating than the collateral damage from military conflicts. "For every soldier returning from Iraq and Afghanistan with symptoms of depression or PTSD, there are around 10 children in the United States who are traumatized by exposure to family violence, sexual abuse, neglect and assault," wrote van der Kolk in a May 2011 *New York Times* article.[5]

Van der Kolk calls child abuse in the United States the nation's "largest public health problem."[6] According to a report from the U.S. Department of Health and Human Services, 3.4 million children in the United States were deemed at risk in 2015 for being victims of domestic abuse and neglect.[7] That number is greater than the entire population of Chicago, the nation's third largest city.[8] The number, which is drawn annually from state child protective service investigations, has climbed steadily over the years from 3.1 million in 2010. The vast majority of these cases involved at least one parent as the perpetrator. "This is particularly tragic, since it is very difficult for growing children to recover when the source of terror and pain is not enemy combatants but their own caretakers," writes van der Kolk in his 2014 book *The Body Keeps the Score*.[9]

Of the 3.4 million children reported to the state agencies in 2015, 1,670 children in the United States died at the hands of their caregivers.[10]

In recent years, van der Kolk has sought to raise awareness about the kind of "chronic trauma" that children experience in dysfunctional households, which almost always leads to what he calls Developmental

Trauma Disorder.[11] While society accepts that PTSD from a horrific isolated event such as war, 9/11 or the Boston Marathon bombing is something that must be treated, van der Kolk believes people want to turn a blind eye to the ongoing effects of Developmental Trauma Disorder. "Yes, it was horrible, and yes those people (affected by the Boston Marathon bombings) are suffering and deserve help," said van der Kolk in a May 2014 article in *The New York Times Magazine*. "But we have tens of thousands of children being traumatized every day, right in the same city (Boston)—a couple million across the country—and no one is offering to help them."[12]

Even though van der Kolk maintains that domestic violence and child abuse is an epidemic in the United States, he has found society is uncomfortable addressing the issue and its myriad causes head on. "We do not really want to know how many children are being molested and abused in our society or how many couples—almost a third, as it turns out—engage in violence at some point in their relationship," he writes in *The Body Keeps the Score*. "We want to think of families as safe havens in a heartless world and of our own country as populated by enlightened, civilized people. We prefer to believe that cruelty occurs only in faraway places like Darfur or the Congo. It is hard enough for observers to bear witness to pain. Is it any wonder, then, that the traumatized individuals themselves cannot tolerate remembering it and that they often resort to using drugs, alcohol or self-mutilation to block out their unbearable knowledge?"[13]

Another misconception about domestic violence—and child abuse in particular—in the United States is that it mainly occurs in minority and/or impoverished homes. But the crime knows no cultural or economic boundaries. Of the 3.4 million children at risk in 2015 for abuse, 43.2 percent were white, 23.6 percent were Hispanic and 21.4 percent were African American.[14] And there are many more abused children who go unreported because they are trapped in outwardly stable looking middle class homes, like the one I grew up in, that fly under the radar of child protective services. Who would have suspected someone like my father, a compassionate doctor and avid churchgoer, was terrorizing his family in secret?

The multitudes of children who experience domestic abuse and receive no help in processing the trauma during their youth will suffer the inevitable psychological effects in adulthood. The brain of a child growing up with chronic trauma becomes like a faulty car engine that misfires when stressed because some of the parts are not assembled correctly. While this has dire implications for the individual, it also results in many negative consequences for society. "Re-enactment of victimization is a major cause of violence," says van der Kolk. "Criminals have often been physically or sexually abused as children."[15] In other words, the United States is entrenched in a self-perpetuating cycle of violence: untreated child abuse victims go on to create more victims.

"Repeated trauma in adult life erodes the structure of the personality already formed, but repeated trauma in childhood forms and deforms the personality," explains Judith Herman M.D. in her 1992 book *Trauma and Recovery: The Aftermath of Violence, from Domestic Abuse to Political Terror.* "The pathological environment of childhood abuse forces the development of extraordinary capacities, both creative and destructive."[16] Herman explains that for children who are chronically abused and have no escape, "fragmentation becomes the central principle of personality organization."

The split self becomes capable of dissociating by going into a "trance state" during sexual abuse, or as in my case, during violent beatings, in order to not only withstand great physical pain, but also to not remember what happened afterward. And, yet, there is the other part of the self that carries what Herman wonderfully calls the sense of "inner badness," the shame of her abuser as well as the belief that she is somehow responsible for his horrific behavior.[17] If she caused it, then her abuser must not be such a bad person after all. For some children and adult abuse survivors, the part of their personality that contains the bottled up shame and anger finds release in committing violence against others. It is the person that Randy called Robert.

Or, paradoxically, in other children "the malignant sense of inner badness is camouflaged by the abused child's persistent attempts to be good…She may become an empathic caretaker for her parents, an efficient housekeeper, an academic achiever, a model of social conformity," writes Herman.

And, thus, the myth that nothing is wrong is perpetuated not only for her parents' benefit, but for the child's own emotional survival. However, such a lie can only go on for so long once the child is grown. "As the survivor struggles with the tasks of adult life, the legacy of her childhood becomes increasingly burdensome," continues Herman. "Eventually, often in the third or fourth decade of life, the defensive structure may begin to break down... The façade can hold no longer, and the underlying fragmentation becomes manifest."[18]

This is delayed onset PTSD, but it is so much more. As Herman notes, and I experienced with raw, terrifying intensity, "survivors fear that they are going insane or that they will have to die."[19]

Women in the 19th century who experienced such an awakening were dismissed as hysterics. Even today, adults who experienced chronic child abuse but can't or won't quite remember it are often misdiagnosed with psychiatric conditions like schizophrenia, generalized anxiety, depression, panic disorder, bipolar disorder, antisocial personality disorder, and dissociative identity disorder. A child who was terrorized and/or neglected by those who were supposed to care for her can, as an adult, experience symptoms of all these conditions. But the only way to find real healing is to address the underlying pain—to comfort the child's wounded soul—so the split mind and spirit can finally become whole.

After I walked out of the Guidance Center and Mary drove me to fill the prescription, I knew none of this. I only knew that I was in a fight for my life.

~~~

It took three more nights and a combination of medications for me to finally get some sleep. After 13 days of being awake most of the time, I slept four hours. The fight to go to sleep was just one battle in the war that I was now fully engaged in with my split self. On one side was the staunch defender of Dad who insisted I was having a hormone-induced nervous breakdown just like Mom and that all the bad thoughts starting to bubble up about my father were a figment of my imagination. This side was shaming me, saying the reason I couldn't sleep was because I was being punished for betraying Dad, my hero. On the other side was the little girl in me who had finally been let loose; she was angry and terrified and way too jacked up to sleep, but she held fast to the truth. And then, thank god, there was a patch of neutral ground—a kind of Switzerland—where the mom in me was unscathed and still managed to care for Austin without interruption.

"Do you remember when we were at that temple in Kyoto and had our fortunes told?" I asked Austin as we ate dinner after my epic day at the Guidance Center. I was feeling a little woozy from the sedative and had ordered pizza to give myself a break from cooking.

"Yeah, why?" replied Austin. He was 13 and had grown up used to his father acting flaky and needy but not me. Now it seemed the little girl inside of me wanted Austin to know that she was not a robot. She had needs, too.

"Well, I think I'm going through that tough time the fortune teller predicted," I said, trying to spin my frightening predicament into a story that I thought Austin could handle. "Grandpa did some bad things when I was little. And I am just remembering them now. That's why I've been having trouble sleeping."

Austin had a way of seeing deep into difficult life situations and finding a Zen-like wisdom that far exceeded his age. "This could be a good thing," he said. "The more you remember, the better you will feel."

But during the first few weeks of outing myself, there was absolutely nothing positive about remembering my past. And it seemed my body knew what was happening well before my mind could summon tangible recollections of the abuse. The nightmares continued but with Dad fully present and glaring at me, like a devil, with fire in his eyes. During the day, I would suddenly get visual flashes of bits and pieces of things: the brown cork table lamp in the den at the Beauregard house, my bedroom late at night, Dad putting his hands on his belt to take it off. With these helter skelter flashes came a gruesome feeling that rattled me as if I had witnessed a horrible car accident but there was nothing to tie it to.

Then I started hearing sounds. There was my dad's grunting when he was swinging the belt and the slapping noise the belt made against my skin. There was also the thud of the buckle when it hit me. I was especially terrorized by the abrupt auditory explosions of what I suspected were the scariest moments of my childhood—the crying and pleading of my mother.

"Felix! Stop! You are going to kill her!"

What? No, I thought, as my eyes filled with tears. That could not have happened to me. How could Dad do that? And then it came again.

"YOU ARE GOING TO KILL HER!"

I never knew when the sounds or images would grab me. It was like I was being swept downstream in a flood and I was periodically pulled below the surface by the circling undertow. I had to frantically fight every single time to get my head back above water before I drowned. My indomitable willpower and tough-as-nails self-image that had carried me through adulthood was completely flattened by these flashbacks.

One afternoon I was sitting on the couch in my house reading. Austin was at a friend's house. Everything seemed calm for a change.

"Mommy?"

The child's voice came from the other room. It must be Austin, I thought. He has come home early. I got up to go look. But no one was there.

I knew immediately whom I'd heard. It was me. The other me. From a long time ago.

I went back to the couch and tried to calm myself. Was I now also becoming schizophrenic?

"Dissociation is the essence of trauma," writes van der Kolk. "The overwhelming experience is split off and fragmented, so that the emotions, sounds, images, thoughts and physical sensations related to the trauma take on a life of their own. The sensory fragments of memory interlude into the present, where they are literally relived. As long as the trauma is not resolved, the stress hormones that the body secretes to protect itself keep circulating, and the defensive movements and emotional responses keep getting replayed…Flashbacks and reliving are in some ways worse than the trauma itself."[20]

Throughout the summer of 2010 I literally trembled with adrenaline every waking moment. I cried almost constantly, as if I was crying for every time that I had willed myself to withhold my tears as a child. My lean body lost 15 pounds and I had non-stop diarrhea. I jumped at shadows and dreaded the death dreams that visited me every night in fitful sleep. Yes, I had survived a violent childhood. But as illogical as it seemed, I feared I would not survive what the memories were doing to me now.

Even though I was meeting regularly with a therapist and had supportive friends I could call on, it was a solitary struggle. My friend Mary who was with me at the Guidance Center left for a yearlong sabbatical in Ireland. And I did not have a spouse or empathetic boyfriend to lean on. It seemed that most of the adults who were close to me wanted to help, but they also didn't really care to know the gory details of what I was experiencing. It was a little too disturbing for people in my tidy middle class life.

My yellow lab Sunny was up for the challenge, though, and she remained by my side—often pressing her body against mine—night and day. And then there was Tomomi. Even though I had temporarily set aside writing about Tomomi and Randy to make sense of what was happening to me, I still found comfort in going through Tomomi's journal and pondering her life. Over the past three years the little girl in her had become best friends with the little girl in me. One day I came across a note she wrote to herself that I had recorded in Yokohama, and now it seemed to speak directly to me.

In my lonely PTSD haze, I had been contemplating where my life should go from here, whether I should try and swim to the shore and walk back up the river to return to who I was before. There were friends and some family members who would likely prefer this. Or should I remain in the river, battle to stay afloat and let the swift and scary current continue to carry me downstream to an unknown destination? The message from Tomomi encouraged me to stay the course; she promised I would not drown.

Trust me. Trust. Trust.

24
Elizabeth

My older sister Elizabeth remembered far more than I did about our childhood. As she raised her own young family in the 1970s and 1980s, the memories weighed on her despite her attempts to leave them behind.

But I was different from Elizabeth. And I thought that difference was my salvation. I was the impervious tomboy. She was the sensitive bookworm. In our youth, I preferred the tree house and roaming in the woods while Elizabeth stayed indoors in her bedroom reading Nancy Drew. She liked cats. I liked dogs. She wore makeup and shaved her legs. I prided myself on not bathing. In adulthood, the disparity continued. I felt that compared to Elizabeth, I was skipping almost weightlessly through life, miraculously untouched by the dark cloud that shadowed her.

"Doesn't it bother you what happened?" Elizabeth used to ask me.

"I don't remember it," was always my smug reply. "Because I am *that* tough," I thought to myself.

So Elizabeth never offered more details, and I was thankful for whatever it was that kept my mind shrouded in safe, selective recollections. This had allowed me to unknowingly twist reality to suit my desired version of how things were: Dad was the tragic hero—happy, gregarious, loving, and always putting his family before himself. And he did have a bit of a temper. Mom was the invalid—a hypochondriac, weak, neurotic, and always consumed with her baseless medical ailments to the detriment of her husband and children.

Elizabeth didn't see it this way at all. In her mind, Dad was an abusive bully and she had been working her entire adult life to heal from the emotional damage he had caused and also to finally reach a point where she could forgive him. Mom was an innocent victim held hostage by Dad's cult-like control of the family. I was a victim, too, or at least I would be, Elizabeth was certain, when the time bomb of memory one day exploded.

These two different versions of our parents had kept Elizabeth and me distant from each other as adults. It was like we were living on opposite banks of a wide river and there was no bridge long enough to bring us together. And as children we had also been on different teams. I was always Dad's advocate and she was Mom's. Maria was unwittingly on my team, mainly because she was the baby and I bossed her around.

Elizabeth and I spent most of our childhoods pitted against each other. But that day in July 2010 when I got home from the Guidance Center without an ounce of toughness left, my big sister was the first person I called. I told her through sobs about my sleeplessness, the nightmares and the PTSD diagnosis. She was not surprised. She had also struggled with PTSD from childhood trauma decades before me.

Elizabeth and I cried together on the phone and she bought a plane ticket to fly from her home in Arlington, Texas to visit me in Flagstaff. Coming to my aid was a tall order for Elizabeth because of her weakened physical state. After Elizabeth got married and moved out of our childhood home in River Plantation at age 17, she and her husband Steve had been together ever since. When they were struggling young parents Elizabeth and Steve joined an evangelical Bible church in Conroe, and Elizabeth found refuge in her faith. It took her years to melt the hatred she had for Dad. Meanwhile, she was diagnosed in her mid-30s with chronic kidney disease.

While Maria and I were moving our parents out of their house and into the Alzheimer's facility in Austin, Elizabeth was in and out of the hospital as her kidneys failed. During a 10-year period, she had two kidney transplants, and the side effects from the anti-rejection drugs left her with a host of ailments, including not being able to walk without a cane. But Elizabeth was ready to rally for me.

Before her visit, Elizabeth sent an e-mail to the therapist I was seeing to share her memories about our childhood. I had asked her to do this in order to fact check myself as I reluctantly began dusting off the cobwebs in this part of my consciousness.

"I remember being terrified of Daddy when he was angry. He was so tall and big, and would take off his belt and hit me with it when I disobeyed or displeased him," Elizabeth wrote. "It seemed Annette tried to provoke Daddy's anger. She didn't want to do something just because someone said so, but only if she wanted to. Annette said she wouldn't cry when Daddy whipped her and that coincides with how I remember it. Daddy would respond by hitting her harder and longer. As we got older I think he hit her often, maybe even daily. She didn't show fear and didn't seem afraid to talk back to him sometimes. Her reactions seemed strange to me because they were so different from mine.

"I'm sorry when I look back now to see that my fear led me to hide out in my room whenever Daddy was whipping her," Elizabeth continued. "I remember Daddy's anger filling our home often in the evenings." There was one incident that Elizabeth recalled in particular because she had tried to stop it. I was about five and getting ready for a bath and Dad forced my leg into scalding water.

Sitting in my house in Flagstaff, nearly four decades after Elizabeth had left our Conroe home as a teenager, we talked about our childhood for the first time ever. Because Elizabeth had not dissociated from her memories the way I did, she had slowly waded years ago to the deep end of the swimming pool that contained our childhood terror and built up the spiritual fortitude to handle the emotional pain as she went. I, however, was suddenly thrown into the deep end and I didn't know how to swim. As Elizabeth came to my rescue, I felt like I was barely able to keep my head above water.

"I'm sorry I was so mean to you," I said one night after dinner. The adrenaline coursing through my body was hot and amplified every sensation, including how guilty I suddenly felt for doing whatever I could to make Elizabeth cry when we were little. I used to pull her hair and would purposely be noisy when Dad told us to be quiet. I remembered feeling angry. Elizabeth remembered feeling scared.

"We were just doing whatever we thought we needed to do to survive," said Elizabeth.

She had not only made peace with our painful childhood but also with the very real possibility that she could die in her 50s from kidney failure. Elizabeth had developed over the years a certain toughness that was very different from mine. Her strength was the spiritual kind and rooted in deep religious faith.

If I did not have Elizabeth by my side to corroborate the memories that were returning, I might have dismissed them as hormone-induced fantasy. But after Elizabeth left and I no longer had a family member to commiserate with, I felt the chasm in myself widening. The child whose leg was forced into scalding water by her father's hand—I did not know that girl. I did not know that man. I was still in shock and my body, which was now on a combination of medications used to treat veterans returning from war in Iraq and Afghanistan, continued to shoot off adrenaline-charged fireworks. On one side, the little girl in me was reliving countless traumatic events while on the other side, the robotic adult sought to increase distance and numbness.

But the flashbacks and nightmares and my thoroughly rattled nervous system were not the worst of it. The true heartbreak came from the realization that Dad was not the wonderful person I thought he was. And because I had always viewed myself as a chip off the old block, I also suddenly felt like I didn't know who I was either.

It would have been so much easier if I had discovered Mom beat me. I could have just added that to the already large pile of things I resented about her. But I had constructed my identity around what I believed were the many positive influences Dad had on me. I was, after all, Daddy's little girl. In adulthood I strove to be like him — a lover of stories, a writer, cheerful, athletic, optimistic, compassionate. I loved Dad so much. Making him proud had always been the wind in my sails.

Now there was no wind. The sails were in shreds. I was adrift.

The pain over losing my hero and facing what he had done to me when I was a defenseless child felt like a mortal wound. It was almost more than I could bear.

~~~

Unlike Elizabeth, who strove in childhood to keep her distance from Dad, I lived dangerously close to him by forming what psychiatrists call a trauma bond. One widely published definition of this sick phenomenon comes from University of British Columbia psychology professor Donald Dutton who describes trauma bonding as a situation in which "powerful emotional attachments are seen to develop from two specific features of abusive relationships: power imbalances and intermittent good-bad treatment."[1]

After Mom had electric shock therapy when I was four and began spending most of her time in bed, I needed a parent who was present, so I turned to Dad. And in our twisted household a pattern was established: I was the child who was closest to Dad, and I was also the one whom he abused most often. "Such an attachment can be understood as the internalized product of repeated experiences in which these children have felt both terrified and, paradoxically, desperately in need of their caregiver, whose protection is felt as essential for their survival," explains trauma expert and psychotherapist Felicity de Zulueta. "Children, and later adults who have lived in fear of their caregiver, will maintain their attachment to their desperately needed caregiver by resorting to dissociation; in other words, they will develop an idealized attachment to their parent by dissociating off their terrifying memories of being abused."[2]

As I read *Trauma and Recovery* by Judith Herman, I identified with her descriptions not only of chronically traumatized children, but also with the treatment of prisoners who experienced torture. It was like that living with someone who beat me nearly every day—probably hundreds of times over about eight or nine years when I was between the ages of three and 12. "In situations of captivity, the perpetrator becomes the most powerful person in the life of the victim, and the psychology of the victim is shaped by the actions and beliefs of the perpetrator," writes Herman. "...he appears to have a psychological need to justify his crimes, and for this he needs the victim's affirmation. Thus he relentlessly demands from his victim professions of respect, gratitude, or even love."[3]

Yes, I gave Dad respect, gratitude and love. And for most of my life I wanted to believe that he gave it back to me. But I also believed both as a little girl and after the PTSD diagnosis that the thing Dad wanted most from me I refused to turn over: my fighting spirit. As the memories came flooding into my consciousness, so did a very entrenched feeling of defiance that had been at my core since childhood. Everyone else in the house was hiding, but I faced the bully. He could not break me. He could not make me cry. I wanted Dad to know there was a part of me that could not be touched by his cruelty. I survived the abuse by dissociating, and also by not caving.

As if waking from a dream, I looked around my house in Flagstaff and saw how I had filled every room with reminders of Dad. It was creepy. My bedroom was the biggest shrine. On the dresser sat his photograph, and on the wall was the crucifix that Dad kept above his bed at Arden Courts. On my dresser was his rosary. Hanging above my bed was a landscape painting of a mountain that used to sit above the mantle in the wood paneled den of our Beauregard home. It dawned on me that these things were subconsciously reinforcing the trauma bond with my father while my conscious mind thought it was connecting me to my hero. The painting was especially disturbing after I remembered through my flashbacks that I had often fixated on it when I was being beaten. I was not in the den. I used to imagine I was hiking up that mountain to a beautiful alpine meadow.

I took down everything in my house that reminded me of Dad and replaced it with pictures of Austin, Sunny, hearts, flowers and birds. At my therapist's suggestion I also started keeping a journal of the extremely unpleasant thoughts and feelings that were spewing forth like vomit after contracting food poisoning. I titled it, "General Thoughts on My Fucked Up Life." In the journal I railed against how I had been treated as a child and was made to feel there was something wrong with me instead of with my parents. The way I failed first grade because I could not read, the poor bladder control, the constant rocking in my rocking chair and the temper tantrums were all classic symptoms of a chronically abused child[4]—not to mention the drawings I did of Dad spanking me with a belt.

I now realized why Dad felt so disturbed around me when he was in the end stage of Alzheimer's at the Peaks. "Daddy, your memory tortured you in your final years," I wrote on July 29, 2010. "I believe that you did love me but you are an asshole. The part of you—the raging, mean bully—did the unforgiveable to your family. Maybe you are suffering now for that? I am suffering, but I am going to get through it."

On an intellectual level, I was starting to get my head around what I would need to do to diminish my PTSD symptoms. I had to see things as they really were and not get stranded in the past. But it was not that simple. I could not just run a new program on the old operating system.

"A single episode of trauma as an adult can have devastating effects," says author and psychotherapist James Finley.[5] "But the younger you were when the trauma happened, the more the perpetrator showed no remorse, the more there was no rescuer and the more it was repeated, the more deeply the trauma becomes internalized into the very infrastructure of yourself...When you are asking [childhood trauma survivors] to give up their symptoms, you are asking them to give up what in their traumatized consciousness is the very thing that gets them through the day."

Finley goes on to explain that children living in abusive or neglectful homes come up with a survival strategy that allows them to feel loved and cared for by the parent—or at the very least to feel that they are not going to be annihilated by the parent. But what is actually parenting the child is the survival strategy. I was parented by dissociation. Tomomi was parented by isolation. Randy was parented by violence. The survival strategies that raised us became our operating systems for functioning in the world—not only as children, but as adults.

"It's not logical at all," says Finley, "but it's the inner logic formed in trauma. And here's the dirty little trick it plays—the ground rules are no one gets away. You get to live as long as you are willing to stay traumatized."

~~~

At Elizabeth's suggestion I made my way to a meeting of a 12-step program called Adult Children of Alcoholics which had helped her years ago. Formed in 1978 as an offshoot of Alcoholics Anonymous, the program started as the next level for recovering alcoholics to address deep issues from their childhood that drove them to drink. But then the program broadened its scope to include anyone who grew up in an abusive home and wanted to apply the 12-step recovery model to "heal the disease of family dysfunction."[6] The term "adult child," according to the official program literature, refers to someone who "meets the demands of adult life with survival techniques learned as children."[7]

The day after Elizabeth flew back to Arlington, I sat sobbing in the musty basement of the Federated Church in Flagstaff at a Tuesday night ACA meeting. I shared my story with a group of child abuse survivors who were not at all surprised by what I said or about how the trauma was now exploding back into my life. Another woman there had been nearly suffocated as a little girl when her mother held a pillow over her face. Other people told of experiences similar to my own at the hands of drunken and raging parents. After the meeting many of the participants gave me a hug and handed me tissues to wipe away my tears. They also gave me their phone numbers and encouraged me to call if I felt overwhelmed by the flashbacks or the immensity of the task ahead.

"I know you may feel like this is the end of the world right now," said a man named Jerry[8] who was molested as a boy by a Catholic priest. "But you will get better. You will get a lot better. I promise."

I bought what ACA members called "the big red book" and started reading and working the steps. ("Step 1: We admitted we were powerless over the effects of alcoholism or other family dysfunction, that our lives had become unmanageable.")[9] The literature about the effects of growing up in a dysfunctional home described me to a tee. Not only was PTSD a textbook symptom, but so were all the other mysterious physical and mental ailments I had wrestled with as an adult: panic attacks, irritable bowel syndrome, heart palpitations, anxiety, hypochondria. I also possessed the key "survival" traits of the Adult Child: workaholism; hypervigilance; always fearing the worst; marrying abusive/addictive partners; confusing codependence with love; stuffing my feelings; dissociating traumatic events; and, perhaps biggest of all, creating a false self that was tough as nails and emotionally numb. Instead of being addicted to alcohol or other substances, I was constantly getting drunk on my monkey mind.[10]

I realized Tomomi was also an adult child. So was Randy. And Billy, and Tetsushi, and my Dad. And, curiously, each of us, except Dad, lost our mothers at age four either to abandonment, neglect, or death.

The goal of ACA is to provide survivors of child abuse and neglect with the tools to break free of trauma bonds and dismantle their false selves—the one constantly reinforcing the unhealthy survival strategies—in order to rebuild and become people who can feel and trust and be emotionally present in their own lives. The program also seeks to address the fractured psyche by "reparenting" the inner child or true self, the person I thought of as my little girl. While ACA is not a religious program, it is a spiritual one. As with Alcoholics Anonymous, a fundamental principle of ACA is that true healing only happens when the job is turned over to a higher power rather than depending on the ego, which is deeply invested in maintaining the false self. ("Step 2: Came to believe that a Power greater than ourselves could restore us to sanity. Step 3: Made a decision to turn our will and our lives over to the care of God as we understand God.")[11]

Although I had stopped practicing the Catholic faith not long after college, I had always believed in the existence of some kind of higher power, what I thought of as God. But I didn't believe I really needed God. Until now. As an adult, my god had been my willpower, my strength and determination that had always gotten me through the toughest times. Now I was powerless. I was afraid. Now I prayed.

For the first time since I was a little girl, I got on my knees at night before going to bed. I prayed for sleep and healing, for guidance and that God would show me the path I should follow. I recited a quote from writer Madeleine L'Engle that Elizabeth had given me in a card: "It's a good thing to have all the props pulled out from under us occasionally. It gives us some sense of what is rock under our feet and what is sand."[12]

I prayed to find my way to the rock. And in this search, I kept working on the story about Tomomi. And it kept working on me.

25
Origins of Violence

A fter our trip to Japan, Austin and I maintained contact with Tomomi's family as if they were distant relatives. Tetsushi wrote brief letters in broken English to Austin asking how he was doing in school. I sent Tetsushi Christmas cards, presents for Blues on his birthday and Austin's school photos. I also sent cousin Konomi letters containing news of our lives in Flagstaff as well as Navajo and Hopi crafts to feed her fascination with Native American culture.

In late August 2010—five weeks into my "emotional sobriety" as it was called in ACA—I went to a Native American arts store in Flagstaff to buy Konomi a gift. She was getting married and I wanted to give her a Hopi katsina doll to hang in her home in Kagoshima. I picked out the Grandmother doll, one of the Hopi's most revered katsinas because the figure represents Mother Earth.[1]

"Do you have a good box?" I asked the man who was ringing me up. "This is going to someone special in Japan."

"Sure. Who?" the clerk asked.

I explained that the katsina was a gift for the cousin of Tomomi Hanamure who was murdered in the Grand Canyon in 2006.

"You know," the clerk said as he rolled the Grandmother in bubble wrap and placed her in a box, "my aunt is the daughter of the woman who was Billy Wescogame's foster mother."

A few years earlier, I would have chalked up this encounter to a fortunate coincidence. Now I felt as if nothing was happening by chance. In the midst of an existential crisis caused by my PTSD symptoms, I had an increasing number of pressing questions that had been moved to the front burner of my conscious mind. I was still on a journalistic mission to investigate Tomomi's life and death, but I was now also researching my own traumatic history that had been triggered by reporting on her murder.

I wanted to know how a father could willfully harm his child, regardless of his own repressed traumatic experiences. And what causes a mother to turn her back on her defenseless little ones? How could such violence and cruelty happen? Just based on the way I loved Austin more than anyone in the world, the circumstances that could drive a parent to do such a terrible thing were inconceivable to me. I needed to understand this for Tomomi's sake and, as it turned out, for my own sake. A chance to get some answers was handed to me along with the wrapped Grandmother katsina.

Two weeks later, as I was weaning myself off the sedative medication that I was afraid of becoming addicted to, I sat trembling in the Tempe, Arizona living room of Raquel and Gustavo Gutierrez. Their small, cinderblock house had no air conditioning and it was 109 degrees outside. Fans hummed all around as their two Chihuahuas smelled my shoes. The darkened room was filled with statues of Mary, crucifixes, Native American baskets, katsina dolls and pictures of foster children who had become part of their extended family.

Raquel was the daughter of the late Eloise Ruiz who had taken care of some 82 foster children during her adult life, one of whom was Billy. Eloise was a licensed foster parent with Arizona's Department of Child Safety (DCS) and after she raised her own children, she began accepting DCS cases, mostly Native American children from the reservation who were abused or abandoned by their parents.

Billy came into Eloise's home around 1967 when he was 10. Before that he had been bounced around in foster care in the Phoenix area and when one foster family said they could no longer manage young Billy, he was sent back to Supai for a year where his mother, Nancy Lee Burro Tilousi, was unable to care for him. His father, Bela Wescogame, wrote a letter to DCS asking that the state take Billy back into the foster care system.[2]

"His mother was an alcoholic," said Gustavo. "She had a lot of problems." Gustavo recalled that Billy's father was an accomplished equestrian and a rodeo champion. But even when Billy's father and mother got back together after a long separation, Bela felt it was in Billy's best interest to stay in the care of DCS.

"Billy called my mother-in-law mom," said Gustavo. "I consider him my nephew."

Gustavo and Raquel, who were both in their late 70s, had been married for 52 years. They used to live just a few miles from Eloise and her husband Cristobal, and visited their home often when it was bustling with foster children many years ago.

"There was Richard, Tony, Bobby Joe, Joseph and Billy," recalled Raquel. "Those boys were like brothers and grew up together. Other foster kids stayed for shorter periods."

Raquel said that despite all the young children running around her mother's home, the house was "immaculate" and the boys were disciplined if they did not follow the rules. "There was never clothes on the floor in their bedroom. Never."

Raquel said money was tight because Cristobal was ill and unable to work. Eloise fed the family mostly beans and potatoes. "Mom kept a tight rein on the kids," she said. "Every boy had chores to do."

"She showed them order. Supai is all disorder," Gustavo mused, letting out a deep laugh from his Santa-sized belly. His blue eyes sparkled beneath long gray hair that was pulled back in a ponytail.

Raquel took a long puff on a cigarette as she thought of her mother who had died in 1994 when Billy was in prison. Raquel had a petite, trim build and short grey hair. She kept a cigarette in one hand at all times while she held a water spray bottle in the other which she used to discipline the Chihuahuas.

"Mom took the boys to Catholic Mass every Sunday," Raquel said. "She also wanted them to learn about their own culture, but there was just no support for that in Phoenix back in those days. The boys knew very little about their own tribe. They never spoke their language; they didn't know their songs or their stories."

Gustavo recalled the time when he hiked down to Supai with Billy in 1975 to attend Billy's father's funeral. The service lasted all night as the tribe sang ceremonial songs. "Billy had a hard time knowing what to do during the funeral because he had forgotten his language," said Gustavo in between chuckles. "I told him he needed to relearn it."

Gustavo said he admired how Billy had assimilated back into his culture in adulthood. "I have a lot of respect for what Billy has done for himself over the years, the way he carries himself, and that he is proud of being a Havasupai. He has made himself a better human being."

Eloise kept records of every child in her care, and she had compiled a scrapbook containing memorabilia about Billy. Raquel handed me the book to flip through while she sprayed the dogs who were barking at a noise outside. There was a school photo of Billy when he was 10 and another photo of him when he was 17, standing proudly as a groomsman in the wedding of one of Raquel's daughters. In fifth grade Billy's artistic talents led him to win a contest for the "best book jacket design."

"Billy was a joker," recalled Gustavo. "He was always smiling and laughing and playing jokes on people."

A May 1965 newspaper story celebrated a field trip made possible by Luke Air Force Base to take Havasupai school children from the reservation "to see the outside world."[3] Billy was living in Supai at the time and was one of 13 first and second graders on the trip. The children toured metro Phoenix, rode a train, went to the circus, ate Mexican food and visited a department store. The Officers' Wives Club gave each child $10 in spending money for a shopping spree "and they knew how to use it," enthused the story. As the 1956 Indian Relocation Act was still very much in force at the time, the message for young Native Americans was loud and clear: Look at the wonderful life you can have if you leave the reservation and abandon your culture.

"Billy had a lot of anger issues, but that is to be expected," said Raquel. "When he started going to school up here, he found out how people didn't like Native Americans. It was very racist. And that just builds up more and more anger."

As I flipped through the scrapbook, I came across a magazine article from the late 1960s written by Ilva T. Schweizer titled, "Supai Billy and the Urban Environment."[4] In one amazingly politically incorrect description after another, the article summed up the twisted world that Billy was subjected to as a child.

Billy lived in Grand Canyon, Schweizer wrote, "with two old medicine men, rough men who cuffed the boy and left him to himself. There was no woman to cook his food...and hug him." The article described how Billy "grew close to the soil" and foraged for food. "Then suddenly he was torn from the friendly earth, transplanted to Phoenix by a welfare agency (that found him to be a neglected child) and grafted precariously to an unlikely stem—a Mexican American family who spoke very little English."

Schweizer described how "this child of nature was tamed by the urban environment," but he could not learn to read "even 10 words" and got into trouble at school. "He was escorted to the office for a private talk with the principal after too forceful an exploration of the mammary protuberance of a playground teacher," wrote Schweizer. The article went on to pine about the wonders of the assimilation policy that Billy and all Native Americans were subjected to at the time. "During the summer, the young warrior was kept from his village and brought closer to the ways of the white man."

Gustavo said that after Billy dropped out of high school, he began drinking and "wandering around." Eloise wouldn't tolerate anyone in her home who used drugs or alcohol. Soon after high school Billy married an Anglo woman and they had a child named Billy Junior.

"Billy has been through various phases," Gustavo added. "He has a short temper, and he can be mean and angry when he's drunk. But everybody has their faults."

But not everybody had to endure what Native American children did between 1860-1978 as they were effectively disenfranchised from two worlds: their own traditional culture and the dominant culture that had placed them in boarding schools or urban foster homes. Even though Billy was teased in Tempe schools for being Native American, he was expected to seamlessly blend with Anglo culture and to be grateful for the opportunity to do so.

"The [Native American] foster kids didn't have any basis for understanding who they were," said Raquel. "And they were at an all Anglo school where kids were mean to them."

The last paragraph of the "Supai Billy" article stated as much in Billy's own words. It quoted an "imagination stretching" essay that Billy wrote as part of a school exercise: "I am a red book. Boys and girls open me and write on me. Sometimes they rip my pages. They put me in their desks and never keep me clean."

~~~

Like a tinder bundle that sometimes sparks and sometimes smolders but never goes out, trauma is passed from one generation to the next. Children unwittingly receive the bundle from their parents, perhaps in the form of physical violence, sexual abuse, abandonment, or simply a complete deprivation of love and affection. But trauma is not just a personal affliction. It can be a global one that infects an entire culture, ethnic group or country.

According to author and psychiatrist Bessel van der Kolk, "The critical difference between a stressful but normal event and trauma is a feeling of helplessness to change the outcome."[5] In this context, being driven from your homeland is a trauma. Genocide, slavery, starvation, epidemic disease and a government policy that seeks to strip an entire people of their cultural traditions all constitute a communal kind of trauma.

As PTSD became an accepted medical diagnosis in the 1980s and researchers identified trauma as a root cause of a spectrum of social problems including substance abuse, domestic violence and other crimes, those studying the condition also broadened the universe of who might be suffering from it. There were war veterans and victims of domestic violence, but also people who survived the Holocaust, Japanese Americans interned in camps during World War II, and anyone who was exposed to life-altering accidents, environmental disasters or political horrors. Researchers found that not only were the survivors of these events suffering from the effects of PTSD but so were their descendants.[6] As van der Kolk pointed out in his publications, the imprint of the original trauma lived on in the victim's mind as he re-experienced it through overwhelming emotions, but it also altered brain chemistry and even the individual's DNA, which was passed on to his children.[7]

When Maria Yellow Horse Brave Heart, a clinical sociologist and member of the Lakota tribe, was doing her doctoral research in the early

1990s, she found the widespread suffering among her people was not accurately described as PTSD. Brave Heart was a descendant of Sitting Bull, and her family heritage was deeply entwined with the 1890 massacre at Wounded Knee. "I became conscious of my own unresolved historical trauma," she said. [8] Brave Heart observed that the modern-day response to trauma among fellow Lakota people took the form of substance abuse, depression, domestic violence and suicide. But she believed the spark that kept the tinder bundle burning was rooted in a cultural history of pain and unresolved grief dating back a century or more. To describe this broader mental health and cultural phenomenon, Brave Heart coined the term "historical trauma."

"Historical trauma refers to cumulative wounding across generations as well as during one's current life span," writes Brave Heart. "For Native people, the legacy of genocide includes distortions of indigenous identity, self-concept and values. The process of colonization and varying degrees of assimilation into the dominant cultural value system has resulted in altered states of an Indian sense of self."[9]

Just as the Havasupais' traditional identity was defined by an intrinsic connection to Grand Canyon and their communal way of life, the Lakota sense of self was intimately bonded with the northern Plains and the collective *Oyate* (Lakota nation). "Being Lakota means carrying the welfare of the *Oyate* in one's heart, making all decisions with the well-being of *Oyate* in mind," explains Brave Heart. "Connection with all of creation, both the present universe and the ancestor spirits, is essential to positive self-esteem. The sense of self and one's identity does not exist apart from the spiritual world, the *Oyate* and all of creation."[10]

When the buffalo were slaughtered to near extinction and the Lakota were corralled onto the reservation, Brave Heart maintains the identity of tribal members became that of victims instead of warriors. And the individual was no longer connected to the spiritual realm of the natural world that had long sustained the tribe. "With the United States government's confiscation of the Black Hills in 1871 and prohibition of traditional spiritual practices in 1881, the Lakota were unable to perform sacred duties in the Black Hills," continues Brave Heart.[11]

The final trauma of that era came in 1890 with the Wounded Knee

Massacre, "a deep psychic wound to Lakota men because they were unable to perform their traditional sacred roles as the protectors of women and children and the guardians of the land and the natural world," according to Brave Heart.[12]

The tinder bundle remained white hot as it was passed on to successive generations in the 20th century. "Lakota grief was denied the necessary open, culturally appropriate communal expression," notes Brave Heart. "...federal policies of forced assimilation were enacted through boarding schools where Indian children were often physically abused, prohibited from speaking their language and forbidden to practice their traditional spirituality...In response to cumulative group trauma, the Lakota developed features of a trauma response and unresolved grief among survivors."[13]

And just as war veterans with PTSD experience flashbacks of past battles as if they are reliving the conflict in the present, people with historical trauma may remember the dark chapters of their ancestry from stories that are passed down, but they also relive the events in their own bodies in real time. The long reach of traumatic memories over generations can negatively impact the way a person's cells respond to stress. Various studies have proven that individuals who are descended from a family tree that is full of nurturing sunshine are on a much longer fuse when dealing with present hardship than people whose grandparents experienced genocide.[14]

"The psychological and even physiological effects of the original trauma of colonization and U.S. Indian policies are not limited to the individuals or generations who actually suffered the traumatic events," explains criminal justice professor M. George Eichenberg in the book *American Indians at Risk*. "The trauma becomes part of the culture, with each succeeding generation experiencing the trauma anew."[15]

And while Anglo culture may view the Ghost Dance movement of the 1880s as a relic of American frontier history, Eichenberg argues the Ghost Dance still carries symbolic power for many tribes and could hold a key to healing current historical trauma among Native Americans. Brave Heart also emphasizes a return to Native American practices and spiritual beliefs, or what she calls "retraditionalization," as the only way for Native Americans to heal from historical trauma.[16]

"The Ghost Dance movement should, perhaps, be seen as a collective, distinctly Native American means of dealing with the trauma caused by European colonialism," writes Eichenberg. "It was an attempt to heal all nations through a return to the security of an idealized past as a means of dealing with historical grief. The Ghost Dance movement failed…Native Americans were left with no collective means for dealing with the trauma of colonialism and thus turned to individual internalization of the pain and rage, manifested through self-destruction (self-victimization through substance abuse and suicide), victimization of one's family (another form of self-victimization), and victimization by outsiders (playing one's historic role)."[17]

~~~

There is a great deal of shame that comes with victimization. Whether it is passed down and internalized from previous generations, comes from being victimized in one's own lifetime, or is born from victimizing others, shame is like a gasoline-soaked rag when waved over a spark of conflict. Any tense situation explodes into flames.

"I believe that the most effective and powerful stimulus of violence in the human species is the experience of shame and humiliation," says author and psychiatrist James Gilligan, M.D., the former director of mental health for the Massachusetts prison system.[18]

Randy is descended from a long line of shame, humiliation and violence. His father, Billy, the man who Randy said he loved most, but who also beat him, was abused by his biological parents, foster parents, a strict brand of Catholicism that demonized his native spirituality, an Anglo school system that denied him his native language, and a century of U.S. government policy that evicted his ancestors from their native land and precipitated starvation of his people through prohibition of hunting.

As for my family history, I would learn from a cousin at my father's funeral wake in 2007 that Dad was probably sexually molested by his mother and also by his brother. He used to tell my sisters and me that he slept in the same bed with his mother until the age of 13. There is, perhaps, nothing more shameful than incest—especially when it has to stay a secret in a shame-based Catholic household. And then there was the Irish potato famine that my ancestors endured followed by poverty, alcoholism and discrimination against Irish Catholic immigrants in the United States.

Does all this violence and trauma explain how a child who is born innocent can become a murderer? Or how a father can brutally whip his young daughter nearly every day for eight years and never show remorse?

"Not all violent adults were subjected to violent child abuse. Nor do all who were subjected to violent child abuse grow up to commit deadly violence," writes Gilligan in his book *Violence: Reflections on a National Epidemic*, which is based on extensive interviews with prison inmates. "Child abuse is neither a necessary nor a sufficient condition for adult violence, any more than smoking is a necessary or sufficient cause for the development of lung cancer. There are, however, plenty of statistical studies showing that acts of actual and extreme physical violence, such as beatings and attempted murders, are regular experiences in the childhoods of those who grow up to become violent, just as we know that smoking is a major, and predictable, cause of lung cancer."[19]

Gilligan goes on to explain how just about all of the men he interviewed for his book who were in prison for violent crimes had been repeatedly and brutally beaten as children. And, as adults, he said they seemed spiritually dead. "How can violence to the body kill the soul, even if it does not kill the body?" he asks. "Having heard hundreds of men describe the experience of being beaten nearly to death, I believe the answer to that question is that violence—whatever else it may mean—is the ultimate means of communicating the absence of love by the person inflicting the violence... The self, starved of love, dies."[20]

Just going by the statistics, I should have turned into a violent adult. I should have been a murderer or, at the very least, a child abuser. But I never felt the slightest urge to lay a hand on my son. I never exploded into a rage as an adult the way my father did. Wondering why this was true was the flip side to the question of why my father beat me. I was my father's daughter after all. And Randy was his father's son. Maybe my ability to dissociate events helped shield me for a time. So did the fact that I had access to a college education and was not from a chronically impoverished community like many Native American reservations.

But there was more to it than that—something far more powerful.

I *was* loved. I experienced copious amounts of love as a child, and I have always known this. It was not from my parents, who were often incapable of giving it, but from the stars, from the trees, from my dog Lucky. I had been touched by violent human behavior, but I also knew that a higher power, the same one that created the Grand Canyon, was taking care of me.

From the first time I went hiking alone in the Big Thicket of East Texas at age eight to my first trip to the bottom of Grand Canyon at age 30, I felt a profound and never-ceasing compassion that emanated from the natural world.[21] With that compassion also came a sense of safety and comfort that was not available to me inside my parents' house or at schools where the teachers didn't ask about my bruises.

Deep in my bones, well beyond the reach of those surface level bruises, I felt the *kami,* the Great Spirit, the God I called a mountain in a childhood poem. The farther I walked into the woods, and the wilder my surroundings got, the safer I felt and the more it fed my soul. It is a world Randy was largely denied as he grew up amid the cement walls and razor wire of the Arizona juvenile correctional system. Even though the Havasupai culture is inherently tied to nature, these bonds were broken for both Randy and Billy in childhood. Tetsushi was separated from the natural world of his childhood as well. And it was a connection Tomomi did not discover until she was an adult.

Nature loved me. *Daishizen.* Nature loved Tomomi. This was the bond, the secret healing handshake, the ultimate source of spiritual life that we shared. I never could have understood this on that first trip to Supai in January 2007. To appreciate what it was that had kept me alive, I had to follow Tomomi down her path that eventually became my path, and face not only what had killed her but, also, what had nearly killed me.

PART VII

26
Momma

M y back was up against the wall. My legs were bent in a chair position and my thighs were beginning to tremble under the strain of being in this uncomfortable pose for several minutes.

"Is it starting?" asked Cheryl. Her voice came through my laptop positioned on the coffee table near where I was squatting in the living room of my Flagstaff home.

"Yes!" I replied, dreading what I knew would be coming next. After another minute my legs were visibly shaking. I felt the vibrations moving up my body like it was a tuning fork and my throat tightened with terror.

I had completed the 12 steps of the ACA program and spent a year and a half in talk therapy as well as being under the guidance of a psychiatrist who prescribed PTSD medications along with numerous helpful books (see bibliography). But on this cold morning in March 2012 when Austin was in school, I was taking my healing to the next level.

Cheryl was a trained trauma therapist who was based in Phoenix but traveled all over the world to places like Africa and Iraq to help victims of horrific, prolonged violence. She specialized in body-based healing techniques called Traumatic Release Exercises and Somatic Experiencing.[1] Talking openly about my abuse was important, but it had not addressed the issue of how my physiology was caught in a kind of traumatic limbo that was hardwired to react with all sirens blaring to any perceived threat. For people who have experienced chronic trauma, the fight, flight or freeze reaction becomes deeply imbedded in the central nervous system and can make the challenge of recovering from PTSD daunting, with no end in sight.

Psychologist and author Peter Levine explains that when people are exposed to mortal danger, an autonomic response kicks in that dates back to when humans were just another mammal species hunted by large predators on the savannah. Mammals are designed to run or fight—or when all else fails and death appears imminent, to freeze. If the mammal survives, it literally shakes off the terrifying experience by trembling and then goes on with its life. Most people who suffer from PTSD are forever stuck in the freeze state because they were not able to experience a resolution when they were in the original life-threatening situation. Part of what Freud called the "repetition compulsion" is driven by a subconscious, evolutionary desire to reach a resolution.

"Traumatic symptoms are not caused by the triggering event itself," writes Levine in his book *Waking the Tiger: Healing Trauma.*[2] "They stem from the frozen residue of energy that has not been resolved and discharged; this residue remains trapped in the nervous system where it can wreak havoc on our bodies and spirits...Drugs may be useful in buying time to help the traumatized individual stabilize. However, when they are used for prolonged periods to suppress the body's own balancing response to stress, they interfere with healing. To complete its biological and meaningful course of action, the organism requires the spontaneous shaking and trembling that we see throughout the animal world."[3]

On this next stage in my journey, I was tackling the trapped energy and redirecting what Levine describes as "animal instincts gone awry."[4] During the past two months, under the guidance of Cheryl (in person and via remote Skype sessions), I had tapped into my body's fear state by inducing trembling and revisited the many times when I was on the receiving end of my father's rage. Unlike talking to a psychologist where I recalled terrifying memories, I was reliving the actual events with Cheryl.

"What's happening?" asked Cheryl. She sensed a shift.

I was still in the chair position and my legs were now trembling violently. My back and arms were vibrating. My vision was going blurry. My head was rattling.

"He's here!" I said as tears started streaming down my face.

I knew I was in my house in Flagstaff, but I had also been simultaneously transported back in time to my childhood home on Beauregard Street. I stepped away from the wall as Cheryl instructed and now my entire body was shaking. Dad's eyes were wild and dark, and he was getting closer. All air had left the room.

"He's taking off his belt," I told Cheryl. Adrenaline was surging through my body. I was getting ready to fight, always fight. But then once Dad settled into his rhythm, I would freeze. I became like stone as he unleashed it all on me. I did not want him to go after Maria. There was no one else to protect my little sister. This time, though, Cheryl wanted me to realize I had some choices.

"What do you want to do?" asked Cheryl.

"I want to get out of here!" I cried.

"Go!"

Cheryl and I had done these sessions again and again. Every time I landed in the terrifying moments from the past, she steered me toward a different outcome. Instead of re-experiencing what actually happened— being trapped, steeling up for the pain, getting beaten, and freezing while I thought I might be killed—I created a new pathway in my mind. Flight.

I hesitated, confused, scared. It was hard to contemplate options when I was so used to having none.

"How would you get out?" Cheryl encouraged.

"Well, I would just walk out the back door," I said, sobbing.

"Go!"

Looking down the dark hallway from the Beauregard house's den to the kitchen, I saw light coming through the window of the back door. The light beckoned me. I walked there as if I was floating, and I put my hand on the brass knob. I slowly, calmly turned it. Yes, I thought, I am turning this knob.

The door opened and I stepped onto the sunlit driveway. Lucky was waiting for me there. We walked across the backyard toward the woods. We walked toward the trees, toward safety.

Mom appeared at the open door. She was distressed.

"Annette! Come back!" she shouted.

I paused for a moment and looked at her. But then I kept walking.

~~~

"Ma'am?"

My mother was trying to get my attention. She did not know me. After 12 years with Alzheimer's disease, she did not know much of anything.

While I was grappling with PTSD symptoms and doing the trauma therapy sessions with Cheryl, I was also caring for Mom at The Peaks in Flagstaff where she had lived for the past six years. At this end stage of Alzheimer's, Mom had become a blob in a wheelchair. She wore diapers, was unable to walk, spoke only a few words and was captivated by the simple movement and flashing lights of a television screen.

After switching off the TV, I sat on the ottoman where Mom's feet were propped. She was wearing her favorite pink sweater that used to be her mother's. The caregivers had painted Mom's nails a matching pink and she was holding a chocolate ice cream cone, which she was forgetting to eat. I put my hand on her leg and looked into her still-sparkling blue eyes.

"Yes?" I said in an attempt to humor myself, as if I was about to get some kind of logical response. But there were no words. She just smiled as the ice cream dripped onto her lap. In this silence at the end of my mother's life I was finally finding out what kind of person she really was.

During the first few years at The Peaks, after I had shipped Dad back to Texas, Mom's neurotic behaviors were in overdrive. I was called to the facility almost daily to mitigate the trouble she was causing. She was in a perpetual panic and monopolizing the caregivers' time with her constant, incoherent requests for their attention. Where was the doctor? How could she eat food that was full of ingredients she was allergic to? She needed to go through the trash, to make phone calls, to sift through other people's stuff, to stay awake all night in case I showed up.

"Oh Annette," she would plead as she chased after me when I tried to slip through the facility's locked door. "You've got to get me out of here!"

Things had not changed much since the days when Mom used to drive me to school wearing a gas mask. And I responded the way Mom had taught me to handle difficult situations—with worry and dread. I hounded doctors about her medications, the kitchen staff about her food, the caregivers about whether or not her teeth were getting brushed daily.

The years dragged on. How long could this nightmare last, I wondered. When I was growing up, Mom almost never laughed or smiled or stopped looking for the next worst-case scenario—although Alzheimer's, or any mental health issue, was never on her long list of what might do her in. After I was tasked with being the lone family member to care for Mom, it seemed that worst-case scenario was, indeed, finally playing out for us both.

And my PTSD diagnosis only added insult to injury. As all the terrible memories from my childhood came flooding back, Mom's memory was disappearing. I was unable to get any answers from Mom even though I was seeing her nearly every day. I wanted to know how she could have let it happen? Why didn't she stop him? Why didn't she pack up my sisters and me and move out? And why weren't my sisters more interested in Mom now? They rarely visited her at The Peaks. I was the family victim all over again. Abandoned by my mother all over again. Why? Why? *Why?*

But gradually the burden lifted and we both stopped asking so many questions. In her final year of life, Mom showed me how to let go. I learned just by being with her hour after hour, day after day, holding hands but not speaking. As I sat there with my hands entwined in hers, I also practiced what Cheryl was teaching me, a skill I had lost long ago: Feeling.

"What are you feeling?" Cheryl would ask during our Skype sessions.

"Well, my stomach feels nauseous and my throat is tight," I would say.

"But think about your emotions," pressed Cheryl. "What are you feeling that is causing your stomach and throat to do that?"

"I am sad, I guess," I would say as tears started to come.

Now, with Mom, I was sad. I was very sad. The sadness was big, full, rising up and overflowing like a bathtub where someone forgot to turn off the faucet. I imagined what kind of mother she could have been under better circumstances. What would it have felt like, I wondered, to have had a mother who was emotionally available, who comforted me and protected me when I was little. Mom smiled at me as I cried. Her blue eyes lit up and she tightened her grip on my hand.

We were both like snakes shedding our skins. The fear-driven adults we had become over so many years slowly fell away. We were returning to who we were, deep down, before the bad things happened. In this way, Alzheimer's was a gift because Mom forgot how to worry. The lines on her face softened. I got to see the sweet, happy woman I never knew as a child.

In the end, Alzheimer's boils people down to their bare essences. There was a woman at the Peaks who sobbed nonstop. Another woman wandered the halls all day saying, "Okay, okay, okay." A man with a Scottish accent launched into screaming tirades, and often directed his rage at Mom, but he was not at the Peaks for long. A rancher wearing Wranglers and a cowboy hat instructed people to clear the halls so the cattle could come through. A woman named Ferle insisted on wearing a wig, makeup and jewelry—all of it askew. Most of the residents just stared blankly into space.

But Mom, she smiled at everyone. She smiled nonstop. She enjoyed wearing fancy hats and wrapping her hair with colorful scarves. She ate chocolate ice cream at every meal, which she had been deathly allergic to until she forgot about such things. Mom stopped asking about doctors and, instead, started talking to the squirrel and blue jay outside her window. I often found her in the grips of an intense dialogue when I stepped into her room.

I also started talking to animals. During my Skype sessions with Cheryl, two doves always sat on a branch outside my window and they greeted me every morning when I went into the backyard. Snakes crossed my path in a way I had never experienced before.[5] It happened so often that I had to watch where I was stepping when I was walking across my yard and hiking in the Grand Canyon or running the trails around Flagstaff. When I took my dog Sunny hiking in the forest above my house, I was visited by hawks, rabbits, foxes and deer at all times of day and all months of the year.

As I continued to heal, I was not changing so much as I was simply returning to my true self, my soul self. It was my relationship to nature that reminded me who that person was. I was the girl who was hugged by trees.

Too often in adulthood my experiences in the outdoors had become a proving ground for how tough I was or were just to get material for stories I was writing. But my research into Tomomi's life helped me connect with my own roots. I knew exactly what she meant as I pored over her journal entries again and again: "This is the Earth!" "Great nature!" "I saw deers." "A hawk visited me." "I cannot find a word for this… so I must make one up: (flower) plus (rainbow)." Every description from her hiking trips, every interview with people she had met along the way, every note she had written to her beloved dog Blues, reminded me that it was Mother Earth who had been the source of inner strength for us both.

When I left Mom's room one afternoon in November 2012 after what would be our last visit, she smiled as I said goodbye. Sunlight streamed through the window and onto Mom's shoulders. She was without a care in the world.

"I love you," I said. I meant it. I felt it. I was no longer the girl who could not love her mother.

"Love you," Mom repeated back.

That night Mom was lifted into bed by a Peaks caregiver named Jesus. She never woke up.

A few days later, after putting Mom's body on a plane back to Texas where she would be buried next to Dad, I went for a long hike in the woods with Sunny. The first snow of winter had fallen that morning and we trudged up a steep hill through the trees. The sky was bright blue and the ground sparkled white in the sun. A fleeting jackrabbit caused Sunny to bound ahead of me.

As I neared the top of the hill, I spotted a large, old doe standing still, frozen, just looking at me. I got closer and she did not run, did not even move. About three feet away from her, I stood there and waited. We locked eyes. She blinked. I started to cry.

"Momma? Is that you?"

27

A Tribe of Women

After Mom's death I felt a sense of empowerment, as if things were getting better for us both. And I thought maybe even Mom had the ability to help me now in a way she couldn't before. It was from this place of emotional stability that I reached out to Randy. I knew I did not have the full story about what was driving him when he attacked Tomomi. I had all the notes from the law enforcement investigation and the audio of his three-hour confession, but there was something missing in all these fact-driven details. I wanted to know what was in Randy's heart.

In January 2014, I sent a letter to the prison in Terre Haute, Indiana where Randy had been transferred from Arizona a few years earlier. The maximum-security facility was for hardened criminals and federal inmates on death row. I had not had any contact with Randy since we visited at the Florence, Arizona prison in February 2007. We did not discuss Tomomi then or the murder because he was still awaiting a possible trial. Now I could tell him about the book, and he could tell me what, if anything, he wanted to share about the murder and his life.

"I never met Tomomi when she was alive but after her death I became drawn to wanting to know more about her," I wrote in the letter to Randy. "I live close to Grand Canyon because that is a very special place to me and where I hike often. I felt that Tomomi might have also been this way. In 2009 I was very fortunate that her family in Japan agreed to help me with this book. My son and I stayed with her father in Yokohama and then we traveled to the Hanamure ancestral home in southern Japan. Since then I have been researching the many places Tomomi traveled to in the United States. She was a very adventurous woman. The book I'm writing will honor her life.

"I have struggled for years over whether or not to contact you for this book," I continued. "Because of what happened, you are connected to Tomomi…I feel the book would be more complete if you had a voice in it."

Randy did not write back, but three months later I got a roundabout reply to my request. Diana Fowles, the counselor in whom Randy had confided when he was in the Coconino County jail, sent me an e-mail message out of the blue. After Randy's sentencing in 2008, Diana had quit her job at the jail and "disappeared" in the words of Detective Larry Thomas. I finally tracked her down through Facebook and sent her a message in January 2012 explaining how I was writing a book. But she didn't respond. I figured the murder and her history with Randy were perhaps things that were too painful or disturbing to talk about.

"Sorry it took so long to reply," she wrote in April 2014. "I've been living in Sedona this whole time. I would love to talk to you. I guess I would have more to say than just about anyone since I spent every day with Randy when he was in jail."

Over the past five years, a tribe of women had stepped up in extraordinary ways to help me tell this story: Tomomi's aunt Tsuyuko, cousin Konomi, Agnes Gray on the Navajo Nation, FBI interpreter Lisa, Karen with the law enforcement team, and now, Diana.

~~~

The next day I was driving to the town of Sedona, 30 miles south of my home in Flagstaff, descending the switchbacks of Oak Creek Canyon with my notebook and tape recorder in the passenger seat. It was Sunday, and Diana wanted to meet on the grounds of Unity Sedona, a New Age church that had become an important part of her life. The service had just ended when I pulled into the parking lot. Diana was out front waiting, peering at arriving cars to see if I was inside. Her hair was red and short. She wore Vibram Five Finger foot glove shoes and black warm-up pants. A pink tank top showed off her tanned, bulging biceps that belied her petite frame.

"They all prayed for me during the service," she said as we made our way through the hundreds of churchgoers toward the garden she wanted us to sit in.[1]

"Oh," I said. "Why?"

"That our meeting would go well," she explained. "I am so nervous to talk about this. I didn't sleep at all last night."

Diana and I were the same age. And the other thing we had in common was that we both had been recovering from traumatic stress over the past several years, which was triggered in part by the murder case. Diana's past was riddled with trauma, including sexual assaults and car accidents. She said she had almost died five times. She wound up working for the Coconino County jail in an attempt to get away from trauma she experienced in Washington state. She wanted to keep her distance from violent offenders and victims to avoid stimulating her own violent memories. But then Diana wound up in the complicated relationship with Randy, and all her personal safety boundaries went down the toilet.

"I was Randy's only advocate," she said. "He wouldn't talk to the therapist at the jail. I became his mom, his nurse, his psychiatrist, everything."

Diana said her involvement with Randy and the murder case had been so disturbing that she resigned from the jail job not long after Randy's sentencing. She was haunted by insomnia, often seeing Randy's dark eyes and scenes from other assaults that drifted like smoke through her nightmares. Diana dropped out of law enforcement and moved to Sedona to try and heal. She had not talked to anyone about the things Randy told her privately beyond what she facilitated for law enforcement officers during Randy's confession. For years Diana feared discussing it would exacerbate her trauma symptoms. But now she was ready.

"Working in the dirt here, just tending the plants, has brought me a lot of comfort," she said.

We were surrounded by a terraced garden of purple irises and other flowers in full bloom that Diana had tenderly nurtured. It was a world away from the windowless, concrete buildings of the Coconino County jail. We sat side by side on a bench bathed in sunlight. People passing by wished Diana good luck. Others looked at us smiling and gave a thumbs up.

"I feel like this is a safe place for me to talk about him," she said as she looked out onto the flowers.

Diana was holding a manila envelope that contained copies of notes and drawings from Randy. She said she came across the envelope recently when she was cleaning her house, and she wondered why she was still hanging on to it. That discovery is what prompted her to reply to my Facebook message from two years earlier. She felt the envelope showing up was some kind of sign.

In addition to my reporting gear, I carried a picture of Tomomi in my fanny pack. It was from January 2002 when she visited Muir Beach in San Francisco with Michael. Tomomi was kneeling in the sand, wearing the hiking boots she bought at the Timberland outlet store. She was beaming with a bright smile, and her arm was around a young Blues with his floppy ear and big puppy paws.

I showed Diana the photo and she handed me the envelope. Aside from the photo displayed at Randy's sentencing and the passport photo that was used in the sheriff's "missing" flyer, it was the first picture Diana had seen of Tomomi, up close and personal.

"She was beautiful," said Diana as she held the framed photo in her hands. "So full of light."

I pulled the papers out of the manila envelope and started going through them.

"I brought those because I just wanted you to see how many times Randy asked for help," Diana said of the stack of inmate request forms. "Over a period of six months he was asking to meet with me every day, sometimes several times a day. He was asking for help, and he was probably getting it for the first time in his life."

We looked at the elaborate picture Randy drew of the peacock that Diana had also saved. In the drawing, flowers were flowing up toward the sky next to the peacock and water was flowing down. I told Diana that "hana" in Hanamure means flower.

"Maybe that's why he drew flowers coming out of the genie's lamp," she said.

Diana told me that when she first started meeting with Randy, she followed security rules and had him shackled with leg and wrist restraints, but then he got so angry, he broke the chains. Many people in her position would have stopped meeting with a prisoner after a potentially dangerous incident like that, but Diana was unfazed. "I never shackled him again," she explained. "Putting him in restraints just made him angry. If I treated him more like a normal person, then he was fine."

Beyond the details of the violent murder, part of what ate away at Diana was her own inner conflict about how she grew to care for Randy. "He was just a kid, just a year older than my own son. I felt so bad for him it made me cry," said Diana. "I would take him something from the commissary and when we talked, he became a normal teenage boy, laughing and joking. Maybe I was the only person who ever saw that potential for kindness in him. Randy had a good side."

Even though Diana interpreted the Sept. 26, 2006 drawing of the peacock as Randy's admission to murdering Tomomi, he did not want to own up to the crime right away. And Diana knew not to press.

"He just wanted me to sit in the cell with him and talk. He said I was the only person in his life who, when he asked for it, took the time to show him compassion," recalled Diana. "I don't know why he wanted to open up to me. He said it was something about my eyes—that he could trust me."

As she spoke, Diana's eyes sparkled like turquoise pools against her bronze skin. She still practiced mixed martial arts and was as physically fit as someone decades younger than her 52 years.

"He couldn't talk to anyone in his family," she said. "Maybe I was like the mother he never had."

Diana said she started taking a pad of paper to her meetings with Randy and he drew pictures to illustrate his feelings, especially about the struggle between good and evil, light and dark. He told Diana stories about Supai and also about all the trouble his best friend, whom he alternately called his cousin, Robert, had gotten into.

"Day by day, there was a little more progress and one day he said it was his best friend who killed Tomomi," recalled Diana. "I was really worn out during those months that we were meeting. Sometimes I would be in Randy's cell for so long that the guards forgot I was there and locked the door shut. But I knew Randy was soul searching, and he really wanted to get [the murder] off his chest."

Diana said she worked the long days and allowed her own trauma symptoms to be triggered because she felt she was probably the only hope for getting justice—both for Tomomi and Randy. "He wanted to get rid of it," she said, "and if he would not have told it to me, he never would have agreed to (formally) confess and he would have walked."

Coconino County Sheriff's Detective Larry Thomas had told me basically the same thing. He said if it were not for the confession along with the fact that Randy pointed detectives to the right t-shirt for obtaining positive DNA evidence from the giant pile of clothing they had confiscated in Supai, Randy might never have been convicted.[2] Even though the murder investigation involved dozens of law enforcement staff from three agencies, solving it ultimately boiled down to one tough, exhausted inmate relations counselor spending as long as it took with Randy as he drew pictures in his jail cell.

~~~

A break for Diana came one day when Randy was talking once again about the bad things his best friend had done.

"You're your friend. You're your best friend, right?" Diana said to Randy. "I'm not a psychologist or anything, but it seems like you have a dual personality from being abused as a child. It's how you survived."

Randy thought about this for a minute and then agreed. It had never occurred to him before. But once Randy admitted that he had been abused, the floodgates opened for telling Diana about his painful, twisted childhood. It was a history that Arizona's Department of Child Safety was well aware of, but something Randy had never shared with anyone. And before he got around to talking about what he did on May 8, 2006, Randy first wanted to tell Diana everything that had happened in his life before that day.

"He showed me scars all over his body where he had been beaten when he was little," recalled Diana. "His father, mother, stepfather, everyone beat him. He was beaten with whatever they could get their hands on—the cable cords from the back of the TV, horse whips, barbed wire, chains. His mom even shot him once in the leg with a .22."

When Randy was a defenseless child, he was ambushed and attacked in a manner similar to the way he would later assault others. It's what psychologist James Finley calls a "ritualistic reenactment of the original trauma."[3] And it seemed the dark side of Randy, his "friend," became the one who got all the attention growing up as he committed more violence, while the sensitive, compassionate side that Diana glimpsed withered without any nurturing.

"I feel like things could have turned out differently if Randy had gotten help early on," said Diana. "But who was going to come to his aid down in Supai? Instead of getting treatment for PTSD, he kept getting locked up because he was violent. Jail became his home. He was safe there. He had three meals a day, a place to sleep, and no beatings."

On Oct. 27, 2006 Randy said he was finally ready to tell Diana what happened. Just as he would later recount for Detective Thomas, Randy first described the murder to Diana as an act committed by his cousin (a.k.a. best friend). Then he eventually admitted that it was himself who did it. "He stood up in his cell and showed me how he put his arm around Tomomi's neck and then threw her to the ground," recalled Diana. "He said he was going to rape her and rob her. He said he didn't actually remember stabbing her."

"Why do you think he stabbed her so many times?" I asked.

"Pure aggression," said Diana. "And the meth didn't help. He was just an angry, angry person."

After Randy admitted he was the killer, Diana asked him if he was ready to make a formal confession. He said he was. Diana contacted the detectives, shackled Randy, and walked him over to a Sheriff's Office conference room where they did what she called "the pizza and candy bar thing."

Diana said Randy was tearful. "He showed remorse. He had good in his heart, but it was just surrounded by rocks and metal," she added.

About a month after his confession Randy was transferred from the Coconino County jail to a prison facility in the central Arizona town of Florence. Diana never visited Randy after that, and the last time she saw him was at his sentencing in June 2008 when he flashed her a peace sign from beneath his shackles.

I told Diana about my visit with Randy in Florence on his birthday. It's possible that when I showed up unannounced in February 2007, Randy thought it was going to be Diana instead of a nosy journalist.

I recalled how Randy said he could get angry like his dad and that he might bust through the glass where we were talking. "He told me the same thing at first," said Diana. "He just had a reputation for violence that he kept putting out there."

I reflected on the simple, grim assessments of Randy from law enforcement detectives, how they described him as a "sociopath" and a "monster."[4]

"Yeah, so if he's a monster, who created that monster?" responded Diana. "Randy had to be that way to survive his circumstances. He didn't have a chance in hell of ever being able to turn his life around."

Diana said she had found release in talking to me about Randy. "It feels good to finally let go of this," she added. "I couldn't discuss my emotions with others in law enforcement and no one else would have understood."

Diana asked me to keep the contents of the manila envelope because she was ready to pass the torch. Not only was she finally in a place where she was able to share this, but I was now in a place to receive it without my own trauma symptoms getting triggered.

We hugged in the Unity parking lot before I got in my car to drive back to Flagstaff. Diana was going to stay behind and work in the garden. She said she felt a burden had been lifted.

"Everybody is better off with Randy in prison, including Randy," said Diana in parting. "But I hope Randy will eventually be able to get on the right path and do something good, maybe help others in prison. I am praying for him to one day see the light within himself."

28
Transcendence

Joy Harjo is a child abuse survivor and member of the Mvskoke [Creek] Nation in Oklahoma.

"I Give You Back"
by Joy Harjo[1]

I release you, my beautiful and terrible fear. I release you. You were my beloved and hated twin, but now, I don't know you as myself. I release you with all the pain I would know at the death of my daughters.

You are not my blood anymore.

I give you back the white soldiers who burned down my home, beheaded my children, raped and sodomized my brothers and sisters. I give you back to those who stole the food from our plates when we were starving.

I release you, fear, because you hold these scenes in front of me and I was born with eyes that can never close.

I release you, fear, so you can no longer keep me naked and frozen in the winter, or smothered under blankets in the summer.

I release you
I release you
I release you
I release you

I am not afraid to be angry.
I am not afraid to rejoice.
I am not afraid to be black.
I am not afraid to be white.
I am not afraid to be hungry.
I am not afraid to be full.
I am not afraid to be hated.
I am not afraid to be loved,

to be loved, to be loved, fear.

Oh, you have choked me, but I gave you the leash. You have gutted
me, but I gave you the knife. You have devoured me, but I lay myself across
the fire. You held my mother down and raped her,
            but I gave you the heated thing.

I take myself back, fear.
You are not my shadow any longer.
I won't hold you in my hands.
You can't live in my eyes, my ears, my voice, my belly, or in my heart
my heart
    my heart my heart

But come here, fear
I am alive and you are so afraid
of dying.

~~~

Two years would pass from the day I walked out of the Guidance Center to being able to believe that I was no longer at risk of going insane, that I could speak the truth of my childhood and not have it destroy me. And after four years, I no longer felt bitter toward my father about what had happened. There was no reversing the past, but I was discovering how to experience peace in the present. Learning about the softer side of Randy from Diana helped me embrace the complicated aspects of Dad—he too had both good and bad sides that had influenced me in myriad ways.

Despite the ugly reality of child abuse, my love for Dad ultimately held steadfast. I figured the part of him that lashed out at me came from the most wounded place in his soul, the terrified, shame-filled little boy. "Felix suffered a lot," said my cousin Ann, who lived with Dad in Galveston when they were children. "He was a very tortured human being."[2]

I reached a kind of détente with Dad where I was grateful for the positive traits he had instilled in me—especially a love for telling stories—but I was no longer his little girl. I was my own person. In this spirit of compromise, I rehung the mountain landscape painting from my childhood, but it went in the laundry room instead of above my bed. Dad's crucifix that hung in his room at Arden Courts went in my back hallway.

I practiced Zen meditation, even as it brought up terrifying memories, and I continued the trauma release exercises that induced more memories. I was purging, purifying, finding solid ground and strength in my brokenness. I was instructed by a Buddhist priest to "make friends with the hungry ghosts" that haunted me. "These ghosts may be with you for some time," she said. "But don't let these memories use you. Use these memories. Our greatest source of pain can also be our greatest gift."[3]

I also had less fear about my unpleasant dreams after my therapist helped me understand them. In the nightmares where I was a spirit floating above my body and bumping up against the doors and windows of a dark room, I was not dead. It was my subconscious mind revisiting all the times I had dissociated and left my body as a child. It was that split part of me seeking escape while the rest of me stayed and endured my father's rage. By the time I arrived at the Guidance Center in July 2010, I had been trapped in that psychologically fractured fight, flight or freeze state for all of my 49 years. Teaching my central nervous system a different way of being and healing my mind and spirit will be a lifelong process.

By the time I reached my early 50s, I came to a deep sense of knowing that I was not being punished for the sins of my father or for the sins of his mother. I was being blessed. It was like walking away from a terrible car wreck and, looking back at the carnage, I am not only grateful to have survived, but I know I am even richer because of what happened. My life's journey is like *kintsugi,* the ancient Japanese art of fixing broken pottery with golden lacquer resin to hold the fractured pieces together. The mended pot is more complex and beautiful than before.[4]

The biggest benchmark for my recovery came in July 2014 on my 53rd birthday when I slept through the night without any medication. During my four years of healing, the sleep aid Ambien had been crucial in giving me rest without being haunted by nightmares and insomnia. I had taken it every single night for 1,358 days, just as my psychiatrist instructed. And then I miraculously no longer needed it.

I am alive. And I am loved. The same love that got me through unspeakably difficult times as a child had also walked me down this new path toward my true self that was on the other side of a deep canyon of pain and sorrow. This, too, was Tomomi's path.

~~~

During the years that I wrestled with my hungry ghosts, Tetsushi moved through his own process of acceptance. He had gained a soulmate in Blues and built his life around caring for his daughter's dog. He came to appreciate Blues' and Tomomi's passions in a way that he never had when his daughter was alive. He became increasingly fit as he walked Blues twice a day. And he reconnected with the outdoors as he took Blues fishing on the weekends.

In 2011 Tetsushi retired from his factory job in Yokohama and moved back to Takarabe, back to the land. He started taking classes in organic farming and learned to grow vegetables on the Hanamure homestead, just as his father, grandfather and great-grandfather had done. The bitterness Tetsushi felt in his heart about the murder diminished with time and he found healing in the open, unpeopled landscape around Okawara Gorge.

It seemed the Havasupai tribe was healing, too. In March 2011 the tribe sent a letter to Tetsushi apologizing for the murder.

"We are mothers," wrote tribal chairwoman Bernadine Jones. "We are ashamed of the murder and we hope this letter does not cause more pain."

But by the time the tribe finally acknowledged the horrific crime committed by one of their own, Tetsushi was beyond the place of needing an apology or an explanation. Reasons simply no longer mattered to him.

I also stopped trying to understand why my father "snapped," as he called it, or why Randy did what he did. "Some people who were child abuse victims simply choose violence. They are ashamed and afraid of being victims, so they victimize others, usually people who can't fight back," explained Robert Emerick, a forensic psychologist who had served as an expert witness over the last 30 years for the prosecution of the most heinous domestic violence cases in Arizona.[5]

"There are many ways to cope with abuse, and some are healthier than others," noted Emerick. He had volunteered to come to my home in July 2012 to help me understand how violence happens and how survivors of violence can find their way out of the weeds. For Tomomi and me, seeking comfort in nature brought healing. But there is also a drive for some child abuse survivors to make sense of their suffering, to find a higher meaning that leads to spiritual enlightenment. Among these people, there is a kinship in strength and determination to transcend the crimes committed against them. They are the warriors. *Bushido.*

I told Emerick how when Randy put the knife to Tomomi's neck, she did not scream. She said, "I respect you."[6]

"Yes, of course," said Emerick as he sat in my living room where the Buddhist prayer beads I held at Tomomi's grave hung on the wall behind his head and my beloved dog Sunny napped at his feet. It was as if he was channeling Tomomi right then, and I was finally getting to know the mysterious Grand Canyon hiker I'd been following for years.

"Here was a woman who could not answer the ultimate riddle of why her mother had left her, but, instead, she found connection far from home with a whole nation of people who had suffered greatly," continued Emerick. "She found kinship in their resolve to practice their belief system and worship the Great Spirit despite all that had been done to them. There was something in Native America that gave Tomomi strength and restored her faith in humanity. When she said 'I respect you,' to Randy, she was probably saying: 'I know your suffering as a people and as an individual. I respect you as a human, with all your faults and challenges on this Earth. You are going to do whatever you are going to do right now; I can't stop that. But I am at peace because I am elevated beyond this physical form. I am a spirit person.' "

After years of searching, I finally understood.

What was Tomomi seeking on her birthday May 8, 2006 when she hiked into Grand Canyon? She had already found it.

I finally understood what Agnes Gray had told me in Monument Valley about what it meant to walk in beauty. "Tomomi was not being reckless," Agnes said. "The Creator was leading her down that path."

Tomomi kept going because she was a spiritual warrior. She hiked into the Grand Canyon for the same reasons I did, again and again. She was returning to her mother, back to the womb, letting nature love her as no one else could.

Tomomi's journey and life were tragically cut short. I wish I could have met her on the trail instead of by writing about her murder. But following Tomomi's path showed me a way out of my own pain. In this new way of living, I am reborn. I am Pure Land.

~~~

On the morning of my 54th birthday I walked across my backyard en route to Mars Hill, a forested park nearby where I hiked almost daily with Sunny. Draped across the concrete step to my garden shed was a perfectly intact snake's skin. I immediately knew the snake that had left it. Over the past several years I had observed this garter snake grow from a skinny juvenile to a healthy adult that was about 16 inches long and probably dined on the mice that lived in the shed. I imagined how earlier that morning, as I slept soundly and the sun warmed the concrete, the snake rested on the step and then moved on, venturing into the world with brand new skin.

I had become more attuned and appreciative lately of the decadent richness in nature, whether I experienced it in my own backyard or at the bottom of the Grand Canyon. The cinnamon sweet fragrance of pine forest duff after a rain, the drum beat of air in a raven's wings, the way the sideways light of the winter sun electrified an alpine meadow—the Earth was full of wondrous presents for the little girl in me.

And now there was this, a beautiful, loving birthday gift from my mother.

I carefully picked up the snake's skin, folded it and put it in my shorts pocket. Then I followed Sunny toward the woods.

Always, forever, toward the woods.[7]

Epilogue
Where They Are Now

Billy Wescogame, Randy's father, continues to live in Supai, where he sells his artwork to village residents and tourists. In 2016, he celebrated 20 years of marriage to his wife Leandra.

Blues, Tomomi's beloved dog that she rescued from South Dakota, died Aug. 14, 2015 at the ripe old age of 14. He lived with Tetsushi in Kagoshima after Tetsushi retired and they often went fishing together. Blues is buried on a mountain near the Hanamure family grave.

Diana Fowles, the former jail counselor who helped Randy, continues to live in Sedona and runs her own home security business. She enjoys spending time with her children and grandchildren.

Elizabeth, the author's older sister, lives in Arlington, Texas with her husband Steve. She continues to struggle with chronic kidney disease and is on her third transplanted kidney. She remains active in her church and leads a women's Bible study group.

Konomi Yanase, Tomomi's cousin, has two young children, a boy and a girl, and works with special needs students at a school in Japan. She hopes to join her uncle Tetsushi on the 13-year anniversary of Tomomi's death with a hike to Havasu Falls in Grand Canyon.

Raquel and Gustavo Gutierrez, members of Billy Wescogame's foster family, both died in 2013 within a few months of each other.

Randy Wescogame is in a high security federal penitentiary in Colorado.

Tetsushi Hanamure, Tomomi's father, is retired and living in his ancestral village of Takarabe. He has not yet built a house on his family property but has spent a lot of time fishing. He misses Blues and Tomomi. He is healthy and physically fit, and plans to hike to Havasu Falls on the 13-year anniversary of his daughter's death to honor her according to his Buddhist tradition.

Tsuyuko Yanase and her husband Shinichi continue to live in Kagoshima. They are proud grandparents of their two daughters' four children.

Acknowledgments

Too often the stories of homicide victims go untold. This is because the telling is too painful for family and friends who must relive the tragedy for the benefit of a journalist. And law enforcement agencies are reluctant to share case files with journalists for fear that the information might be mishandled.

I was only able to tell Tomomi's story because I was fortunate enough to have the extraordinary cooperation of FBI and Coconino County sheriff's detectives, as well as the participation of Tomomi's family and friends.

I am especially indebted to Coconino County Sheriff's Detective Larry Thomas and former FBI Special Agent Doug Lintner. They patiently put up with my persistent questions and were generous in sharing their investigative work. I am also grateful for the help of Coconino County Sheriff's Evidence Technician Tom Ross and the Bureau of Indian Affairs police officers in Supai. And thank you to forensic psychologist Robert Emerick for his sage-like wisdom.

If there is an unsung hero in Tomomi's murder investigation, it is Diana Fowles. She showed courage and grace behind the scenes in obtaining Randy's confession. And she selflessly relived the traumatic experience to share it with me so I could accurately write about what happened. Thank you.

Getting to know Tomomi's family and friends while reporting this book was an honor. After the devastating loss of his daughter, Tetsushi Hanamure opened his heart and home to me. This was, indeed, a very *bokkemon* thing to do. I am forever grateful to Tetsushi for allowing me the privilege of telling his daughter's story. I am also indebted to the rest of Tomomi's family: Tsuyuko, Shinichi, Haruno, Konomi, Sali and Makoto, as well as to Tomomi's many friends who met with me in Japan.

This book began with the story I wrote in 2007 for *Backpacker* and the narrative took shape under the masterful storytelling skills of my editors: Peter Flax, Dave Howard and Jon Dorn. I am indebted to the *Backpacker* staff for guiding me in reporting and writing "Freefall," as well as for taking on such a complicated, controversial topic in the first place.

In regard to the *Backpacker* story, I am also grateful to Billy Wescogame for the courage he showed in speaking with me. He had the guts to come forward, not only out of concern for his son and his tribe, but also out of compassion for Tomomi.

As the story evolved into a book, I was guided by my brilliant literary agents Jeremy Katz and Zach Schisgal. They coached me through several painful revisions and, as Jeremy once said, managed to "get me out of the weeds" when I felt lost in the daunting proposal process.

Ultimately, *Pure Land* became a reality because of my publisher Aquarius Press. I am forever grateful to Aquarius co-founder and owner Heather Buchanan for believing in this book. Also thank you to my talented editor Monica Prince, along with Randall Horton and the rest of the Aquarius team.

During nearly five years of writing this book, I was blessed to have a village of friends who gave input on the evolving manuscript and tirelessly proofread what I wrote. Thank you to MaryEllen Arndorfer, Karen Fella, Karen Pugliesi, Jeff Berglund, Shawn Skabelund, Aaron Skabelund, Angie Moline, Ann Cummins, Tom Martin, Tom Myers, Barbara Aurnou, Elaine Thomas, Melissa Rhodes, Barbara Larkin, Margot Murphy, Cari Clark, Angele Anderfuren, Naomi Sasaki and Zuni Ishikawa. I am especially thankful to Nicole Walker, Larry Hendricks and Michelle McManimon for their editorial prowess.

While writing *Pure Land* was one of the most amazing experiences of my life, it was also one of the most terrifying. Revisiting childhood trauma in order to describe it in a visceral way felt like I was walking on a six-inch wide ledge in the Grand Canyon that dropped 1,000 feet into the abyss. It was hard not to freak out. I could not have navigated this perilous path without the support of gifted mental health professionals and spiritual guides. Thank you to my counselors and healers: Mary Delduca, Niki Sachs, Sousan Abadian and Cheryl Sanders. Also thank you to Annabelle Nelson and my Zen sangha for their comforting presence.

To my dearest friends, Monica Brown, Leilah Danielson, Mary Tolan, Laura Camden and Betsy Aurnou, who always had my back, offering endless moral support, chocolate and wine—thank you. I am lucky to have friends who love me like a sister. Also, to my real sister, Elizabeth: Thank you for encouraging me to tell our family story and for setting a big sister example of what spiritual strength and emotional health looks like. And thanks to my little sister, Maria, for sharing my love of the outdoors and storytelling, and for cheering me on to fulfill the dream of writing this book.

Finally, I am grateful to my son Austin. A large portion of his childhood unfolded during the decade I worked on *Pure Land*. Austin was with me every step of the way, hiking to Supai, staying in the Navajo hogan in Monument Valley, and journeying across Japan. Many children would complain under such circumstances, but not Austin, not once. He was always upbeat and ready for the next adventure. If there was any single inspiration driving this book, it was the joy of being Austin's mother. Amid so much darkness, Austin has been the brightest, most heavenly light.

NOTES

Epigraph quote from Suzuki: D.T. Suzuki, *Buddha of Infinite Light: The Teachings of Shin Buddhism, the Japanese Way of Wisdom and Compassion* (Boston: Shambhala Publications, 1998).

1 "Hiking In"

1. "Havasupai Reservation," Grand Canyon National Park, accessed July 1, 2016, http://www.nps.gov/grca/planyourvisit/havasupai.htm
2. Annette McGivney, "Freefall: Tragedy in the Grand Canyon," *Backpacker,* June 2007.
3. Lawrence Czarneki, telephone interview by author, February 2007.
4. Tom Myers, telephone interview by author, February 2007.
5. Michael Ghiglieri and Thomas Myers, *Over the Edge: Death in Grand Canyon,* 2nd ed. (Flagstaff: Puma Press, 2001).
6. "Official web site of the Havasupai Tribe," accessed July 2, 2016, http://www.havasupai-nsn.gov/index.html
7. Larry Hendricks, "Murder Suspect Had Troubled Past," *Arizona Daily Sun,* 13 December 2006.
8. "2010 Census," U.S. Census Bureau.
9. Bureau of Indian Affairs officers Kendrick Rocha and Henry Kaulaity, interview by author, Supai, AZ, January 2007. Also, Federal Bureau of Investigation agent Doug Lintner, interview by author, Supai, AZ, January 2007.
10. Stephen Hirst, interview by author, Flagstaff, AZ., January 2007.
11. Damon Watahomigie, interview by author, Supai, AZ, January 2007.
12. Leonard Peltier is a Native American activist and leader of the American Indian Movement (AIM). In 1977 he was convicted and sentenced to two consecutive terms of life imprisonment for first degree murder in the shooting of two FBI agents during a 1975 conflict on the Pine Ridge Indian Reservation in South Dakota.
13. The Havasupai tribe filed a lawsuit against the state of Arizona's university system: "Havasupai Tribe of Havasupai Reservation v. Arizona Board of Regents; Court of Appeals of Arizona, Division 1, Department D," http://caselaw.findlaw.com/az-court-of-appeals/1425062.html.
14. Billy Wescogame, interview by author, Supai, AZ, February 2007.
15. The Supai Group is comprised of exposed beds of red sandstone dating from the end of the Paleozoic era. The Wescogame, Manakacha and Watahomigi sub-groups are each named after nearby landmarks and reflect the main Havasupai tribal names encountered by F.E. Matthes of the U.S. Geological Survey when he was conducting field research for the 1902 Bright Angel quadrangle topographic map. Source: "The Supai Group: Subdivision and Nomenclature," Geological Survey Bulletin 1395-J, U.S. Department of the Interior, 1975.
16. Roland Manakaja interview by author, Supai, AZ, February 2007.
17. Since 1986, the Havasupai tribe and environmental groups have fought against the establishment and operation of the Canyon uranium mine, which is located on Coconino National Forest lands at the sacred Havasupai site of Red Butte and six miles from Grand Canyon National Park's South Rim. In April 2015, a federal judge overturned the latest appeal by the tribe and the U.S. Forest Service approved a mining plan. Source: Center for Biological Diversity, "Federal Judge Oks Uranium Mining Next to Grand Canyon

National Park," http://www.biologicaldiversity.org/news/press_releases/2015/uranium-mining-04-08-2015.html

18. Given the popularity of rap music in Supai at the time, this graffiti was likely an homage to the 1988 protest song, "Fuck the Police," by the gangsta rap group N.W.A.

19. "Man Charged with Killing Japanese Tourist at Grand Canyon," *Associated Press,* 8 December 2006.

2 "Earth and Sky"

1. Agnes Gray, interview by author, Monument Valley, AZ, October 2009.

2. *In Beauty I Walk: The Navajo Way to Harmony,* DVD, Sherri Brenner Productions (Berkeley: Berkeley Media, 2006).

3. Letters from Tomomi to Konomi were given to the author during a July 2009 visit with Tomomi's family in Japan.

4. Callie Rennison, "Violent Victimization and Race, 1993-98," Bureau of Justice Statistics Special Report, U.S. Department of Justice, (March 2001). See also: Steven Perry, "American Indians and Crime: A BJS Statistical Profile, 1992-2002," Bureau of Justice Statistics, U.S. Department of Justice, (December 2004).

5. Debra Weyermann, "And Then There Were None: On the Navajo Reservation, a passion for blood sport," *Harper's,* April 1998.

3 "Nation of the Willows"

1. Frank Cushing, *The Nation of the Willows,* (Flagstaff: Northland Press, 1965) 34-35.

2. Ibid., p. 43.

3. Stephen Hirst, *I Am The Grand Canyon: The Story of the Havasupai People,* 3rd ed. (Grand Canyon: Grand Canyon Association, 2007), p.32. Also called Skeleton Man, Masauwu was the Spirit of Death, Earth God, door keeper to the Fifth World, and the Keeper of Fire. He was also the Master of the Upper World, or the Fourth World.

4. Cushing, p. 75.

5. Hirst, p. 32.

6. Roland Manakaja, interview by author, Supai, AZ, February 2007.

7. "U.S. Census rolls," http:/archive.org/stream/indiancensusroll178unit#page/n173/mode/2up

8. *The Sacred Oral Tradition of the Havasupai,* eds. Frank D. Tikalsky, Catherine A. Euler and John Nagel (Albuquerque: University of New Mexico Press, 2010), p. 21.

9. Karl Jacoby, *Crimes Against Nature: Squatters, Poachers, Thieves and the Hidden History of American Conservation* (Berkeley: University of California Press, 2001), p. 162.

10. Ibid., p.175.

11. Ibid., p.176.

12. Ibid., p.163

13. John F. Martin, "Changing Sex Ratios: The History of Havasupai Fertility and Its Implications for Human Sex Ratio Variation," *Current Anthropology,* 35 (June 1994): 3.

14. Hirst, p. 70-71; Jacoby, p. 165.

15. *Havasupai Habitat: A.F. Whiting's Ethnography of a Traditional Indian Culture,* Steven A. Weber and P. David Seaman, eds. (Tucson: University of Arizona Press, 1985), pp. 137-138.

16. Betty Leavengood, *Grand Canyon Women: Lives Shaped by Landscape,* 2nd ed. (Grand Canyon: Grand Canyon Association, 2004), p. 226.

17. Hirst, p. 106.

18. Ibid., p.158.

19. Jacoby, p.188.

20. Hirst, p. 163.

21. Hirst, p. 181.

22. Florence Barker, "Rev. Harris baptizing Jim Crook," image from Florence Barker Collection (Flagstaff: Northern Arizona University Cline Library Special Collections, 1938).

23. Hirst, p. 191.

24. Hirst, p. 193.

25. Ilva T. Schweizer, "Supai Billy and the Urban Environment," (article from unknown publication was clipped by Billy Wescogame's foster mother in Tempe, AZ and placed in a scrapbook that she collected).

26. Raquel Gutierrez, interview by author, Tempe, AZ, Sept. 16, 2010.

27. Gustavo Gutierrez, interview by author,Tempe, AZ, Sept. 16 2010.

28. Billy Wescogame, interview by author, Supai, AZ, February 2007.

4 "Nature Traveler"

1. Explanation of Japanese slang word *bokkemon* comes from Aaron Skabelund, a history professor at Brigham Young University, who specializes in Japanese history. Interview by author, Flagstaff, AZ, November 2009.

2. Konomi Yanase, interview by author, Kagoshima, Japan. July 2009.

3. Sioux refers to the indigenous peoples of the Great Plains region that roamed in what is today North Dakota, South Dakota, Montana, Wyoming and Nebraska. The Great Sioux Nation encompasses the Lakota (which has seven sub-tribes, including Oglala), Nakota, Dakota and other smaller tribes. Sioux refers to those speaking the Siouan language and the word originated from a name given to the Lakota by the Chippewa Nation who was, historically, enemies of the Lakota. Because it means "snake" in Chippewa and was adopted by European invaders, some modern-day Native Americans view the use of the word Sioux as a slur. The author apologizes for its use in this book but she found it hard to avoid in some cases as it remains the official name of many Plains Indian tribes, places and historic events; it is also used by the tribal members themselves.

4. Luther Standing Bear, *Stories of the Sioux*, 2nd ed. (Lincoln: University of Nebraska Press, 2006).

5. Information from Tomomi Hanamure's personal journal obtained by author from Tomomi's father in July 2009.

6. Tim Nelson, telephone interview by author, September 2009.

7. Notes from Coconino County Sheriff's investigation into Tomomi's murder; detectives conducted interviews with Phantom Ranch employees and National Park staff in the summer of 2006.

8. Barbara Nixon, *Mi' Taku'Ye-Oyasin: Letters from Wounded Knee* (Bloomington: Xlibris Publishing, 2012), p. 75.

9. Paul Hedren, *Fort Laramie and the Great Sioux War* (Norman: University of Oklahoma Press, 1998).

10. Winona LaDuke, *All Our Relations: Native Struggles for Land and Life* (Cambridge: South End Press, 1999).

11. *Henry B. Whipple Papers*, 1833-1934; Minnesota Historical Society manuscripts collection, http://www2.mnhs.org/library/findaids/P0823.xml.

12. LaDuke, p. 141.

13. Dee Brown, *Bury My Heart at Wounded Knee: An Indian History of the American West* (New York: Open Road Media, 2012).

14. "History and Culture," Mount Rushmore National Memorial, accessed July 9, 2016, http://www.nps.gov/moru/learn/historyculture/index.htm

15. "The Burkett Plaque," National Park Service, accessed July 9, 2016, http://www.nps.gov/moru/learn/historyculture/upload/THE-BURKETT-PLAQUE.pdf.

16. Timothy Williams, "Sioux Racing to Find Millions to Buy Sacred Land in Black Hills," *The New York Times,* 4 October 2012.

17. "National Register of Historic Places Registration Form," United States Department of the Interior, accessed July 9, 2016, http://focus.nps.gov/pdfhost/docs/NHLS/Text/66000719.pdf.

18. "2010 Census," U.S. Census Bureau.

19. Nicholas Kristof, "Poverty's Poster Child," *The New York Times,* 9 May 2012.

20. Erik Eckholm, "Gang Violence Grows on an Indian Reservation," *The New York Times,* 14 December 2009.

5 "Dad"

1.   The Great Famine, also called the Great Hunger, in Ireland lasted from 1845-1852 and was a period of mass starvation, disease and emigration from the country, then a colony of Great Britain. A fungus that traveled on ships from North America ravaged the Irish potato crop, which was the sole food source for peasant Irish farmers. More than 1 million people died and another 1 million migrated to North America and other parts of Europe during the famine.

2.   The Great Galveston Hurricane, also called the "1900 Storm," is the deadliest natural disaster to ever strike the United States. The storm made landfall Sept. 8, 1900 and the storm surge washed over the Gulf Coast island of Galveston, which did not yet have a seawall. An estimated 8,000 people were killed.

3.   Houston population figures from 1950-1970 from U.S. Census Bureau.

4.   Disdain for Irish Catholics has an official name: Hibernophobia. Negative attitudes toward the Gaelic Irish dates back to the Middle Ages but it intensified in the 18th and 19th centuries when the island was a colony of Great Britain and the English gentry looked down on the clan-centric lifestyle of Irish Catholics who lived in a communal culture that relied on farming a single crop, potatoes, and most families lived in single room huts. The protestant English viewed Irish Catholics as backward and lazy. That bias crossed the Atlantic and caused Irish immigrants to be discriminated against in the United States in the 19th century, although it pales in comparison to what Native Americans and African Americans experienced during that era. In 1836, well known British politician and writer Benjamin Disraeli wrote: "[The Irish] hate our order, our civilization, our enterprising industry, our pure religion. This wild, reckless, indolent, uncertain and superstitious race have no sympathy with the English character. Their ideal of human felicity is an alternation of clannish broils and coarse idolatry. Their history describes an unbroken circle of bigotry and blood." Source: Wikipedia, "Anti-Irish Sentiment," last modified June 10, 2016, https://en.wikipedia.org/wiki/Anti-Irish_sentiment.

5.   The McGivney Hemorrhoid Ligator was patented in 1964 by John Q. McGivney M.D. It used a rubber band to cut off circulation to a hemorrhoid, which a few days later would slough off, eliminating the need for surgical removal.

6.   Valium was introduced in 1963. By 1974, 60 million Americans filled prescriptions for the addictive tranquilizer. For more, see: Robin Marantz Henig, "Valium's Contribution

to Our New Normal," *The New York Times,* 29 September 2012.

6 "Child of Supai"

1. Hirst, p. 17.

2. "P.L. 93-620," also called the Grand Canyon Enlargement Act, was championed for years by Arizona Senator Barry Goldwater and supported by the Nixon administration. It was signed into law by President Gerald Ford Jan. 3, 1975.

3. "Testimony by Havasupai Chairman Lee Marshall presented before the Subcommittee on Parks and Recreation of the Committee on Interior and Insular Affairs," United States House of Representatives, Nov. 12, 1973, Washington D.C.

4. "Carletta Tilousi, et al. v. Arizona Board of Regents," Arizona Court of Appeals, Maricopa County Superior Court No. CV2005-013190, http://www.azcourts.gov/portals/89/opinionfiles/cv/cv070454.pdf.

5. Billy Wescogame, interview by author, Supai, AZ, February and March 2007.

6. Ibid.

7. Ibid.

8. "Separation Agreement," Havasupai Tribal Court, September 1993.

9. John Dougherty, "Trouble in Paradise," *High Country News,* 27 May 2007.

10. Anonymous, interview by author, Flagstaff, AZ, February 2007. The identity of this source was withheld to protect her privacy.

11. Letter from Carla Crook to Havasupai Tribal Court, April 26, 1996.

12. Havasupai Tribal Court hearing, Sept. 20, 1996.

13. Letter from Leila M. Parker, Substance Abuse Program Specialist, U.S. Department of Health and Human Services, to Havasupai Tribal Court, Sept. 16, 1996.

14. "In School Suspension Referral Form," Supai School, September 1996.

15. "In School Suspension Referral Form," Supai School, Oct. 10, 1996.

16. Anonymous, interview by author, Flagstaff, AZ, February 2007. The identity of this source is withheld to protect her privacy.

17. Anonymous, telephone interview by author, November 2015. The identity of this source is withheld at his request to protect his privacy.

18. Letter from Billy Wescogame to Havasupai Tribal Court, June 8, 2000.

19. Letter from Carla Crook to Havasupai Tribal Court, Jan. 15, 1999

20. Anonymous, telephone interview by author, November 2015.

21. Raquel Gutierrez, interview by author, Tempe, AZ, Sept. 16, 2010.

22. Billy Wescogame, interview by author, Supai, AZ, February 2007.

23. "Incident Report" for "verbal sexual abuse," Supai School, Feb. 19, 1998.

24. Handwritten note from Supai School teacher Geoff, undated.

25. Letter from Carla Crook to Billy Wescogame, Dec. 3, 1997.

26. Letter from Billy Wescogame to Havasupai Tribal Court Judge Shirley Nelson, May 3, 1998.

27. Letter from Carla Crook to Havasupai Tribal Court, Jan. 15, 1999.

28. Havasupai Tribal Court Custody Order JV98-23, May 15, 1999.

29. Havasupai Elementary School "Discipline Referral Form," Sept. 28, 1999.

30. Letter from Ronald E. Arias, principal of Havasupai School, to Billy Wescogame, Oct. 15, 1999.

31. Letter from Carla Crook to Havasupai Tribal Court, Oct. 14, 1999.

32. Havasupai School memo from Havasupai Special Education Department, Jane Carl, May 2000.

33. Letter from Billy Wescogame to Havasupai Tribal Court, June 8, 2000.

7 "Child of Conroe"

1. The Big Thicket is a heavily forested expanse in southeast Texas and is historically one of the most bio-diverse regions in North America, including more than 100 species of trees and shrubs, and, possibly, the extinct ivory-billed woodpecker. The Big Thicket was once 2 million acres in size but it was consumed in the 20th century by housing developments and the timber industry. Today, 109,000 acres is protected in the Big Thicket National Preserve.

2. Grogan's Mill ceased operation in the 1970s and the homes and mill were razed to make way for an upscale subdivision. Today, the Grogan's Mill subdivision includes a golf course, country club and shopping center with a gourmet grocery store.

3. This name is an alias in order to protect her privacy.

4. The author discovered in the process of researching this book that the club name Red Bandit was actually a mistake; it should have been Red Baron. When the author was a child she meant to name the club after the Peanuts cartoon series about Snoopy and his nemesis the Red Baron. The series included a popular 1966 song "Snoopy vs. Red Baron," that was featured on "Snoopy's Christmas" TV special.

5. Jean Craighead George, *My Side of the Mountain,* 3rd ed. (New York: Penguin Putnam Books, 2001).

6. Technically, the author's mother was not wearing a gas mask but a half-face respirator with dual cartridges and disposable filters.

7. According to the Mayo Clinic, fibromyalgia is a disorder characterized by widespread musculoskeletal pain accompanied by fatigue, sleep, memory and mood issues. Many people also have tension headaches. Women, especially in middle age, are far more likely than men to suffer from this condition. Fibromyalgia, now more commonly called Chronic Fatigue Syndrome, is frequently associated with psychiatric conditions such as depression, anxiety and posttraumatic stress disorder.

8. The childhood poem "My Mountain" by the author reads: "To many people a mountain is just a hunk of rock. But to me it seems to talk. It seems to speak from its mighty peak and say in a quiet and kind way, 'I was here in the beginning. I will be here in the end. I am here to stay.' To me God is like a mountain. He is strong and steady and here to stay. But different from a mountain, his love is like a fountain. And I drink from it every day. Anyone can drink from this fountain and God will be their mountain, and he will shade them from sin, if they will give their heart to him."

8 "Michael"

1. Matthew Power, "Ghosts of Wounded Knee," *Harper's Magazine,* December 2009.

2. Jamie Sams and David Carson, *Medicine Cards: The Discovery of Power Through the Ways of Animals* (New York: St. Martin's Press, 1999), p. 41.

3. This story from Tomomi was retold by her cousins Konomi and Sari during a July 2009 interview with the author in Kyoto.

4. *Jodo Shinshu* Buddhism, also called Shin Buddhism, is "the essence of Pure Land teaching." It was founded in the 13th century by Tendai Japanese monk Shinran and is the most widely practiced branch of Buddhism in Japan. For more information, see Wikipedia, "Jodo Shinshu," last modified June 1, 2016, https://en.wikipedia.org/wiki/Jōdo_Shinshū.

5. The names of Tomomi's stepmother "Fukuyo" and stepbrother "Eito" are aliases at the request of Tetsushi Hanamure who wanted to protect their privacy.

9 "Mountains and Canyons"

1. James B. Gillet, *Six Years With the Texas Rangers, 1875-1881* (Lincoln: University of Nebraska Press, 1976).

2. Eve Ball, *In the Days of Victorio: Recollections of a Warm Springs Apache* (Tucson: University of Arizona Press, 1970).

3. "2010 Census," U.S. Census Bureau.

4. Testimony of Kathleen Kitcheyan, chairwoman of the San Carlos Apache Tribe, to the United States Senate Committee on Indian Affairs, April 5, 2006, for Oversight Hearing on "The Problem of Methamphetamine in Indian Country."

5. Ghiglieri and Myers.

10 "Blues"

1. Bob Jorgensen, telephone interview by author, December 2011.

2. Crazy Horse Memorial is a mountain monument under construction on privately held land in the Black Hills of South Dakota, 14 miles from Mount Rushmore. It is intended to be approximately 27 feet taller than Mount Rushmore and depicts Crazy Horse, an Oglala Lakota warrior, riding a horse. The statue was designed by Polish sculptor Korczak Ziolkowski who worked on the massive project from 1948 until his death in 1982. As of July 2016 only the face of Crazy Horse had been completed.

3. Sigmund Freuid, *Beyond the Pleasure Principle* (Mineola: Dover Publications, 2015), p.12.

4. Inazo Natobe, *Bushido, the Soul of Japan: An Exposition of Japanese Thought* (North Clarendon: Charles E. Tuttle Company, 1969).

5. Phillip P. Arnold, "Black Elk and Book Culture," *Journal of American Academy of Religion* 67 (1999) 1.

6. John Neihardt, *Black Elk Speaks: Being the Life Story of a Holy Man of the Oglala Sioux* (New York: Pocket Books, 1972), p. 36.

7. Henry Warner Bowden, *Dictionary of American Religious Biography,* 2nd ed. (Westport: Greenwood Press, 1993), p. 628.

8. James Mooney, "The Ghost Dance Religion and Sioux Outbreak of 1890," *14th Annual Report of the Bureau of Ethnology, Part 2* (1894).

9. Vinson Synan, *The Origins of the Pentecostal Movement* (Tulsa: Oral Roberts University, 1996).

10. Neihardt, p. 230.

11. Tetsushi Hanamure, interview by author, Yokohama, Japan, July 2009.

12. Neihardt.

13. When reviewing Tomomi's trip photo albums during a July 2009 visit to her home in Japan, the author observed photos Tomomi had taken of wolves in Yellowstone, and the wolves were approximately 100 feet away.

14. Tetsushi interview.

15. Letter from Carla Crook to Havasupai Tribal Court, April 28, 2001.

16. Dougherty, "Trouble in Paradise."

17. Letter from Billy Wescogame to Havasupai Tribal Court, Nov. 7, 2001.

11 "Panic"

1. Reid Wilson, *Don't Panic: Taking Control of Anxiety Attacks,* 3rd ed. (New York: Harper Perennial, 2009).

2. "Psalm 102," *Bible,* King James Version.

12 "Route 66"

1. By 1946, following the surrender of Japan after World War II, 350,000 U.S. personnel were stationed in Japan as the United States occupied the country for nearly a decade. The 24th Infantry Division occupied Kyushu in southern Japan. Three U.S. Army bases remain in operation today, with the largest being Fort Buckner in Okinawa on the southernmost tip of Japan where there are also U.S. Navy and Marine bases. There are still 13 Marine bases in Japan and four Naval bases. Many Japanese citizens resent the ongoing U.S. military presence in their country.

2. Chester Burnett (June 10, 1910-Jan. 10, 1976), also known as Howlin' Wolf, was an African-American Chicago blues singer, guitarist and harmonica player; he was originally from Mississippi. In 2004, *Rolling Stone* magazine ranked him No. 51 on its list of the "100 Greatest Artists of All Time."

3. Route 66, often called the "Main Street of America" or the "Mother Road," was established in 1926 and was one of the first interstate highways in the U.S. Highway System. It extended for 2,448 miles from Chicago through Missouri, Kansas, Oklahoma, Texas, New Mexico and Arizona before terminating in Santa Monica, California. It was officially decommissioned from the U.S. Highway System in 1985 but many sections of the road have been adopted by state highway systems and have received National Scenic Byway designations or historic designations. A free driving guide and map to the entire route can be found at http://www.historic66.com.

4. John Steinbeck, *The Grapes of Wrath* (New York: Viking Penguin, 1989), p. 160.

5. John Steinbeck, *Travels With Charley: In Search of America* (New York: Viking Penguin, 1986).

6. Ibid, p. 161

7. Vikki Oritz Healy, "Illinois Towns on Route 66 Vie for Foreign Tourists: In Europe It's Very Much the Epic American Road Trip," *Chicago Tribune,* 15 October 2001.

8. Peter B. Dedek, *Hip to the Trip: A Cultural History of Route 66* (Albuquerque: University of New Mexico Press, 2007), p. 4.

9. After World War II, starvation was a threat across Japan but so was widespread disease. Between 1945-1948 some 650,000 people contracted cholera, dysentery, typhoid fever, diphtheria, epidemic meningitis, polio and other communicable diseases and some 100,000 people died. However, tuberculosis was the biggest killer. In 1947 alone, some 150,000 people became infected with TB and two thirds of the victims died. In 1947, the infant mortality rate in Japan soared to 77 deaths per 1,000 births, compared to 5 per 1,000 four years later. Source: James L. McClain, *Japan: A Modern History* (New York: W.W. Norton, 2002).

10. The Japanese concept called *wa* translates into English as harmony. It implies a unity and conformity within a social group and has been prized in traditional Japanese culture in much the same way Americans value individualism. The kanji character for *wa* is even a name used for Japan. A popular saying in Japan that exemplifies *wa* is "a nail that sticks out gets hammered."

11. According to American anthropologist John Embree, who studied a village in southern Japan in the 1930s, "With such an emphasis on co-operation the most striking type of misfit is an individualist. The commonest solution for such a man is to emigrate." Source: John F. Embree, *Suye Mura: A Japanese Village* (Chicago: The University of Chicago Press, 1939). p. 174.

12. *Postwar Japan as History,* ed. Andrew Gordon (Berkeley: University of California Press, 1993).

13. James E. Roberson, *Japanese Working Class Lives: An Ethnographic Study of Factory Workers* (New York: Routledge, 1998).

14. James L. McClain, *Japan: A Modern History* (New York: W.W. Norton, 2002)

13 "Randy"

1. "Failure to thrive in elderly persons is defined by The Institute of Medicine as weight loss of more than 5 percent, decreased appetite, poor nutrition, and physical inactivity, often associated with dehydration, depression, immune dysfunction, and low cholesterol. Failure to thrive is not a single disease or medical condition; rather, it's a nonspecific manifestation of an underlying physical, mental, or psychosocial condition." Source: "Failure to Thrive in Elderly Adults," Medscape, accessed July 8, 2016, http://emedicine.medscape.com/article/2096163-overview.

2. Carla Crook, interview by author, Supai, AZ, February 2007.

3. Randy Wescogame, interview by author February 2007. Because the author did not take notes or record her conversation with Randy, she immediately dictated her recollection of the interview into a tape recorder as she left the Florence prison grounds.

4. Larry Thomas, Coconino County Sheriff's Detective, interview by author, Flagstaff, AZ, July 2009.

14 "Desperation"

1. Mari Motooka, interview by author, Yokohama, Japan, July 2009.

2. Rena (last name withheld for privacy), interview by author, Yokohama, July 2009.

3. Tetsushi Hanamure, interview by author, Yokohama, July 2009.

4. Midori Takagi, interview by author, Yokohama, July 2009.

5. Rena, interview by author, Yokohama, July 2009.

6. E-mail from Akiko Copland to author, October 2009.

7. Paul Rubin, "Indian Givers: The Havasupai trusted the white man to help with a diabetes epidemic. Instead, ASU tricked them into bleeding for academia," *Phoenix New Times,* 27 May 2004.

8. According to U.S. Department of Justice figures, crime on Native American reservations grew by 50 percent between 2000-2010 but the number of suspects being investigated for violent crimes on Indian lands decreased by 3 percent during that same time period. Additionally, reservations patrolled by the Bureau of Indian Affairs had 3,462 full-time police personnel in 2000. But in 2012 that number had dropped to 3,000 despite the steady increase in crime. Source: Timothy Williams, "Washington Steps Back from Policing Indian Lands, Even as Crime Rises," *The New York Times,* 12 November 2012.

9. Dougherty, "Trouble in Paradise."

10. Bureau of Indian Affairs officer Henry Kaulaity, interview by author, Supai, AZ, January 2007.

11. The account of Sarah Maurer's assault draws from a telephone interview with Maurer conducted by Coconino County Sheriff's Detective Larry Thomas in June 2006 and also from a Skype interview with Maurer conducted by the author in March 2016.

12. FBI Detective Doug Lintner, interview by author, Flagstaff, AZ, July 2010.

13. Billy Wescogame, interview, Supai, AZ, February 2007.

15 "Yokohama"

1. Last Rites is a Catholic ritual performed by a priest to prepare a person for death. The three sacraments of Anointing of the Sick, Penance and the Holy Eucharist are administered as *Viaticum,* which is Latin for "with you on the way."

2. Annette McGivney, "Freefall: Tragedy in the Grand Canyon," *Backpacker,* June 2007, accessed July 10, 2016, http://www.backpacker.com/survival/freefall-tragedy-in-the-grand-canyon/.

3. Debbi Kirkpatrick wrote a reader e-mail to Backpacker in response to McGivney's "Freefall" article that said, in part: "My first sign of despair came when we all watched a local Supai native purposely pushing a horse over the edge of the switchbacks!"

4. "Lisa" is an alias. The identity of this source is being withheld at her request in order to protect her privacy.

5. Bowing is a deeply ingrained part of Japanese culture that started around the 6th century when Buddhism became prevalent. Bowing is the primary way to greet someone and also to show reverence to a superior or someone older. Bowing is also used to show thanks, remorsefulness, greeting others at the beginning and ending of a meeting, when asking for a favor or apology and when worshipping. Each of these situations generally requires a unique kind of bow, but one always bows by hinging forward from the hips, with a straight back (never hunching) and with arms at the side of the body. The person who is younger or in a position that is less senior should bow lower. For more, see: "Bowing in Japan," Tofugu, accessed July 10, 2016, https://www.tofugu.com/japan/bowing-in-japan/.

6. Homicide rates for Japan and the United States are 2013 figures compiled by the United Nations Office of Drugs and Crime. Source: *Business Insider,* accessed July 10, 2016, http://www.businessinsider.com/oecd-homicide-rates-chart-2015-6.

7. According to FBI statistics the homicide rate on the Navajo Nation of 18.8 per 100,000 people in 2012 was more than four times greater than the United States average. In 2013 there were 42 homicides among a reservation population of 180,000. Source: "Murders on Navajo Nation Spiked Above National Rate in 2013," *The Guardian,* 28 April 2014.

8. Japan's suicide rate in 2005 was 19.4 individuals per 100,000 people, nearly double the rate in the United States and among the highest in the world. Source: "World Suicide Rates By Country," *The Washington Post,* accessed July 10, 2016, http://www.washingtonpost.com/wp-srv/world/suiciderate.html.

16 "The Land of Wa"

1. Andrew Cobbing, *Kyushu: Gateway to Japan* (Folkstone, UK: Global Oriental, 2009), pp. 1-16.

2. The Kojiki, meaning "record of ancient things," was compiled under the direction of Japanese emperors between 500-700 A.D. with the intent of chronicling Japan's mythic history and the divine origins of its rulers. It is a primary source for early Shinto beliefs.

3. Shinto gods are collectively called *yaoyorozu no kami,* which means 8 million kami. Japan is often referred to by Japanese as a land of myriad gods.

4. The Chinese kanji character originally used for "wa" means "stunted." The Japanese adopted a new meaning with a different character to connote "harmony, peace, balance" and it is used conceptually to be synonymous with the word "Japan."

5. Paul Varley, *Japanese Culture,* 4th ed. (Honolulu: University of Hawaii Press, 2000), pp.7-8

6. Although the Tokugawa period in Japan that enforced Confucian social order by class ended in 1867 when it was replaced by the Meiji Restoration period, isolated rural villages enforced the traditional class structure into the early 20th century. Farmers, or peasants, held stature because they provided food to the community and their descendants

were expected to carry on the family tradition. Merchants and artisans were in a class below farmers.

7. This description of Takarabe is simulated from the extensive accounts by John Embree of village life in Suye Mura located not far from Takarabe in the Kumamoto prefecture of Kyushu. See Embree in the "Bibliography" for his book *Suye Mura*.

8. The Toroku mine located near the town of Takachiho in the Miyazaki District of Kyushu emitted arsenic into the air as part of its routine operations from 1920-1941 and 1955-1962. A 1973 report published by Japan's Kumamoto Medical Society documented arsenic poisoning in area residents. The pollution was especially toxic in surrounding valleys because arsenic-laced air settled into low-lying areas.

9. For the full text of the three Pure Land sutras, see: "The Pure Land Sutras," Cloud Water Zendo, accessed July 10, 2016, http://www.cloudwater.org/index.php/pure-land-buddhism/reading-the-sutras.

10. Statistics on Japanese population migration from rural areas to cities is from "Urban Population," the World Bank, accessed July 10, 2016, http://data.worldbank.org/indicator/SP.URB.TOTL.IN.ZS.

17 "Havasu Falls"

1. Tetsushi Hanamure, interview by author, Yokohama, Japan, July 2009.
2. Mari Motooka, interview by author, Yokohama, July 2009.
3. Coconino County Sheriff's Office, "Incident Investigation Report," May 2006.
4. Hirst, p. 71.
5. This description is based on what the author witnessed during her hike in January 2007 and also from the accounts of other hikers who visited Supai in 2006.
6. Coconino County Sheriff's Office, "Incident Investigation Report," May 2006.
7. Mari Motooka, interview by author, Yokohama, July 2009.
8. Tetsushi Hanamure, interview by author, Yokohama, July 2009.
9. Rena, interview by author, Yokohama, July 2009.
10. Konomi Yanase, interview by author, Osaka, Japan, July 2009. Also, Tomomi "necha" is nickname used by sisters as a term of endearment.
11. Coconino County Sheriff's Office, "Incident Investigation Report," May 2006
12. Randy Wescogame interview by Coconino County Sheriff's Detective Larry Thomas, Flagstaff, AZ, Oct. 2006.
13. Billy Wescogame, interview by author, Supai, AZ, February 2007.
14. Coconino County Sheriff's Office, "Incident Investigation Report," May 2006.
15. Ibid.
16. A t-shirt Randy was wearing bearing the image of the Looney Tunes character, the Tasmanian Devil, "Taz," would become a critical piece of evidence in the murder investigation.
17. Randy Wescogame interview by Coconino County Sheriff's Detective Larry Thomas, Flagstaff, AZ, Oct. 2006.

18 "Flashback"

1. This particular beating was punishment for an incident where the author accidentally allowed her dog Lucky to eat four sirloin steaks that were just off the grill and sitting on the kitchen counter waiting to be served to dinner guests. Lucky was jumping at the back door wanting to come inside. The adults were occupied in the living room. The author opened the back door and before she knew it Lucky had inhaled the steaks.

19 "Search for the Killer"

1. Coconino County Sheriff's Office, "Incident Investigation Report," May 2006.

2. Coconino County Sheriff's Office "Evidence/Property Receipt, May 11, 2006.

3. Coconino County Sheriff's Office, "Incident Investigation Report," May 2006

4. Coconino County Sheriff's Detective Larry Thomas, interview by author, Flagstaff, AZ, July 2009.

5. Coconino County Sheriff's Office, "Incident Investigation Report," May 2006.

6. Ibid.

7. BIA Supai police officer Henry Kaulaity, interview by author, Supai, AZ, January 2007.

8. Coconino County Sheriff's Office, "Incident Investigation Report," May 2006.

9. Ibid., transcription of interview with Sage Manakaja.

10. Ibid., transcription of interview with Denise Watahomage

11. Coconino County Sheriff's Detective Larry Thomas, interview by author, Flagstaff, AZ, July 2009.

12. Coconino County Search and Rescue member Joe Rommel, interview by author, Flagstaff, AZ, January 2007.

13. Coconino County Sheriff's Detective Larry Thomas, interview by author, Flagstaff, AZ, July 2009.

14. Digital photograph of t-shirt taken by Coconino County Sheriff's Evidence Technician Tom Ross, Supai, AZ, May 14, 2006.

15. Coconino County Sheriff's Detective Larry Thomas, interview by author, Flagstaff, AZ, July 2009.

16. Ibid.

17. Excerpt from digital audio file of interview with Randy Wescogame conducted by Thomas and Cornish, Supai, AZ, May 13, 2006, as part of homicide investigation.

18. FBI Special Agent Doug Lintner, interview by author, Flagstaff, AZ, January 2007.

19. Coconino County Sheriff's Office, "Incident Investigation Report," May 2006, transcription of interview with Yvette Slack.

20. Excerpt from digital audio file of interview with Randy Wescogame conducted by Thomas and Lintner, Supai, AZ, May 14, 2006, as part of homicide investigation.

21. Coconino County Sheriff's Office, "Incident Investigation Report," May 2006.

22. Coconino County Search and Rescue member Joe Rommel, interview by author, Flagstaff, AZ, January 2007.

23. Tsuyuko Yanase (Tomomi's aunt), interview by author, Kagoshima, Japan, July 2009.

24. The hyoid bone in the neck is significant according to Buddhist spirituality because it the place where a person's voice emanates and the bone structure resembles a seated Buddha. In traditional Japanese funerals, which mix Shinto and Pure Land Buddhist practices, family members use chopsticks to pick out the hyoid bone from the partially cremated body and place it in a special urn. One chopstick is made from bamboo and the other from willow to signify the transference from the physical to the spiritual worlds.

25. Tsuyuko Yanase, interview by author, Kagoshima, Japan, July 2009.

26. Mark Shaffer, "Havasupai Perplexed by Killing of Tourist," *Arizona Republic,* 24 July 2006.

27. FBI Special Agent Doug Lintner, interview by author, Flagstaff, AZ, January 2007.

28. Ibid.

29. BIA Supai police officer Henry Kaulaity, interview by author, Supai, AZ, January 2007.

30. Coconino County Sheriff's Office, "Incident Investigation Report," May 2006.

31. Sarah Maurer, Skype interview by author, March 2016.

32. Excerpt from digital audio file of telephone interview with Sarah Maurer conducted by Thomas, June 2006, as part of homicide investigation.

33. Coconino County Sheriff's Detective Larry Thomas, interview by author, Flagstaff, AZ, July 2010.

34. FBI Special Agent Doug Lintner, interview by author, Flagstaff, AZ, July 2010.

35. Coconino County Sheriff's Detective Larry Thomas, interview by author, Flagstaff, AZ, July 2009.

36. Tsuyuko Yanase, interview by author, Kagoshima, Japan, July 2009.

37. Tetsushi Hanamure, interview by author, Yokohama, Japan, July 2009.

20 "Confession"

1. Rapper Crunchy Black was arrested and convicted in April 2015 for possession of meth as well as previous domestic violence charges. Source: Colin Stutz, "Three 6 Mafia Member Arrested for Meth Possession," *Billboard,* 15 April 2015.

2. Coconino County Sheriff's Detective Larry Thomas, interview by author, Flagstaff, AZ, July 2009.

3. "Coconino County Detention Facility Inmate Request Form" from Randy Wescogame, September 23, 2006.

4. "Investigation Report" from FBI Special Agent Doug Lintner, October 11, 2006.

5. Diana Fowles, interview by author, Sedona, AZ, April 2014.

6. Ibid

7. This is an observation by the author after seeing the binder of Billy Wescogame's drawings of his many tattoos and comparing that to Randy's drawings collected by the Coconino County Sheriff's Office.

8. Memo from Diana Fowles to detectives, "CI Division Supplemental Report DR#S06-01256," October 26, 2006.

9. Diana Fowles, interview by author, Sedona, AZ, April 2015.

10. Memo from Diana Fowles to detectives, "CI Division Supplemental Report DR#S06-01256," October 26, 2006.

11. A copy of this drawing is included in the Coconino County Sheriff's Office "Incident Investigation Report," May 2006.

12. E-mail from Diana Fowles to Doug Lintner, Sept. 26, 2006.

13. Kwan Yin is also spelled Guan Yin, Kuan Yim, and Kwan Im. These are the short form for Kaun-shi Yin meaning, "observing the sounds (or cries) of the (human) world." In Japanese Buddhism, Kwan Yin or Guan Yin is synonymous with the Bodhisattva Avalokitesvara, the pinnacle of mercy, compassion, kindness and love.

14. Diana Fowles, interview by author, Sedona, AZ, April 2014.

15. Memo from Diana Fowles to detectives, "CI Division Supplemental Report DR#S06-01256," October 26, 2006.

16. Unless otherwise noted, the conversation between Randy, Thomas and Fowles is drawn from a transcription of the interview conducted by Thomas on Oct. 28, 2008 at the Coconino County Sheriff's Office in Flagstaff.

17. Coconino County Sheriff's Detective Larry Thomas, interview by author, Flagstaff, AZ, July 2009.

21 "Punishment"

1. Coconino County Sheriff's Detective Larry Thomas, interview by author, Flagstaff, AZ, July 2009.

2. Tetsushi Hanamure, interview by author, Yokohama, Japan, July 2009.

3. Coconino County Sheriff's Evidence Technician Tom Ross, Flagstaff, AZ, April 2016.

4. Coconino County Sheriff's Office, "Incident Investigation Report," May 2006.

5. FBI Special Agent Doug Lintner, interview by author, Flagstaff, AZ, July 2010.

6. Coconino County Sheriff's Detective Larry Thomas, interview by author, Flagstaff, AZ, July 2009.

7. United States District Court District of Arizona, "CR-06-1077-MHM Plea Agreement," Sept. 18, 2007.

8. Descriptions of the sentencing event come from the author's first-hand observations.

9. Tetsushi Hanamure, interview by author, Yokohama, Japan, July 2009.

10. Dennis Wagner, "Havasupai Reborn Year After Disastrous Flash Flood," *Arizona Republic,* 16 August 2009.

11. Havasupai Tribal Council "Declaration of Emergency —Havasupai Resolution 26-08," Aug. 18, 2008.

12. Betty Reid, "Hundreds Evacuated Near Grand Canyon After Flooding," *Arizona Republic,* 17 August 2008.

22 "Return to Supai"

1. Tetsushi Hanamure, interview by author, Yokohama, Japan, July 2009.

2. Thich Nguyen Tang, "Buddhist View on Death and Rebirth," Urban Dharma, accessed July 11, 2016, http://www.urbandharma.org/udharma5/viewdeath.html.

3. "Karen" is an alias used in order to protect the identity of this source for professional reasons.

4. Coconino County Sheriff's Detective Larry Thomas, interview by author, Flagstaff, AZ, July 2010.

5. Diana Fowles, interview by author, Sedona, AZ, April 2015.

6. Dougherty, "Trouble in Paradise."

7. The monkey mind is a term sometimes used by the Buddha to describe the agitated, easily distracted and incessantly moving behavior of ordinary human consciousness. In this analogy, the Buddha described humans grasping for one thought after another just as monkeys constantly grab branches on trees. Source: "Monkey Mind, The," Guide to Buddhism A to Z, accessed July 11, 2016, http://www.buddhisma2z.com/content.php?id=274.

8. Supai tribal police, interview by author, Supai, AZ, May 2010.

9. Amy Harmon, "Tribe Wins Fight to Limit Research of it DNA," *The New York Times,* 22 April 2010.

10. In the Pure Land Sutra *Namu Amida Butsu* means "total reliance upon the compassion of Amida Buddha." For more on the sutra and Pure Land history, see *Wikipedia,* "Pure Land Buddhism," last modified on June 5, 2016, https://en.wikipedia.org/wiki/Pure_Land_Buddhism.

11. Shunryu Suzuki, *Zen Mind, Beginner's Mind* (Boston: Shambala Publications, 2006).

12. Ibid., page 28

13. According to Merriam-Webster, a sociopath is one "who behaves in dangerous or violent ways toward other people and does not feel guilty about such behavior."

14. Suzuki, p. 135.

23 "Collapse"

1. According to the *Merck Manual of Psychiatric Disorders,* "Dissociative Amnesia is a type of dissociative disorder that involves inability to recall important personal information that would not typically be lost with ordinary forgetting. It is usually caused by trauma or stress...Although the forgotten information may be inaccessible to consciousness, it sometimes continues to influence behavior."

2. Sigmund Freud first used the term "repetition compulsion" in a 1914 article published in German titled, "*Erinnern, Wiederholen und Durcharbeiten*" ("Remembering, Repeating and Working-Through"). He further explored the concept in a 1920 essay "Beyond the Pleasure Principle."

3. Alice Miller, *The Drama of the Gifted Child: The Search for the True Self* (New York: Basic Books, 1996) pp. 9-10.

4. The fifth edition of the *Diagnostic and Statistical Manual of Mental Disorders* has changed the official name of "delayed onset post-traumatic stress disorder" to "delayed expression PTSD." For more, see "PTSD History and Overview," National Center for PTSD, U.S. Department of Veterans Affairs, www.ptsd.va.gov.

5. Bessel van der Kolk, "Post Traumatic Childhood," *The New York Times,* 10 May 2011.

6. Bessel van der Kolk, *The Body Keeps the Score: Brain, Mind, and Body In The Healing of Trauma* (New York: Viking Penguin Books, 2014), p. 150.

7. U.S. Department of Health and Human Services Administration for Children and Families, Children's Bureau, "Child Maltreatment 2015."

8. According to the U.S. Census Bureau, the estimated population of Chicago in 2015 was 2.7 million.

9. van der Kolk, *The Body Keeps the Score,* p. 21.

10. U.S. Department of Health and Human Services Administration for Children and Families.

11. Chronic trauma in childhood is a specific condition referred to as Developmental Trauma Disorder by Bessel van der Kolk and his colleagues. They maintain it is distinctly different from PTSD in terms of pathology and treatment needs. They lobbied unsuccessfully in 2010 to have DTD added to the Diagnostic and Statistical Manual of Mental Disorders.

12. Jeneen Interlandi, "A Traumatized Mind?: Bessel van der Kolk wants to revolutionize the way we treat PTSD—by starting with the body," *The New York Times Magazine,* 22 May 2014.

13. van der Kolk, *The Body Keeps the Score,* p.11.

14. U.S. Department of Health and Human Services Administration for Children and Families, Children's Bureau, "Child Maltreatment 2015."

15. Bessel A. van der Kolk, "The Compulsion to Repeat the Trauma: Re-enactment, Revictimization and Masochism," *Psychiatric Clinics of North America,* Vol. 12 No. 2 (June 1989) pp. 389-411.

16. Judith Herman, *Trauma and Recovery: The Aftermath of Violence, from Domestic Abuse to Political Terror* (New York: Basic Books, 1992) p. 96.

17. Ibid., p.105.

18. Ibid., p.114.

19. Ibid, p.114.

20. van der Kolk, *The Body Keeps the Score*, p.66

24 "Elizabeth"

1. Donald D. Dutton and Susan Painter, "The Battered Woman Syndrome: Effects of Severity and Intermittency of Abuse," *American Journal of Orthopsychiatry*, Vol. 6 No. 4 (October 1993), pp.614-622.

2. Teresa Descilo, "Understanding and Treating Traumatic Bonds," *Healing Arts*, accessed July 11, 2016, http://www.healing-arts.org/healing_trauma_therapy/traumabonding-traumaticbonds.htm.

3. Herman, p.75.

4. van der Kolk , *The Body Keeps the Score*, pp.168-169.

5. Caroline Myss and James Finley, *Transforming Trauma: A Seven Step Process for Spiritual Healing*, audio CD (Louisville, CO: Sounds True Inc., 2009), session4.

6. Adult Children of Alcoholics World Service Organization official website, http://www.adultchildren.org.

7. Adult Children of Alcoholics, *ACA Fellowship Text* (Torrence, CA: Adult Children of Alcoholics World Service Organization, 2006), p. 94.

8. Jerry is an alias used in accordance with the rules of anonymity of the ACA program.

9. *ACA Fellowship* Text, pp.92-93.

10. Ibid, "The Laundry List," p.5.

11. Ibid pp. 92-93.

12. Madeleine L'Engle, "The Summer of the Great-Grandmother," *Crosswicks Journal*, Book 2, January 1984.

25 "Origins of Violence"

1. For the Hopi, the Grandmother Katsina is among the most cherished, "The Mother of all Katsinam" (a title she shares with Crow Mother). Grandmother Katsina could be thought of as the Mother Earth of the Hopi people. Her Hopi name is *Hahay-i wu-uti*, which translates into "pour water woman." In many paintings and carvings, she is shown pouring water out of a gourd from one hand. This represents the pouring of life around the world. In her other hand, the Grandmother Katsina is often holding an ear of corn, a symbol of the nourishment she provides to all beings.

2. Raquel and Gustavo Gutierrez, interview by author, Tempe, AZ, September 2010.

3. "Havasupai Children Visit Luke," *Jet Journal* (weekly publication of Luke Air Force Base in Glendale, Ariz.), 14 May 1965.

4. Ilva T. Schweizer, "A Vignette: Supai Billy and the Urban Environment," publisher and date unknown. Raquel thought the article was from the Sunday magazine of the *Arizona Republic*.

5. Bessel van der Kolk, "In Terror's Grip: Healing the Ravages of Trauma," *Cerebrum* (January 1, 2002), pp.34-50.

6. Maria Yellow Horse Brave Heart, "The Historical Trauma Response Among Natives and Its Relationship to Substance Abuse: A Lakota Illustration," in *Healing and Mental Health for Native Americans*, eds. Ethan Nebelkopf and Mary Phillips (Lanham, MD: Altamira Press, 2004), pp.7-15.

7. van der Kolk, *The Body Keeps the Score*.

8. Maria Yellow Horse Brave Heart, "Wakiksuyapi: Carrying the Historical Trauma of the Lakota," *Tulane Studies in Social Welfare*, 2000.

9. Hilary N. Weaver and Maria Yellow Horse Brave Heart, "Examining Two Facets of American Indian Identity: Exposure to Other Cultures and the Influence of Historical Trauma," *Journal of Human Behavior in the Social Environment*, Vol. 2, No. 1-2 (1999), p.22

10. Ibid., pp.22-23.

11. Ibid., pp.23.

12. Maria Yellow Horse Brave Heart, Jennifer Elkins, Greg Tafoya, Doreen Bird and Meina Salvador, "Wicasa Was'aka: Restoring the Traditional Strength of American Indian Boys and Men," *American Journal of Public Health*, Vol.102, No. S2, supplement 2 (2012), p. S179.

13. Weaver and Brave Heart, p.23.

14. Dan Hurley, "Grandma's Experiences Leave a Mark on Your Genes," *Discover Magazine*, May 2013.

15. M. George Eichenberg, "Criminal Victimization of Native Americans," in *American Indians at Risk*, Vol. 1, ed. Jeffrey Ian Ross (Santa Barbara: Greenwood/ABC-CLIO, LLC, 2014) p.49.

16. Roxanne Struthers and John Lowe, "Nursing in the Native American Culture and Historical Trauma," *Issues in Mental Health Nursing*, 24 (2003) pp. 257-272.

17. Eichenberg, p.50.

18. James Gilligan, *Violence: Reflections on a National Epidemic* (New York: Vintage Books/Random House, 1996) p. 223.

19. Ibid., pp.45-49

20. Ibid., p. 47

21. Beyond the emotional and spiritual benefits of being in nature, various studies have documented the positive effects on neurobiology. A study published in the December 2015 issue of the *International Journal of Environmental Research and Public Health* even documented that simply showing stressed study subjects pictures of unremarkable natural scenes (such as a forest) caused their parasympathetic nervous system to kick in, lowering heart rates and reducing stress. When the subjects were shown pictures of urban settings, there was no stress-lowering response.

26 "Momma"

1. According to the official TRE website traumaprevention.com: "TRE® (Tension, Stress & Trauma Release Exercise) is a…series of exercises that assist the body in releasing deep muscular patterns of stress, tension and trauma. Created by Dr. David Berceli, PhD, TRE® safely activates a natural reflex mechanism of shaking or vibrating that releases muscular tension, calming down the nervous system." Somatic Experiencing ® is also a body-oriented approach to healing trauma that was developed by Peter Levine and is taught through the Somatic Experiencing Trauma Institute.

2. Peter A. Levine, *Waking the Tiger: Healing Trauma* (Berkeley: North Atlantic Books, 1997), p. 19.

3. Ibid., p. 38.

4. Ibid., p. 32.

5. According to Native American and shamanic cultures, encounters with snakes, both in real life or in dreams, deliver powerful medicine. Snakes symbolize rebirth or transmutation of life's hardships into wisdom. "The transmutation of the life-death-rebirth cycle is exemplified by the shedding of the snake's skin," according to authors Jamie Sams and David Carson. "It is the energy of wholeness, cosmic consciousness and the ability

to experience anything willingly and without resistance." Source: Jamie Sams and David Carson, *Medicine Cards: The Discovery of Power Through the Ways of Animals* (New York: St. Martin's Press, 1999), p. 61.

27 "A Tribe of Women"
1. Diana Fowles, interview by author, Sedona, AZ, April 2014.
2. County Sheriff's Detective Larry Thomas, interview by author, Flagstaff, AZ, July 2010.
3. Caroline Myss and James Finley.
4. During a June 2010 interview, FBI Agent Doug Lintner described Randy as a sociopath. During a July 2010 interview, Coconino County Sheriff Detective Larry Thomas described Randy as a monster.

28 "Transcendence"
1. Joy Harjo, "I Give You Back," in *Unsettling America: An Anthology of Contemporary Multicultural Poetry,* eds. Maria Mazziotti Gillan and Jennifer Gillan (New York: Penguin Books, 1994), pp. 370-371. This poem is reprinted with permission from Joy Harjo.
2. Author's cousin Ann Hamilton, telephone interview by author, August 2010.
3. Susan Weimer Roshi, Zen Master in the Diamond Zangha, interview by author, Flagstaff, AZ, March 2011.
4. Kintsugi means to "repair with gold" in Japanese. Rather than viewing broken ceramics as something to be discarded, the repair highlights the brokenness of the object and this history becomes part of the aesthetic. According to *kintsugi* philosophy, that which is flawed or imperfect is beautiful.
5. Robert Emerick, interview by author, Flagstaff, AZ, July 2012.
6. Tomomi's last words, according to Randy, are excerpted from a transcription of the confession interview conducted by Detective Larry Thomas on Oct. 28, 2008 at the Coconino County Sheriff's Office in Flagstaff.
7. On her 55th birthday the author finished writing this book.

BIBLIOGRAPHY

Books
Adult Children of Alcoholics, *ACA Fellowship Text.* Torrence, CA: Adult Children of Alcoholics World Service Organization, 2006.

Ball, Eve, *In the Days of Victorio: Recollections of a Warm Springs Apache.* Tucson: University of Arizona Press, 1970.

Brown, Dee, *Bury My Heart at Wounded Knee: An Indian History of the American West.* New York: Open Road Media, 2012.

Cobbing, Andrew, *Kyushu: Gateway to Japan.* Folkstone, UK: Global Oriental, 2009.

Cushing, Frank, *The Nation of the Willows.* Flagstaff: Northland Press, 1965.

Dedek, Peter, B., *Hip to the Trip: A Cultural History of Route 66.* Albuquerque: University of New Mexico Press, 2007.

Embree, John, F., *Suye Mura: A Japanese Village.* Chicago: The University of Chicago Press, 1939.

George, Jean, Craighead, *My Side of the Mountain,* 3rd ed. New York: Penguin Putnam Books, 2001.

Ghiglieri, Michael and Thomas Myers, *Over the Edge: Death in Grand Canyon,* 2ⁿᵈ ed. Flagstaff: Puma Press, 2001.

Gillet, James, B., *Six Years With the Texas Rangers, 1875-1881.* Lincoln: University of Nebraska Press, 1976.

Gilligan, James, *Violence: Reflections on a National Epidemic.* New York: Vintage Books/Random House, 1996.

Gordon, Andrew, ed., *Postwar Japan as History.* Berkeley: University of California Press, 1993.

Hedren, Paul, *Fort Laramie and the Great Sioux War.* Norman: University of Oklahoma Press, 1998.

Herman, Judith, *Trauma and Recovery: The Aftermath of Violence, from Domestic Abuse to Political Terror.* New York: Basic Books, 1992.

Hirst, Stephen, *I Am The Grand Canyon: The Story of the Havasupai People,* 3ʳᵈ ed. Grand Canyon: Grand Canyon Association, 2007.

Jacoby, Karl, *Crimes Against Nature: Squatters, Poachers, Thieves and the Hidden History of American Conservation.* Berkeley: University of California Press, 2001.

LaDuke, Winona, *All Our Relations: Native Struggles for Land and Life.* Cambridge: South End Press, 1999.

Leavengood, Betty, *Grand Canyon Women: Lives Shaped by Landscape,* 2ⁿᵈ ed. Grand Canyon: Grand Canyon Association, 2004.

Levine, Peter, A., *Waking the Tiger: Healing Trauma.* Berkeley: North Atlantic Books, 1997.

McClain, James, L., *Japan: A Modern History.* New York: W.W. Norton, 2002.

Miller, Alice, *The Drama of the Gifted Child: The Search for the True Self.* New York: Basic Books, 1996.

Caroline Myss and James Finley, *Transforming Trauma: A Seven Step Process for Spiritual Healing,* audio CD. Louisville, CO: Sounds True Inc., 2009.

Nixon, Barbara, *Mi' Taku'Ye-Oyasin: Letters from Wounded Knee.* Bloomington: Xlibris Publishing, 2012.

Roberson, James, E., *Japanese Working Class Lives: An Ethnographic Study of Factory Workers.* New York: Routledge, 1998.

Sams, Jamie and David Carson, *Medicine Cards: The Discovery of Power Through the Ways of Animals.* New York: St. Martin's Press, 1999.

Standing Bear, Luther, *Stories of the Sioux,* 2ⁿᵈ ed. Lincoln: University of Nebraska Press, 2006.

Steinbeck, John, *The Grapes of Wrath.* New York: Viking Penguin, 1989.

Steinbeck, John, *Travels With Charley: In Search of America.* New York: Viking Penguin, 1986.

Suzuki, D.T., *Buddha of Infinite Light: The Teachings of Shin Buddhism, the Japanese Way of Wisdom and Compassion.* Boston: Shambhala Publications, 1998.

Suzuki, Shunryu , *Zen Mind, Beginner's Mind.* Boston: Shambala Publications, 2006.

Tikalsky, Frank, D., Catherine A. Euler and John Nagel, eds. *The Sacred Oral Tradition of the Havasupai.* Albuquerque: University of New Mexico Press, 2010.

van der Kolk, Bessel, *The Body Keeps the Score: Brain, Mind, and Body In The Healing of Trauma.* New York: Viking Penguin Books, 2014.

Varley, Paul, *Japanese Culture,* 4ᵗʰ ed. Honolulu: University of Hawaii Press, 2000.

Weber, Steven, A. and P. David Seaman, eds., *Havasupai Habitat: A.F. Whiting's Ethnography of a Traditional Indian Culture.* Tucson: University of Arizona Press, 1985.

Wilson, Reid, *Don't Panic: Taking Control of Anxiety Attacks,* 3ʳᵈ ed. New York: Harper Perennial, 2009.

Articles

Brave Heart, Maria, Yellow Horse, "The Historical Trauma Response Among Natives and Its Relationship to Substance Abuse: A Lakota Illustration," in *Healing and Mental Health for Native Americans,* eds. Ethan Nebelkopf and Mary Phillips. Lanham, MD: Altamira Press, 2004.

Brave Heart, Maria, Yellow Horse with Jennifer Elkins, Greg Tafoya, Doreen Bird and Meina Salvador, "Wicasa Was'aka: Restoring the Traditional Strength of American Indian Boys and Men," *American Journal of Public Health,* Vol.102, No. S2, supplement 2 (2012).

Donald D. Dutton and Susan Painter, "The Battered Woman Syndrome: Effects of Severity and Intermittency of Abuse," *American Journal of Orthopsychiatry,* Vol. 6 No. 4 (October 1993).

Dougherty, John, "Trouble in Paradise," *High Country News,* 27 May 2007.

Eichenberg, George, M., "Criminal Victimization of Native Americans," in *American Indians at Risk,* Vol. 1, ed. Jeffrey Ian Ross (Santa Barbara: Greenwood/ABC-CLIO, LLC, 2014).

Eckholm, Erik, "Gang Violence Grows on an Indian Reservation," *The New York Times,* 14 December 2009.

Harmon, Amy, "Tribe Wins Fight to Limit Research of it DNA," *The New York Times,* 22 April 2010.

Hurley, Dan, "Grandma's Experiences Leave a Mark on Your Genes," *Discover Magazine,* May 2013.

Healy, Vikki, Oritz, "Illinois Towns on Route 66 Vie for Foreign Tourists: In Europe It's Very Much the Epic American Road Trip," *Chicago Tribune,* 15 October 2001.

Henig, Robin, Marantz, "Valium's Contribution to Our New Normal," *The New York Times,* 29 September 2012.

Interlandi, Jeneen "A Traumatized Mind?: Bessel van der Kolk wants to revolutionize the way we treat PTSD—by starting with the body," *The New York Times Magazine,* 22 May 2014.

Kristof, Nicholas, "Poverty's Poster Child," *The New York Times,* 9 May 2012.

McGivney, Annette, "Freefall: Tragedy in the Grand Canyon," *Backpacker,* June 2007.

Power, Matthew, "Ghosts of Wounded Knee," *Harper's Magazine,* December 2009.

Reid, Betty, "Hundreds Evacuated Near Grand Canyon After Flooding," *Arizona Republic,* 17 August 2008.

Rubin, Paul, "Indian Givers: The Havasupai trusted the white man to help with a diabetes epidemic. Instead, ASU tricked them into bleeding for academia," *Phoenix New Times,* 27 May 2004.

Shaffer, Mark, "Havasupai Perplexed by Killing of Tourist," *Arizona Republic,* 24 July 2006.

Struthers Roxanne and John Lowe, "Nursing in the Native American Culture and Historical Trauma," *Issues in Mental Health Nursing,* 24 (2003).

van der Kolk, Bessel, "Post Traumatic Childhood," *The New York Times,* 10 May 2011.

van der Kolk, Bessel, "The Compulsion to Repeat the Trauma: Re-enactment, Revictimization and Masochism," *Psychiatric Clinics of North America,* Vol. 12 No. 2 (June 1989).

Wagner, Dennis, "Havasupai Reborn Year After Disastrous Flash Flood," *Arizona*

Republic, 16 August 2009.

Weyermann, Debra, "And Then There Were None: On the Navajo Reservation, a passion for blood sport," *Harper's,* April 1998.

Williams, Timothy, "Sioux Racing to Find Millions to Buy Sacred Land in Black Hills," *The New York Times,* 4 October 2012.

Williams, Timothy, "Washington Steps Back from Policing Indian Lands, Even as Crime Rises," *The New York Times,* 12 November 2012.

Court Documents and Government Reports

"Havasupai Tribe of Havasupai Reservation v. Arizona Board of Regents; Court of Appeals of Arizona, Division 1, Department D," http://caselaw.findlaw.com/az-court-of-appeals/1425062.html.

Henry B. Whipple Papers, 1833-1934; Minnesota Historical Society manuscripts collection, http://www2.mnhs.org/library/findaids/P0823.xml.

"Child Maltreatment 2015," U.S. Department of Health and Human Services Administration for Children and Families, Children's Bureau, http://www.acf.hhs.gov/programs/cb/research-data-technology/statistics-research/child-maltreatment.

ADDITIONAL RESOURCES

In addition to the literature cited in the Bibliography, the author found these non-profit organizations and books helpful in understanding and treating trauma, as well as how to heal the spiritual and emotional wounds of domestic violence and neglect:

EMDR International Association: Links to therapists and information on the proven PTSD treatment protocol called Eye Movement Desensitization and Reprocessing Therapy: www.emdria.org.

National Child Traumatic Stress Network: A resource for parents, educators, judges and others who are helping children cope with the effects of domestic violence and neglect: http://www.nctsnet.org/.

The Trauma Center at JRI: This is the organization run by psychiatrist Bessel van der Kolk. Its website offers extensive resources in terms of research articles and treatment options: www.traumacenter.org.

Trauma Incident Reduction: Resources on alternative PTSD treatments, including research articles and therapists: www.healing-arts.org.

Chodron, Pema, *When Things Fall Apart: Heart Advice for Difficult Times.* Boston: Shambhala Publications, 1997.

Finley, James, *Christian Meditation: Experiencing the Presence of God.* San Francisco: Harper Collins, 2004.

Hanh, Tich Nhat, *Finding Our True Home: Living in the Pure Land Here and Now.* Berkeley: Parallax Press, 2003.

Harjo, Joy, *Crazy Brave: A Memoir.* New York: W.W. Norton, 2013.

Tolle, Eckhart, *A New Earth: Awakening to Your Life's Purpose.* New York: Plume/Penguin, 2005.

Williamson, Marianne, *A Return to Love: Reflections on the Principles of a Course in Miracles.* New York: Harper Collins, 1992.

About the Author

Annette McGivney is an award-winning journalist and the longtime Southwest Editor for *Backpacker* magazine. In addition to *Backpacker*, her writing has appeared in *Outside, Arizona Highways,* and *Sunset* magazines. Her June 2007 *Backpacker* article "Freefall" about the murder of Tomomi Hanamure won a Maggie Award in 2008 from the Western Magazine Publishers Association for Best News Story. McGivney is the author of the previous books, *Resurrection: Glen Canyon and a New Vision for the American West* (Braided River, 2009), and *Leave No Trace: A Guide to the New Wilderness Etiquette* (The Mountaineers, 2003). She teaches journalism at Northern Arizona University and lives in Flagstaff, Arizona.

Turning *Pure Land* into a Cause

One of Annette McGivney's primary motivations in writing *Pure Land* was to raise awareness about family violence and Developmental Trauma Disorder, and to help those affected find healing. In conjunction with the book, McGivney has established a public outreach campaign called I Am Pure Land that includes a non-profit organization aimed specifically at immersing child victims in the healing power of nature. A portion of the author's royalties from *Pure Land* will support guided wilderness river trips for child victims of domestic violence in a program created by McGivney called The Healing Lands Project. These trips include mental health professionals who continue to work with the children after the wilderness journey is over. For more information on Healing Lands, as well as other outreach initiatives of I Am Pure Land go to: www.iampureland.com.

CPSIA information can be obtained
at www.ICGtesting.com
Printed in the USA
BVHW081455270819
556814BV00006B/1297/P